DOUBLE MINDS

Books by Terri Blackstock

TERRI BLACKSTOCK

DOUBLE MINDS

A Novel

ZONDERVAN®

ZONDERVAN.com/
AUTHORTRACKER
follow your favorite authors

ZONDERVAN®

Double Minds
Copyright © 2009 by Terri Blackstock

This title is also available as a Zondervan ebook.
Visit www.zondervan.com/ebooks.

This title is also available in a Zondervan audio edition.
Visit www.zondervan.fm.

Requests for information should be addressed to:

Zondervan, *Grand Rapids, Michigan 49530*

Library of Congress Cataloging-in-Publication Data

Blackstock, Terri, 1957-
    Double minds / Terri Blackstock.
       p. cm.
    ISBN 978-0-310-31842-2 (hardcover, jacketed)
     1. Musicians—Fiction. 2. Young women—Crimes against—Fiction. 3. Nashville
(Tenn.)—Fiction. I. Title.
PS3552.L34285D68 2005
813'.54—dc22

                                  2008038645

Scripture quotations are taken from the *New American Standard Bible,* © Copyright
1960, 1962, 1963, 1968, 1971, 1972, 1973, 1975, 1977 by The Lockman Foundation. Used by
permission.

Interior design by Christine Orejuela-Winkelman

Printed in the United States of America

09 10 11 12 13 14 • 24 23 22 21 20 19 18 17 16 15 14 13 12 11 10 9 8 7 6 5 4 3 2 1

This book is lovingly dedicated to the Nazarene

ACKNOWLEDGMENTS

While I was writing *Double Minds,* a book about a struggling singer/songwriter, I had the privilege of meeting Erica Lane. Erica is an up-and-coming Christian singer who writes her own songs. She's the subject of a reality television show that documents her challenges as she tries to get a record contract and build name recognition. Meeting her and watching her program (which airs on FamilyNet, JCTV, and other channels) inspired me, and I was able to get ideas for Parker's character through watching her. Thanks, Erica, for being a genuine Christian in a tough world. I pray that your influence will reach far and wide.

I also want to thank my husband, Ken, for all the years of support he's given me. I thank someone in every book, but he's often left out because we take for granted those who are always there for us. It shouldn't be that way. Ken provides a lot of fuel for my books, because he says such quippy and clever things, and no matter how tough things get in this crazy household of ours, he always finds ways to make me laugh. He's generous and kind, and his Bible-based wisdom gives me a strong sense of security. Ken is the greatest representative on earth of the love Christ has for me. Thanks for being there for me, honey. I love you very much.

CHAPTER ONE

Emergency, Parker! Call me!

The text on Parker James's iPhone almost broke her rhythm. She focused on the piano keys and tried to ignore it. Her brother could wait. Didn't he realize she was in the middle of a concert?

She never should have set the phone on the music rack where she could see it. Now, in the middle of her best song, she was distracted by the vibration — as well as the message. She forced her mind back to the lyrics she'd written.

It was rare to have the undivided attention of fifty middle schoolers. Tonight, as she'd played piano and crooned her songs, they actually stopped whispering and shoving each other. Instead, they sang along, a beautiful chorus of a cappella praise.

The phone vibrated again as more voices joined the song. Jaded young faces held sweet, teary-eyed expressions, far removed from eighth-grade mini-dramas. Many of them closed their eyes … and they weren't nodding off. They lifted their hands but weren't waving to friends. They were *in the zone* — that special place where all performers pray they'll take their audience. No way was she going to stop to answer the phone.

Red bangs fell in front of her eyes and she shook them back. "Sing it with me," she whispered into the microphone.

"Flying, dying,
This life is trying ...
My fingers prying
   Your hand away.
But You are bigger ...
You grasp with vigor ...
   And get me through another day."

Another text flashed onto the screen.

Parker, there's been a murder. Call immediately.

Now he had her attention.

The sound of soft voices rose and swelled, but the phone had snagged her thoughts. A murder? Her brother Gibson was a homicide detective, but he'd never reported a murder to her before. It had to be someone she knew. Someone close to her.

She stopped playing, letting the voices carry the song. Slipping off her stool as the teens kept singing, she stepped over to Daniel Walker, the youth minister, who strummed a guitar on the stage next to her. "Could you take over for a minute?" she whispered.

He nodded reverently, continuing to sing, and she slipped into the hallway and called Gibson. He answered after half a ring.

"Parker?"

"Yeah, what's wrong?" she whispered.

"I'm at Colgate. There's been a shooting."

The chorus continued on the other side of the door:

"Flying, dying,
This life is trying ..."

She plugged her ear. "A shooting? Who?" She heard Gibson talking to someone in the background. *"Gibson?"*

The phone cut off, and she punched the button to call him back. It went straight to voicemail.

She stared at the backlit screen of the phone in her hand. Had the phone company lost the call, or was Gibson in trouble? And *who'd been shot*? Her other brother, LesPaul, worked as a recording engineer at the complex, but she was pretty sure he wasn't in a session tonight.

The singing stopped, and she touched her pounding chest, trying to decide what to do. She had to tell someone she was leaving. She wasn't finished with her concert. What would they think?

She cracked the door open as Daniel took the microphone. "Wow," he said in an intimate rumble, "that was great. And isn't it just like Parker James to forego the applause and adulation, and step out quietly in the middle of our worship, to let God have all the glory?"

She stepped back and closed the door as she heard the applause and adulation she really had come here for.

"Follow that example, guys," he went on. "She's a real woman of God, and I'm humbled by what she did here tonight."

Now she couldn't go back in, even if she wanted. What could she do? Tell Daniel that he had her all wrong? That she wanted to sing another half-hour and work them into a standing ovation?

No, she couldn't. She had to get to Colgate Studios. She started walking away, then heard Daniel's voice again. "The thing about Parker is that she doesn't have a voice that draws big crowds."

Her ego took the blow and splattered on the ground. It was worthy of a chalk outline.

"But man, can she tell a story with her songs and lead us right to the throne of God."

She told herself it was a compliment, not a criticism, but the words still hurt. Crestfallen, she headed out to her V-dub. No time now for hurt feelings, not when someone she knew might be dead. What could have happened? Had some band members gotten into a fight? Even though Colgate Studios was a drug-and-alcohol-free zone, and mostly catered to Christian record labels, the musicians, engineers, and producers weren't always drug-free — and they didn't always behave differently from the secular musicians who'd given the industry its reputation for sleaze and self-indulgence.

Occasionally there was an incident. But never anything requiring a homicide investigation.

Dread washed through her as she tried to remember who was recording there tonight. Clayton Marks, who'd been in Studio G all afternoon, had seemed depressed since his new album had tanked. Rumor was that he'd tried to take his own life once already. Maybe he'd succeeded tonight.

Would Homicide be called in for a suicide? Yes, of course. They probably had to investigate just in case it was a murder. But would Gibson call her out of a concert to tell her that? Besides, he'd specifically called it a murder.

By the time she hit 16th Avenue South, part of legendary Music Row, she had the heavy, sad certainty that she'd be attending the funeral of someone close to her. As she passed Sony Music, a million blue flashing lights illuminated the road in front of Colgate Studios. She drove straight for the roadblock and stopped behind a squad car.

A cop she didn't know approached her as she got out. "Ma'am, you can't park there."

She strained to see the building a few doors down. "I work at Colgate Studios. What happened?"

"I need you to move your car."

She turned to the crowd. "Somebody tell me ... what happened?"

"Somebody got shot," a teenager on a bicycle said.

The officer stepped between them. "Ma'am, if you don't move this car — "

Parker turned back to him. "Please. Who was shot?"

"Get back in your car!"

She'd had enough. "I'm Detective Gibson James's sister. I'm here because he asked me to come. Please call him and tell him I'm here."

"I don't know who he is."

"He's a homicide detective!" She dug her phone out of her bag.

Pressing Gibson on speed dial, she waited for him to answer. It rang once, twice, three times.

"Parker, are you here?"

"Yeah, but they won't let me through the barricade!" She read the officer's nametag. "Could you tell Sgt. Foster to let me in?"

"Let me talk to him."

She thrust the phone at the unyielding cop. "He wants to talk to you."

The man took the phone, listened, then handed it back. He gave her a look that made her wrists hurt. No doubt he was one move away from slapping the cuffs on her. "He said he'd meet you at the tape," he said through clenched teeth.

"Thank you." She pushed between two squad cars and headed for the crime-scene tape, which crossed the street in a diagonal out from the building, creating a triangular perimeter. A crowd of press people were already there, snapping pictures as cops came and went out of the Colgate Studios building. The front glass was pierced with bullet holes, near where her reception desk sat. Every light in the building was on, and people moved around in the front room near her desk.

She stopped on the street, needing to keep some distance between herself and the evil inside.

A reporter from NewsChannel 5 was doing a live remote. "John, sources tell us that the murdered woman was a receptionist at Colgate Studios ..."

A receptionist? *She* was the receptionist! Who had been watching the front desk tonight? Erin? Cat? Andy? Heat pounded in her face.

She couldn't wait for Gibson. She ducked under the tape and bolted for the door. Another cop almost tackled her, but she twisted away. "Gibson!"

Her brother emerged then. "Let her go. She's a witness."

A witness? She hadn't witnessed anything.

"Who is it?" she cried as she went toward him.

Gibson crossed the grass and took her arms. She stared up into his face. "Brenna Evans."

Her mouth fell open, but her throat closed so tight she thought she might choke. Why had the intern even been here so late? The Belmont University student had only been working here for three months, mostly in the afternoons after her classes.

She was dead? So pretty and so young…

"Good Tidings was recording in Studio C," Gibson said, "and Ron Jasper came out and found her dead on the floor."

Brenna shot dead … while Good Tidings recorded their hymns in the booth down the hall? She tried to grasp it, but madness swirled in her head. From somewhere in the fog, she asked, "Did he see who did it? Did they catch them?"

"No, he didn't see. She was dead when he found her. Since the booths are soundproof, no one heard the gunfire. She was apparently shot by someone outside, through the window. She was at your desk."

Horror clutched her throat. "It could have been me … I'm usually here …"

"Parker, I know this is tough for you, but I need your help. I can't take you into the building, but I need for you to look at some pictures and see if anything is missing from your desk. We haven't ruled out robbery. Rayzo's checking the security tape to see if anyone went in after the shooting."

"Pictures? Yes, show me."

He pulled the digital camera out of his coat pocket and turned it on. She watched as he clicked through the pictures he'd taken of the body. Parker's lungs seemed to shut down. She couldn't catch her breath. The young girl with the Bohemian style lay on her back where she'd fallen, between Parker's computer case and her file cabinet. She wore a long, flowing skirt — lavender, the color of calm — and camel-colored Uggs. She lay on her back, her long, wavy blonde hair matted with blood.

Parker's chair had fallen back with her, and Brenna's legs seemed tangled in it.

She turned away, unable to look. "Look at this one, Parker," he said finally. "Your desk. Everything in place? Anything missing?"

She shook the terror out of her thoughts and focused on the image. Brenna's textbook lay open, next to a binder with notebook paper in it. A pen lay on top of a blank sheet. A can of Diet Coke sat next to her books. On the other side of the L-shaped desk sat Parker's laptop — right where she'd left it. Next to that lay Brenna's backpack, beside Parker's mug of pens.

"Parker! Did they take anything?"

She ripped her mind from Brenna's things and forced herself to scan her desk. "No ... although these pictures are too small to tell for sure. Everything looks normal."

He clicked through several more pictures of her desk taken from different angles, some zoomed in on the stacks of papers, the pens in their container, the contents of her top drawer.

Think, she told herself. *This is important. There's a person with a gun out there, and they could come back.* She said, "Did you check for the keys to the studios?"

"The ones in the second drawer?"

"Yeah."

He clicked through more photos and found one of the contents of that drawer. The keys were still there.

"What are the musicians saying?"

"They all say either you or Cat were at your desk when they checked in. None of them saw Brenna."

"Brenna wasn't on the schedule tonight. Cat relieved me. She was here when I left."

"I just talked to her. Cat says Brenna showed up and wanted to relieve *her.* Cat was glad to have the night off."

"That doesn't make sense. Brenna's an unpaid intern. Why would she want to work extra hours?"

"Cat said Brenna thought it was a quiet place to study."

"It's not, though. People come and go, talking loud. The phone rings constantly. People hang out in the kitchen and lounge." Of course, Gibson knew that as well as she did. He worked on the side as a studio musician. He'd done dozens of sessions at Colgate.

"George is here. I'm about to talk to him. We'll see if he can shed any light."

George Colgate had opened Colgate Sound Studios ten years ago and built a reputation for keeping the latest and most state-of-the-art equipment in every booth. Major labels rented time for their artists to record here, and Colgate had a staff of house engineers who were the best in the business. Parker had come to work here as a way to network, pay her bills, and get coveted studio time to record her own songs for free.

She'd never counted on bullets flying toward her desk. She wiped her face and realized her hands were cold.

"Nothing's been stolen or vandalized, according to George," Gibson said. "But he's pretty shaken up. The control boards and all the equipment are intact, as far as I can see."

Cold wind whipped across the parking lot, slapping her hair into her face.

Her gaze drifted back to that bullet-pierced window, where camera lights flashed as the crime-scene investigators recorded the scene in all its cruel detail. She should have been here. If she had, that girl who had no stake in this company — wouldn't have been killed. But then Parker herself would have been sitting there ...

Parker glanced back at the crowd just outside the crime-scene tape. WSMV had a camera crew here, and their lead reporter was lit up like a hologram in the dark night.

There were people to be notified. Brenna's parents, her room-mate, her boyfriend ... It was wrong to just leave her on the floor like that while the media vultures circled around the crime tape, the window lit up. "Why can't you close the shades? Everyone's looking."

"They can't see her on the floor," Gibson said. "And we can't close them, because there might be evidence on the windows or the shades, just like they are."

Of course. She'd helped Gibson study for his homicide detective exams. She knew the procedure. Blood spatters were important. One stray drop of blood could tell them about the angle of the gun, the caliber, the distance from which it was fired. "Gibson, who's going to tell her family?"

"We'll have an officer go."

She ran her fingers through her hair. "What about her roommate and the people who know her at school?"

"We only notify next of kin." He clicked off his camera. "I've got to get back in."

She stood frozen in the cold night and watched her brother cross the yard back into the building. The night strobed with blue-and-white lights. The media snapped pictures of her, like she was somebody. She didn't want to talk. If they didn't have Brenna's name yet, maybe the parents could be notified first. She thought of Brenna's roommate and boyfriend. They would hear it on the news, probably soon.

Parker thought of going to Belmont, less than a mile away, to notify them herself. But she didn't even know which dorm Brenna lived in. She'd never asked Brenna her roommate's name. Brenna's boyfriend had come by once or twice to bring her lunch when she was working during the day. He looked young and untarnished. Almost innocent. Way too innocent to have a murdered girlfriend. What would it do to him?

On the other hand, maybe *he* was the killer. Maybe this was about a failed relationship. She turned on her phone and pressed her brother's number again.

He answered quickly. "Yeah?"

"Gibson, I just remembered she has a boyfriend. His name is Chase something. Kind of an Irish last name. Mac-something."

"Okay, we'll talk to him."

"It shouldn't be hard to find him. Check her phone's speed dial."

"Parker, I know how to do my job."

"I know. It's just . . ." She knew she'd better just let him handle it. But he could be flakey sometimes, and he was new at this. Since he'd been promoted to Homicide, he'd only had to solve three cases, all of them pretty cut and dried. This one might be different.

She turned off her phone and stood there a moment, unable to move or think. Tears rushed to her eyes and she put her hand over her mouth. How could this happen? She'd never dreamed Gibson would be investigating the death of someone she knew.

Turning, she walked through the night of blue strobes, cameras flashing like paparazzi.

"Ma'am, could you tell us your name?"

"Did you know the victim?"

"Do the police know who killed her?"

She ignored the reporters and ducked under the tape, and went back toward her car. Tomorrow she'd wind up in the paper with a caption that said "Unidentified Woman Weeps at Door of Colgate Studios."

"Ma'am, can you confirm the victim's name?"

Parker looked at the reporter dressed in a black Armani suit, his face painted for his close-ups. She wiped her eyes. "Please don't give her name tonight. Just keep that out of it until her family and friends are told."

The man kept pressing. "We're told that it's Parker James in there. That she's the receptionist at Colgate. Can you confirm that?"

Parker's heart jolted, and she opened her mouth to correct them. But then she thought of Brenna's eighteen-year-old friends watching the news while waiting for David Letterman, and learning that she'd been murdered on Music Row. What if Brenna's parents weren't notified before newscasters began broadcasting her name? Would people call them, crying, wanting to know if it was true?

No, she couldn't let that happen, not if she could help it. Brenna had been at Parker's desk when she died. The least Parker could do was to confuse the media's reporting. She cleared her throat. Her voice sounded far away. "I can confirm that Parker James is the receptionist."

Gleefully, the reporter backed away, ready to do his standup for the audience at home. He would probably broadcast that Parker had been murdered. Soon the other channels would be announcing that, too.

What a mess.

She got into her car, sick with the thought that *her* family and friends would be devastated now. What had she been thinking? She clicked on her phone, pressed her mother on speed dial. Her voicemail quickly took over, which probably meant she was on the phone. Lynn James couldn't abide Call Waiting.

"Mom, this is Parker, alive and well." She sniffed and looked around her car for a Kleenex. "I wanted you to know that the rumors of my death have been greatly exaggerated." Her mother would love that she'd quoted Mark Twain. Parker found a tissue and dabbed at her nose. "Seriously, I'm alive. Don't believe what you see on the news. It wasn't me who was murdered. It's just a stupid … misunderstanding."

She hung up and sat for a moment. Her mother would let LesPaul, her other brother, know. But Parker would need to call her dad.

A reporter knocked on her window, and others began to surround her car. She punched the lock button, then dug in her purse for her keys and couldn't find them. A camera flashed through the windshield — as if they thought *she* was the murderer, or maybe Brenna herself, risen from the dead after dusting herself off.

How could she get rid of them? She thought of all the ways she'd managed to help her famous friend Serene avoid reporters. A flash of brilliance struck her, and she rolled her window down. "They're going to be moving the body out in the next few minutes," she yelled.

Suddenly she was history. They lit out for the story unfolding at the door of Colgate — hounds on the scent of a corpse.

CHAPTER TWO

Lynn James wasn't aging well. Her fiftieth birthday was on the horizon, but she wished she could slide under it without a mention. Why celebrate a day like that with gifts? It was a day when she needed condolences. People coming by with meals. Sympathy cards. Whispered lies, like I-know-how-you-feel and you-don't-look-half-as-bad-as-you-think.

She transferred the cheese and crackers to the platter, wondering how much more the girls of her Bible study could eat. They'd ripped through her meatballs and finger sandwiches like death-row inmates at their last meal. Oh, for the metabolism of the young!

One day she'd been cute ... and the next, her jowls were sagging and her eyelids were heavy and loose. In pictures, her features looked blurred and hangy, like someone had taken a clay sculpture of her and slid their fingers down it.

What she hated most about herself was her vanity. Why did she care how she looked? Her beauty should have nothing to do with outward adornment, at least according to the apostle Peter. But tell that to the other hip middle-agers in Nashville, who'd begun nipping and tucking when they were thirty-five.

If she could just lose ten pounds, maybe her skin would

tighten up. Her double chin wouldn't need liposuction. Her knees wouldn't sag.

Or maybe they still would. Why eat healthy for no good reason?

It was ridiculous, dwelling on her appearance like a twenty-year-old. She had seventy-year-old friends who would kill to look like her. By the time *she* was seventy, her chin would be slapping her knees.

Maybe if she invited women her own age over instead of her former college students, she wouldn't be having these thoughts. But the girls seemed to enjoy the weekly Bible studies.

The phone rang as she pushed through the door into the living room, where the noise level reminded her of a wedding shower. Whoever was calling would have to leave a message. She set the platter down. "Sorry about the phone. I forgot to turn the ringer off."

"Don't you want to answer it?" Sarah Stover, her favorite ex-student, asked.

It stopped ringing and went to voicemail. "Too late now. Kristy, will you check the caller ID?"

Twenty-five-year-old Kristy, sitting next to the phone, lifted it from its charger. With the technical savvy of a ten-year-old, she quickly found the name. "It was your daughter, Parker."

Lynn smiled. "She had a concert tonight. She probably wants to tell me about it. Anybody need more tea?" Several of them had empty glasses, so the peach-flavored iced tea was a hit. She pushed back into the kitchen, but before she grabbed the pitcher, she picked up the phone and punched the numbers for her voicemail.

Parker's voice came across the line. "Mom, this is Parker, alive and well."

She sounded stopped up. Was she crying? Lynn forgot about the pitcher. Her daughter had her full attention now.

"I wanted you to know that rumors of my death have been

greatly exaggerated. Seriously, I'm alive. Don't believe what you see on the news. It wasn't me who was murdered — "

Lynn's heart stumbled. Still clutching the phone, she went back into the living room. Sarah looked up at her. "Dr. James?"

She swallowed hard. "Turn on the TV. Someone's been murdered." Forgetting her guests as the television came on, Lynn dialed Parker's number.

CHAPTER THREE

Her mother's phone call came as Parker turned onto Wedgewood.

"What do you mean, *rumors of your death*? Why would someone think you've been murdered?"

As Parker related the night's events, she felt her mother's fear rippling like static through the phone line. "Parker, that could have been you!"

One of her mother's true gifts — stating the obvious. "Tell me about it. Did you know her, Mom? She went to Belmont."

"No, she wasn't in any of my classes. Do you have any idea who did it?"

"No. But Gibson's working the case."

Her mother didn't sound comforted by the thought. She'd never warmed to the idea that her firstborn was a cop, and the idea of him chasing killers kept her up nights. "You shouldn't have lied to that reporter. Now everyone's going to think you're dead. My phone'll ring off the hook. That's a little creepy, don't you think?"

"Yes, it was creepy. But I didn't lie; I just confirmed that I was the receptionist. I know it was stupid." Someone beeped in, and she glanced at the phone. "Mom, I have to go. Dad's on the other line, and he probably just heard the report."

"Oh, God help him. This'll drive him to drink."

"Yeah, well — everything does. I'll call you later." She glanced down at the Answer and Ignore buttons, and clicked Answer. "Dad?"

"Parker? Parker, is that you?" His tongue sounded thick. There was crowd noise behind him, a Garth Brooks song wailing in the background.

"Yes, it's me, Dad. Where are you?"

"At home."

She knew it was a lie. He was obviously sitting at some bar that happened to have the news playing on its television.

"The press is wrong. Really, I'm okay." She went into the story again — knowing he couldn't hear it all. Still, she heard relief and joy in her father's voice.

"Actually, this is genius. Think about it, Parker. Now the press will be digging through their files to find out who you are. People will know your name."

"Yeah, as a dead person. I don't think that kind of publicity will do me a lot of good."

The noise behind him faded, and she imagined him stepping outside. "Of course it will. The name will stick with them. That's why I named you Parker. People don't forget it."

Parker braked at a stoplight. "So, you think I should just roll with it and accept the posthumous fame that will come with being murdered?"

He was silent for a moment. "No, I'm not saying that."

"Whew, that's a relief. I was thinking I'd have to go into hiding. Do they have some kind of murdered-person-protection program?" Another creepy thing to say. Why did she joke when she was squinting through tears? Brenna was dead.

She heard his deep raspy chuckle. "Good one. But seriously. Even one mention on the news will do you good. Any idea what TV exposure like that would cost if you had to pay for it? I hope your website is up to date."

Holding the phone with her shoulder, she turned off West End onto Murphy Road. "I didn't really want them to learn about me this way."

"Doesn't matter how they learn your name. Just that they do. You're not getting any younger."

Her dad always said just the right thing. "Yeah, I know. Twenty-six. I'm almost ready for dentures."

"Passes faster than you think."

Pete James's life had passed him by, that was for sure. He'd missed most of it in a drunken stupor. He'd spent his life chasing dreams, then sabotaging them. Now he dreamed of his children's musical careers as if he were their manager. Even in their mother's womb, he'd named them after guitars. Parker was glad his hobby wasn't reptiles. She might have been named Iguana.

His marketing zeal was inappropriate now, so she managed to wriggle off the phone, then retreated into silence for a moment. But the image of the dead girl was still in her head when she got home. She pulled into her carport as the motion light came on. Sitting in the car for a minute, she stared at a bird spot on the windshield and wondered if Brenna had suffered. Had she endured moments of agony before her life bled out of her? Had she prayed?

Parker's phone buzzed yet again, startling her. She pulled it out of her pocket and saw Serene's pampered made-for-TV face. She wasn't in the mood to talk to her needy friend right now. But she'd probably seen the news, too. She clicked it on. "Hello?"

"Parker, where are you?"

"In my carport. I guess you heard about the murder."

"What murder?"

And Parker was off again, repeating the story for the third time. About halfway through, she realized Serene was talking to someone with her, relaying the conversation to them.

"Serene? Serene!"

Serene checked back in. "I'm here. Listen, are you sure you want to be alone tonight? I mean, what if they meant those bullets for you?"

Parker hadn't wanted to dwell on that thought. She didn't have any enemies. Was there someone out there who wanted her dead? She looked at the door to her house, suddenly aware that she was vulnerable sitting here in her open carport. She checked her car door. Still locked.

"Just come sleep over at my house tonight," Serene said. "I'd feel better knowing you were safe."

Good idea. She thought of going in to get a few things first, but now she was too frightened. "All right," she said. "I'll come. But why were you calling?"

Serene hesitated. "We'll talk about it when you get here."

"No, go ahead. I want to know."

Serene paused and Parker grew uneasy. Serene's pauses usually bulged with unasked favors. "I need your help."

"Help with what?"

"Long story. I'd rather talk to you in person. It's *huge*. We have some decisions to make."

"Decisions? About what?"

"About my album. Please, Parker."

She sat a moment, then shifted her car into reverse. "All right, I'm coming."

"Great. Butch wants to talk to you."

She waited as Serene's manager got on the phone. "Hey, Parker, on your way would you swing through Wendy's?"

She mashed the volume button on her phone. Had she heard him right? He wanted her to make a food delivery?

"She hasn't eaten in a couple of days," he said. "She says if you bring her something, she'll eat."

Without doubt, Serene was malnourished. The idea of getting her to eat moved the favor into the life-or-death category. "She only eats protein bars. What will she eat from Wendy's?"

"Just get two number-one combos with Cokes."

Two? So Butch was hungry too. She wondered if Serene had really agreed to eat such a high-fat meal. If she ate it, she'd go purge within minutes. But if there was a possibility that her friend might get *some* nourishment … "Okay, I'll bring it, but she has to digest it."

She clicked her phone off. To calm her nerves, she used her thumb to navigate to her iTunes. She found her Parker Playlist, all songs she'd written and sold to Serene. She clicked on the rough cut of the song she'd most recently recorded — "Double Minds."

Serene sang it well in her belt-out voice, even though Parker doubted she grasped all its meanings. It had come from the passage in James 4:

> Draw near to God and He will draw near to you. Cleanse your hands, you sinners; and purify your hearts, you double-minded. Be miserable and mourn and weep; let your laughter be turned into mourning and your joy to gloom. Humble yourself in the presence of the Lord, and He will exalt you.

She'd told a story in the song — the story of a man who'd lost his way and groped blindly through life, looking for light in dark bars, while his spirit longed to find the path he'd once been on. Two people in one, fighting over the same spirit, sharing the same double-mind.

Only when she'd finished writing the song did she realize she'd told her father's story. In fact, he was the subject of a lot of her songs.

Serene loved it and planned to release it as the first single from her new album.

Draw near to God and He will draw near to you …

The words of the chorus warmed her spirit like a balm. And tonight, when she couldn't escape the reality of the murder, she needed that balm.

It could have been her. She could have been sitting there behind that counter, talking on the phone or tweaking her latest song on her MacBook. She could have looked up and seen headlights through the window, slowing down as the killer took aim …

Gibson could have been investigating *her* death on the floor of

Colgate Studios. Her gratitude at being spared battled with her sorrow that Brenna hadn't been. Aware that her guilt was irrational, she tried to chase it away.

At Wendy's, she circled the building to the disembodied voice and ordered two number-one combos. She thought of ordering herself something, as well, but she couldn't focus enough to decide what she wanted. She was thirsty from crying, but she'd just get water when she got to Serene's house.

The line was long for this time of night, but Nashville wasn't a town that retired early. With four colleges in a ten-mile radius, West End was just coming alive at ten p.m. She looked at the people standing in the parking lot, students mostly. She imagined a murderer walking up to her car and lifting his gun. Had the killer been expecting to find her? Or had he known she wouldn't be there?

Maybe it had been someone specifically targeting Brenna. But if so, why had he done it on the rare night she was working at Colgate, especially when she wasn't even scheduled to work?

Her mind rolled through tapes of people she'd seen over the last few weeks. She knew of at least four people who were angry that they hadn't been able to book adequate studio time. One guy had bolted in last week demanding to see George Colgate, but after he'd stormed through the building and looked in George's office, the man had finally accepted that he wasn't in.

Not that that was unusual. The CEO of Colgate owned several record labels, so he was hardly ever on site. Some claimed Parker ran the place, since she booked all the sessions and assigned house engineers. But she got along with most of the clients and had an uncanny knack for diffusing tense situations. She couldn't think of anyone angry enough to murder her.

The car in front of her moved up, so she took her foot off the brake and rolled forward. This could be a long wait. She dialed George Colgate's cell number, doubtful that he'd answer. But he did.

"Colgate." His voice was subdued. She could hear voices around him.

"George, it's Parker."

"Did you hear what happened?" he asked.

"Yes, I just left there. They wouldn't let me in. Are you there?"

"Yeah, in the building, sitting in the lounge. They've been questioning me since I got here."

The cars moved again, and she made her boss hold while she placed Serene's order. He would think she was callous, popping through a fast-food line after something so life-shattering. "Sorry," she said as she rolled her car forward. "Serene gave me a life-or-death request for food. She probably hasn't eaten a bite in days." That didn't need explaining. It was clear from Serene's frightening thinness that she had a problem. "George, do you have any idea who did this?"

"None."

"Do you think he was after one of us?"

"I don't know," George said, "but I think I'll get a hotel tonight. If it's me he's mad at, I don't want to be home. By the way, did you know the press thinks it's you who died?"

She moved up and paid at the first window. "Yeah, I know. They'll figure it out eventually." She rolled to the second window. Whispering thanks, she dropped the bag on her passenger seat, then reached for the drinks.

When she hung up, she turned the stereo back up and listened as Serene belted the words of another of Parker's songs — one she'd written the night of September 11th. She'd lain awake, listening to her mother down the hall, quoting Psalm 46 like a prayer: "God is our refuge and strength, a very present help in trouble. Therefore we will not fear, though the earth should change, and though the mountains slip into the heart of the sea; though its waters roar *and* foam, though the mountains quake at its swelling pride ..."

Scripture wove itself into her song, as it so often did. That chorus had become famous; now it was sung in multitudes of churches on Sunday mornings.

My refuge, my strength, my helper, my King
Cease striving and know forevermore
That I am Lord, That I am Lord.

The chorus wasn't one of her flashes of brilliance, but the songs that made it seldom were. It had been a flash of brilliance for King David, who'd penned it. She had just reframed it. Serene had decided to record it after hearing it just once. The song propelled her to the top of the Christian Top 20 for thirty-two weeks. It had made her more money than any of her other songs. Now Serene lived among the wealthy in the Franklin area.

Parker still lived in her little home in West End, but she wasn't complaining. She loved her house with all its charm and age. She'd bought it three years ago at the age of twenty-three, an act that had taken her from childhood to adulthood in one fell swoop, all financed by the selling of a few special songs. She loved all 700 square feet of it.

She only hoped the killer didn't have her address.

CHAPTER FOUR

Parker didn't like being dead.

The television was on in Serene's den, and Serene and her Svengali, Butch, sat in front of the wide flat-screen as the local news covered the murder. Butch, Serene's manager, leaned forward with rapt fascination. It may have been the first sincere emotion she'd ever seen on his pale face.

Butch was an unlikely manager for a rising Christian recording artist. He walked around in raggedy shorts and an oversized T-shirt. He had a round belly and a bald head and was usually sucking on a Tootsie Pop that would have rotted his teeth if it weren't for his porcelain veneers. But he was a genius with music.

The reporter Parker had "tipped off" stood in front of the camera, rattling off the "facts" surrounding the murder at Colgate Studios.

"Parker, check this out," Butch said.

Parker dropped the bag of food on the coffee table and handed Serene her Coke. "Yeah, I know. I'm dead, allegedly."

She let her gaze settle on the screen. There was her brother, coming out of the studio with bags of evidence. She hoped they'd found fingerprints. Even now, Gibson could be showing up at the killer's house, ready to take him into custody.

Serene sat on the floor with her legs crossed, looking nothing like the star she was. She had the body of a fourteen-year-old boy — a scrawny one at that. At five-five and ninety-five pounds, she had no curves or comfort, just sharp angles. She had no trouble shopping at the stores in Nashville that only carried sizes zero and two. But that was the way America wanted their celebrities these days. Parker was content to be a size ten and made no apologies for it.

She watched Serene tear into the bag and unwrap the burger. Her friend had probably not eaten more than half a piece of cantaloupe or some chicken broth in the last few days. And what she did eat she didn't keep down. She'd been taught well in the School of Skinny.

But Serene didn't bite into the burger. Instead, she opened it up and began peeling off the pickles and lettuce and onions.

"Just eat the stupid thing," Butch said.

"I just want the patty."

"You promised you'd eat it."

"I am going to eat it. It's a big patty."

Parker should have known.

Serene took a tiny bite of the patty. "So that girl who was killed. I only saw her a couple of times, never talked to her. She was always filing or something. What did Gibson tell you about the murder?"

Parker sat on the arm of the sofa. "Nothing. Just asked me a few questions about the office and the stuff on my desk. Wanted to know if anything was missing."

"Was it?"

"I don't think so. Computers were still there, sound boards and engineering equipment seemed fine."

Serene tasted her drink, wrinkled her nose, and set it on the coffee table. Too much sugar, no doubt. Parker should have gotten her a diet drink. "Do they have any idea who killed her?"

"If they do, he didn't tell me." Parker's dull eyes settled on the screen, and that sick feeling came back. Why had she let them think she was dead? She thought of those kids she'd been leading in worship when she got the call. Would they hear on the news that she'd been murdered? Maybe she should call their youth minister, Daniel. He might even still be there with them, hanging out, playing ping-pong in the rec room before they went home for the night. She didn't want them posting blogs about her death on MySpace while she collected her press clippings. She wasn't eager to read a thousand eulogies and watch as teenagers picked her life apart and pasted it on websites for all to see.

Hearing her name drew her thoughts back to the wide screen over Serene's fireplace mantel.

"Sources tell us that Parker James was twenty-eight years old —"

"Twenty-*six*," she muttered.

"She'd been working at Colgate Studios as receptionist for the past five years. The deceased has a website that describes her as a singer/songwriter, as well. In fact, the site claims that she penned most of Christian artist Serene Stevens's songs."

Serene collapsed in laughter. "You're gonna be more famous than I am!"

Butch threw his head back and howled. "Girl, get a grip. You don't let people think you're dead just to make another family feel better."

She could never make him understand. "They would have broadcast Brenna's death on TV. Her parents would have found out that way."

"But *that* was true!" Serene said. "You're crazy, you know that?"

Parker closed her eyes and leaned her head back. "I know. I panicked and just threw it out there. I kept thinking of her family —"

"Never mind yours."

"I've been in touch with them. They know I'm not dead."

"What about all your friends? Don't you realize people are probably crying over their poor murdered friend right now?"

Parker looked at Serene. Was that true? Would there be people grieving her supposed loss? She did have a lot of friends and acquaintances, though none as close as her family or Serene. Maybe there would be tears shed . . .

She hoped so. It would be a terrible thing to have your death pass without a tear.

She caught herself and looked back at the news. What was she thinking? What kind of self-centered diva was she to crave that kind of mourning? She'd been so worried about Brenna's friends finding out in the dorms that she hadn't even considered her own. "What should I do? Go back and talk to the reporters?"

Butch chuckled. "Probably no need. If it helps any, the other two stations are reporting that it was Brenna."

She grunted. "You could have told me that before making me feel like a jerk."

"I'm just messing with you," he said.

She took the remote and changed the channel. Just as he'd said, Brenna's name was on the screen, along with her age and the fact that she was a Belmont student. So Parker's pretense had been unnecessary. Serene and Butch were right. She *was* a fool.

Disgusted, she got up. "I think I'll go home, after all."

"Why?" Serene asked. "I told you you could stay here."

"I don't really feel like company tonight. I think I'll take my chances."

"We didn't mean to laugh at you," Butch said, still chuckling. "Don't go."

Parker scowled back at him. "What do you care?"

"He cares because we need you, Parker."

"Why?"

"We need some rewrites . . . like, tonight."

Parker stared at her. Did Serene expect her to write at a time like this? "I'm not in the mood."

"There's nothing you can do for Brenna."

"I'm not trying to *do* anything. I just don't want to be around people right now."

"But you've *got* to help me." Serene's hair was pulled up in a ponytail, and strands of it fell into her eyes. She wore a great big sweatshirt with the name of some college Parker had never heard of, and a pair of baggy gym shorts. She stood there barefoot, her hundred-dollar pedicured toenails in living color. She had that look on her face — the one that broadcast her need for another stupid favor, like driving through Wendy's after a friend had been murdered. "Parker, I didn't want to tell you on the phone because you were upset."

Parker braced herself.

"Jeff Standard is trying to buy out my contract."

"Jeff Standard? The guy who owns Standard Entertainment Corporation?"

"That's him."

Parker stared at her. The CEO of the record giant owned several other entertainment companies as well. She'd seen his picture on the cover of *Rolling Stone* last month. Something about his stellar skill in picking artists that made him millions.

"Wow," she said. "How does he know about you?"

Butch leaned back. "There's a lot of money in Christian music. And with the success of 'Trying,' she got his notice."

Parker lifted her eyebrows. This *was* huge. "But if he's only interested in Christian music for the profit — "

"Don't be naïve," Butch said. "Christian record execs are in it for profit, too. They'd go under if they didn't make money."

"Right now I have one song on the secular charts." Serene's eyes sparkled. "What if *all* my songs crossed over? Think how many people I could reach."

Parker could see her point. She always meant for the songs she wrote to reach a broad audience. If they drew larger numbers to worship ... well, that was success, wasn't it? "So what do you need my help with?"

"I need you to rewrite all the songs on the album."

Parker caught her breath. "What? I thought you were almost finished recording. You're going to rerecord *everything*?"

"Not everything. The musical tracks are fine. He just wants us to tone down the lyrics for the general market."

Parker brought a hand to her chest. "What does 'tone down' mean?"

Serene sighed. "Now, don't go all judgmental on me, Parker. He just wants to make it a little more ... what was the word?"

"Ecumenical," Butch provided.

Parker knew that word. *Ecumenical* meant that no one stood for much of anything.

"I've got a hard deadline," Serene said. "The tour is booked and there's a street date for the album's release in the stores."

"The *Christian* stores," Parker pointed out.

"That's right. But Jeff Standard owns the biggest chain of record stores in the country. If this works out, he'll get them into the secular stores. He's got the money to get the airplay on the radio stations. If that happens, Parker, we'll both be rolling in money."

Parker sighed. It wasn't supposed to cost money to get airplay on radio stations. Payola was against the law. But the big money knew lots of ways around the law. They hired promoters to schmooze and cajole program directors into putting their songs in their lineups.

"Come sit down. Let's talk about it," Serene said.

Parker dropped onto a chair. Slipping off her shoes, she pulled her feet beneath her. Serene turned off the television and stood in front of it, the star of the room. "Parker, think of it. You could live in a house like this. I could buy an even bigger one."

"I don't want a house like this, Serene. I'm perfectly content with my own little house. I don't write to get rich."

"Of course you don't, but you wait salivating for every royalty check that comes."

"Sure, I take the money and pay my bills with it. It's not wrong to be paid for what I do. But being a millionaire isn't my goal."

"I know, I know," Serene said, lifting a hand like she'd heard it a thousand times. "You're in it for ministry. I totally get that. But what if you didn't have to work as a receptionist? What if you could just spend all your time writing and living life?"

Parker had to admit that sounded good. "Still, if we take out the lyrics that could point them to God … if we're making them worship the wrong thing —"

"Not every song has to be about worship, Parker."

"But every song is." She got up and turned on the stereo, tuned the radio to a country station. "Listen to this. This guy's worshiping the girl in the black dress sitting at the bar."

"No, he's not," Serene said.

Parker flipped to a rap station. "This one's worshiping guys with diamond grills on their teeth." She turned it to a rock station. "A girl named Roxanne." Another country station. "A little boy's daddy."

Butch spread his arms on the back of the couch. "That's not worship. That little boy isn't *worshiping* his daddy. He just misses him. Those songs are pointing out the human condition, and that's not wrong."

"Okay, but I'd still say ninety percent of songs are worshiping something. The other ten percent are sappy cry-in-your-beer songs about some perverted *version* of the human condition."

"Where do you get those statistics?" Butch asked. "I don't remember that question on the last copyright application."

"She pulls them out of the air," Serene said. "A song can't worship, anyway. *People* worship."

"Whatever the statistics, I want the songs I write to help fill the voids those other songs talk about."

"They will, Parker. They just won't be so in-your-face."

"In-your-face is what got you to the *Billboard* charts. 'Trying' is in-your-face."

"But I need love songs. They'll get me played on secular stations, so people will buy the albums. Then they'll hear the worship songs." Serene got on her knees in front of Parker. "Remember when we were kids, Parker, dreaming of being famous?"

"You are famous. You got your dream."

"Not like I'd be if Jeff Standard buys my contract. And don't get all holier-than-thou on me. You've auditioned twice for *American Idol*. If you got on that show you wouldn't hesitate to sing whatever they told you to — from the Beatles to Diana Ross. You'd be giving it a shot like the rest of them, not balking that the songs weren't Christian songs."

Serene knew her too well. "Doesn't matter. I'll never get on that show." Daniel's words tonight about her not having a voice that drew crowds played back through her mind. The *American Idol* producers apparently agreed with him.

Her songwriting ability wasn't in question, however. She liked her songs the way she'd written them. She didn't want to change them. "Look, I know this is a big thing for you, and I don't want to shoot you down. But if I rewrite them, would I still be able to perform the original ones?"

"Of course you could," Butch said.

Parker pictured herself in front of a youth group — or a church full of people — singing the songs the way she intended them. Even if she told them how songwriting worked — that you wound up being a surrogate mother, delivering the songs over to someone who would perform them the way they wanted — wouldn't they think her version was cheesy? If Serene's version was what they knew, her performances of the originals would fall flat.

"What if I wrote some new songs for your album?"

"There isn't time to rerecord everything. We've already recorded the musical tracks. It has to be these songs."

She leaned her head back on the seat and looked up at the ceiling. "Then you could rewrite them without me."

Serene smirked. "And you're willing to split the royalties with another songwriter, or give them up entirely?"

She hadn't really thought of that. She did need the money, and she deserved to have those songs added to her catalog. Why couldn't Serene just be happy with them the way they were?

Butch sat next to Parker. "Your song 'Double Minds' could easily be a love song if you changed a few words. The story about the guy looking for light in a dark bar could be about a guy mourning a lost love."

Parker winced. When she'd written that song, she'd thought of her father, trapped in darkness. How could she massage it into something else? "But I thought that was the title song. You named the album after it."

"We can still keep that title," Butch said. "If we could just go over the songs again, you could rewrite the lyrics in a flash. I've seen you write. We could knock it out tonight. We want your genius, Parker. Serene wants you to get full credit as the writer."

Her throat was dry, and she wished for water.

Serene got that whine in her voice. "Parker, if we get this done on time, I won't have to cancel any tour dates. I'll still be playing to my fans. But Jeff Standard can get us bigger venues and more dates. I won't just be playing in churches."

"What's wrong with churches?"

"They don't generally hold that many people. Stadiums and coliseums hold more."

Butch went to the stereo and plugged his iPod in, and the rough cut of "Double Minds" began to play. Parker closed her eyes and listened to the song swelling over the speakers. Serene's voice transformed simple words and crude melodies into works of art.

She wondered who the real genius was.

Parker listened as the words of Scripture played across the chorus, weaving itself through the song. How could she untangle that to remove it? The song had been birthed in Scripture.

Serene sat on the coffee table. "These are the songs we're going to use, because they're fabulous, Parker. We're a killer team."

She couldn't deny that.

Butch pulled out a sheet with the lyrics written down. He thrust it at her.

She took it and looked down at it. He'd crossed through God, sinners, cleansing hands ...

"If we do all this we'll have to take the double-minded references out. That doesn't even make sense as a love song."

"Sure it does," Butch said. "The guy wants to get back with his girl, but he can't give up his old ways — double minds. It works."

She brought her dull eyes back up to Serene. "How sure are you that Standard's going to buy your contract?"

"I'd say ninety percent. He's in negotiations with the label now."

"And you think NT is going to let you go?" That didn't seem likely to Parker. NT Records had a tremendous investment in Serene.

"If Jeff Standard pays them enough, they will. And he seems pretty set on making this happen."

That sounded serious. "What if I say no?"

Serene's eyes rounded. "You're my best friend, Parker. Like a sister. I want to take you where I'm going. You could ride the wave with me. It could be your ticket."

Serene's clichés were the reason she didn't do her own writing. "*My* ticket? To where?"

"If my records get into the hands of millions more people, then artists all over the place will be fighting for your songs."

"Most people buy records as mp3s these days," Parker said. "They won't even see the liner notes."

"I'll tell them on my interviews. We'll be like Elton John and Bernie Taupin."

She didn't doubt that Serene would do that. But it wasn't enough to sway her. "I wrote those songs in worship ... some while I was praying. I just did a concert tonight, and everybody was into it. The Holy Spirit was working. They were lifting up their hands and singing — kids with twenty-second attention spans. That's why I write, Serene. That's why I perform."

"Who are you kidding, Parker? You know you want to do more than youth groups!"

Parker let out a long breath and realized how tired she was. It had been a long day, and a girl lay dead. "You know, tonight's not a good time to talk about this. Let me sleep on it and we'll talk tomorrow."

"You're not going to sleep on it," Butch said. "You're going to be up all night thinking about Brenna."

"Maybe," she snapped, "but that's nobody's business but my own."

"Parker, come on!" Serene blurted. "You know you're not safe going home."

Maybe she should go to her mother's. Her mom would be glad to have her there, especially in the aftermath of her recent fake death. Parker got up, feeling weariness aching down her spine. She picked up her heavy handbag and slipped it over her shoulder. "Tomorrow we'll talk."

"This is urgent! I have to get this done right away."

"No one's going into the studio tonight. In fact, Colgate might be closed for days. It's a crime scene now."

Butch groaned and looked at Serene. "I told you you needed to put a studio in your basement like everybody else in Nashville."

While they argued about it, Parker made it back to her car.

CHAPTER FIVE

As she drove back to West End, Parker wondered about the wisdom of going home. But her mother's house probably still swarmed with her Bible study group, and Parker didn't feel like being pumped for behind-the-scenes information. Gibson had called as Parker left Serene's and asked if he could talk to her again tonight. He preferred that she not be at their mother's, since Mom would freak if she saw the other pictures he needed to show Parker.

Parker already felt sick. "Will you meet me at my house?"

"Can't," he said. "Not yet. I'm on my way to talk to Brenna's parents. Don't be afraid. I really don't think the guy was after you."

But what did *he* know? He'd been in this job for all of a month. His first case had been a domestic violence case. The wife, who'd been beaten, had shot her husband, then called the police and turned herself in. The second had been a barroom brawl with dozens of witnesses. And the third was a DUI accident that left a child dead. None had been difficult to solve.

It wasn't that she doubted her brother's competence as a detective — there was no doubt involved. She was *certain* he didn't know what he was doing. He probably wouldn't know a murderer if he waved a gun in his face.

If only she hadn't helped him study for the exams, she would be able to trust in his instincts.

Gibson's history was one of gut impulses and bad choices. He'd flunked out of college because he attended more frat parties than classes. Then he had to get a job. He lost his first two sales jobs because he couldn't drag himself out of bed to show up. His womanizing had left a trail of heartbroken ex-girlfriends who thought they could change him.

Lynn finally pushed him out of her nest, praying he'd sprout wings. He picked himself up and joined the army. They made him an MP and sent him to Afghanistan in the first wave after 9/11. That was where he embraced Christ and vowed to turn his life around.

The military gave him a sense of discipline and purpose. When he got out a few years later, he joined the police department and began working nights as a studio musician — a good fit, but his ups and downs kept the family from trusting him just yet.

Parker was a firsthand witness of how poorly prepared Gibson had been for the homicide detective exam. He'd gone to take the test with hope and a prayer, and she sat at home waiting for word that he'd failed. When he passed, she wondered if the examiner got his test mixed up with someone else's. But apparently he'd passed fair and square. And as much as she doubted his investigative abilities, she did value his protection. At six-three and 225 pounds, Gibson made a good bouncer.

If he couldn't meet her at home yet, she could drive around until he was ready. She could spend that time praying for Brenna's family. But why burn up all that gas? She tried to think of an all-night Starbucks, but there weren't any.

Finally, she went home and sat in the car in her carport, letting the engine idle so she could whip it into reverse if anyone jumped out of the shadows. After a while, she realized that was crazy. She turned the key off, slid out of the car, and closed the door quietly. Then she bolted for her side door. She fumbled for the key, stuck it in the knob, and went inside.

She turned on the light. No one moved out of the shadows or pounced from behind the refrigerator, and there weren't that many places for full-grown humans to hide. Her small kitchen stood to the left of the door she'd come in, her counter separating it from the living area, which was just big enough for a couch and a small easy chair, an entertainment wall with surround-sound, and a baby grand piano in the corner. She'd sunk more money into the piano and entertainment system than she had in all her furniture combined, since hearing her songs at their best was a priority.

She hurried through the kitchen and down the hall. She'd converted her extra bedroom into a music room, where she had an electric keyboard, a desktop computer, and several guitars. Though the room was full, there were no hiding places. She looked in the open closet in which she'd wedged a desk and shelves. Nothing had changed.

Her bedroom looked the way she had left it. Her bed was high off the floor, and nothing hunkered beneath. She breathed a sigh of relief.

Then it hit her that it might not be wise to let people know she was home. Even though her car sat in the carport for anyone with a flashlight to see, she worried that the media might come knocking, hoping to clear up the confusion. Better if the lights were out. She went back through the house, turning out all the lights, then felt her way back to her bedroom.

She lay back on the bed, staring up at the dark ceiling. This was ridiculous. She had things to do. She couldn't allow herself to be made a prisoner in her own home. And anyway, this couldn't be about her. She wasn't important enough at Colgate Studios for anyone to want dead.

She forced her thoughts away from herself to Brenna's parents. She prayed for them, imagining their anguish.

After a while, she heard a car coming up the street, saw headlights turning across her curtains. She sat up. Someone was pulling into her driveway.

She slid off the bed and went to the window, peered out through the curtains. Thankfully, it was Gibson's Bonneville. She watched as he turned his lights off and got out, slamming the door with no regard for the neighbors who had probably gone to bed long ago, oblivious that their neighbor had been pronounced dead. He ambled up the driveway as if nothing had happened tonight.

She flipped on her bedroom light and hurried through the house to the kitchen. She met him as he came in the door from the carport. "Did you talk to her parents?"

Her brother shrugged out of his coat and tossed it over the arm of her couch. "Yeah. They were in shock. Her mother was a wreck. Really sad."

"Did they know why Brenna was at Colgate tonight?"

"No. They thought she was studying. She had a test coming up. Hey, did you know that her mother is Tiffany Teniere?"

Parker's jaw dropped. Tiffany Teniere was a Christian star as big as Amy Grant. She'd been riding the Christian charts for over twenty years. "Why wouldn't Brenna tell me a thing like that?"

"You know how teenagers are about their parents."

"Yeah, but that's relevant. We're in the music business." She caught her breath when it hit her who Brenna's father was. Tiffany Teniere was married to Nathan Evans, who owned a couple of major labels. A star-maker, he had taken several unknown artists and catapulted them to fame. "Okay, now I'm really confused. Why would Brenna work for Colgate as an unpaid intern when she could have gotten all the experience she could ever want working in her father's record company?"

"Good question."

Parker frowned and tried to remember her first conversation with the girl. "When she called about applying for our internship, she said she was a Music Business major and just wanted a chance to learn."

"Maybe she just wanted to get to know the people who recorded there." Gibson went to her refrigerator and stared inside.

"Yeah, maybe. "

"Maybe her dad is one of those tycoons who makes his children come up through the ranks."

"Still, why wouldn't she mention it?"

"Probably thought it would be a distraction. Maybe she wanted you guys to know her for herself and not for her famous parents."

Yes, Parker supposed that made sense. "So, are they okay?"

He closed the refrigerator door without getting anything out. "They're in horrible shape. A doctor came while we were there and sedated her mother. Her father's grief was different, though."

"Different how?"

"He was angry. Really, really angry. Snapping at everyone. Shooting questions at me like he thought I'd killed her. We get that sometimes. People grieve differently."

Yes, Parker could only imagine how grief like that could twist and cut like barbed wire, making people strike back.

"Hey, can I use your printer?"

She didn't know why he even asked. Gibson had long ago made her house his home-away-from-home. He couldn't stand his room-mate, so half the time he slept on Parker's couch. "Sure, go ahead. What do you need it for?"

"I want to print out these pictures. Look at them enlarged."

"You don't have printers at the police station?"

"Yeah, but I don't want to go there to do this. Too much pres-sure. Besides, I need to talk to you. I need you to tell me everything you've ever known about Brenna, starting with the day you met her. Did she come to Colgate through Belmont's internship program?"

"No, she was a freshman, and that program's for upperclassmen. She didn't want credit hours — just experience. So she offered her-self as an unpaid intern. She didn't want anything in return. Hard to pass up free help, so I finally put her through to George."

The one-by-one-inch display on her printer ran through the pic-tures quickly, a tease of images of Brenna dead on the floor. Parker turned away.

Gibson ignored her and fumbled with the printer until it began printing. "I'm doing them in eight-by-tens," he said. "That way we can see the details better."

"I'm not sure I have enough ink for that." But she knew she did. She'd recently changed the cartridges. It had cost her whole honorarium for the youth group concert she'd done the week before last.

The printer began to hum. Parker looked back. As the pictures rolled out of the machine, she saw Brenna's legs over the fallen chair. She turned away again as Brenna's face came into view.

More headlights moved across her curtains. Another car door slammed. "Who's that?"

"Probably Rayzo. He wants to talk to you, too."

Kyle Rayzo was Gibson's partner. Parker had a feeling that the rough and brusque forty-year-old didn't much like her. She didn't know why. Maybe he just didn't relate well to women.

She opened the door as he started to knock. "Hi, Detective Rayzo. Nice to see you."

"You too," he said, not even meeting her eyes. The big man lumbered in, a poster child for high blood pressure and diabetes and all the side diseases that came from being overweight. He'd gained all this weight after being shot in the leg a year ago. The leg had healed, but the inactivity had puffed him up like the Pillsbury Doughboy.

Gibson pulled the pictures out of the printer. "I'm printing these out. Parker was just telling me about Brenna."

Rayzo went to the refrigerator as if it were his own. "Got anything to drink?"

"Sure," she said. "Some water and cranberry juice. A little bit of milk."

He grabbed the bottled water, drank it down, then headed to the tap for a refill.

Gibson took the pictures emerging one at a time from the printer and laid them out on the coffee table. Parker forced herself to go sit down on the couch. She scanned the photos that would have looked benign if she hadn't known that a dead girl lay just out of frame. How did one get comfortable when two detectives stood in her living room, poring over pictures of their crime scene?

"I've got some pictures here of her bedroom. You should see that house. It's like a palace or something. Parents are stinking rich."

Rayzo sat on the couch at the opposite end from Parker. Gibson was still adding pictures to the display on the table as they rolled out of the printer.

"You okay, Sis?"

"Yeah, fine."

"Keep talking. When Brenna started working there, did any friends show up? Phone calls? Weird incidents?"

She tried to think. "No. Her boyfriend, Chase, came by a time or two, just for a minute. She introduced me. He was nice. Mostly she was quiet and just worked hard. She picked things up really fast. We had her doing filing, vacuuming the studios, that kind of thing. After a couple of weeks I let her fill in for me during my lunch hour and stuff."

Gibson sat in the easy chair. "I want you to pick up each picture of your desk and study it one more time. Anything out of place? You know how you left it this afternoon, right?"

"I ... I don't want to see ..."

"Her body's not in the ones I'm showing you."

Parker blinked back the tears burning her eyes and forced herself to take the pages. She studied the pictures of her desk, her drawers, her tabletop.

The pictures were bigger and easier to see than they'd been in the two-by-four inch display on Gibson's camera. But she saw nothing out of place. She'd left her MacBook on, its screen saver flashing across the display in colorful strands of light. It was still doing that when Gibson took the pictures.

"That your laptop, is it?" Rayzo asked.

"Yes."

"Amazing nobody's snatched it."

"I don't usually leave it there, but tonight I had my hands full when I left. I decided to come back for it after the gig. Cat was there when I left, so I knew it was safe."

She stared at the photos of the contents of each of her drawers. Everything was as she'd left it. "I just can't see anything wrong. Brenna's stuff is there, but that's the only thing different."

She reached for the pictures of the studios, saw the messes left by musicians in the throes of production — guitars left on their racks, baseball caps and tossed coats, drink cans and shoes kicked off. The sessions lasted hours, and the bands usually made it their home for the duration. The police must have made them clear out and leave everything just as it was.

"Where were you at the time of the murder?" Rayzo asked.

Parker looked up. "At a concert at Savior Church. I didn't leave until Gibson called me to come to Colgate. I had to cut the concert short."

Rayzo made a note of it in his wilted notebook. "All the studios were full except one tonight," he said. "Your calendar said some dude was booked there, but your log book didn't show he'd checked in."

"Johnny Jackson," she said. "He couldn't get the musicians he needed, so he cancelled at the last minute."

"Any way he could have shown up, after all?"

"Not with a gun." Johnny Jackson was a sixty-year-old Christian country singer who would give his own life to lead someone to Christ. No way he'd usher them into heaven with a bullet. Then again, she really didn't know him that well. "He's a really nice guy. Besides, when he called he said he was having dinner out with his family. I'm sure that can be verified."

She hoped Rayzo wasn't taking her brother on a wild goose chase, hunting down good people and trying to make killers out of them.

Gibson went back to the printer and pulled the next dozen out. He looked so young, so over his head. He was twenty-eight, two years older than she, yet she *felt* older, and somehow responsible for him. What was he doing in Homicide, this man who never listened? How would he ever solve a murder?

She went through the rest of the pictures but had nothing to offer them. Finally, Rayzo got up.

"Where are you going?" Gibson asked.

"Home, to bed."

"But the case is still hot."

"That's what I got a young partner for. Do what you can. I'll call you in the morning."

Gibson followed him to the door. "What do you think I should do next?"

"Search the dumpsters in the area for a gun."

"In the middle of the night?" Parker asked.

"Like the man said, the case is still hot. I ain't crawlin' in no dumpsters. I've paid *my* dues." Rayzo ambled out toward his car.

Gibson looked a little pale. "Well, guess I'd better get on it." He took the stack of pictures and looked around for his keys. Eventually, he realized they were in his pocket. "I gotta go."

She suddenly felt the chill of vulnerability. She didn't want to be here alone. "Do you think you'll be back tonight?"

"Doubtful. I have a lot to do. You're not scared, are you?"

She didn't want him to know she was. She'd spent a lot of time proving to her family how independent she was. "Should I be?"

"Maybe. You need to load that gun I bought you."

She hated guns, and when he'd given it to her for her last birthday, she'd kept it in the box, refusing to put ammunition in it. In fact, he had forgotten to give her bullets — or rounds, or whatever they called them — so the gun was useless, just as she wanted it.

"Yeah, I still have it."

"Well, don't be afraid to use it if anything happens," he said. "You should get a dog."

"I don't usually need one. I have a cop who sleeps on my couch."

She watched as he left, then turned the light back off and went to her room, changed into some sweatpants and a T-shirt, and slipped under her covers. She would leave the lamp on in the living room.

She tried to sleep, but she dreamed of dead bodies, a brain-movie scored by a melody she'd never heard. When she woke, she was in a cold sweat. She went into the living room to see if Gibson had come in. The couch was empty.

As she often did when she woke in the night, she went into her music room and fired up her computer. Opening her recording software, she picked out the melody she'd heard in her dream. Slowly, she began to flesh it out with lyrics — a song about the fragility of life, the sudden ending of innocence, the shock of a life ripped away.

Though she attributed her gift of ideas and talent to God, she saw many of her songs through the eyes of a character named Lola, whom she'd created years before. No one knew about this alter-ego who lived out Parker's emotions. She never mentioned Lola in the songs, but her quiet friend came to her at night in fits of brilliance and urged her to write songs that Serene could record. Lola had experienced divorce and brutal breakups, the death of a child, the grief of a mother. She had been so happy that she wanted to dance, had praised God so intensely that she could almost fly. She'd been suicidal, brokenhearted, grief-stricken, and abandoned. She had commitment issues, control issues, anger issues, and she battled loneliness and passion. She'd been in love more times than Parker could count.

Lola was insecure yet confident, strong yet fainthearted, courageous yet unruly, and she always seemed to land on her feet. Lola provided Parker a way of holding her problems at bay so she could observe them from every angle.

Tonight Lola had been treading through Parker's dreams, and now the after-effect, the composing of a song that might be one of her best yet, gave Parker a little satisfaction. This one she would keep for herself, for her own CD. This one might actually put her on the map.

By the time Gibson came in, scruffy, starving, and dying for sleep, Parker found that she was exhausted as well. She tossed Gibson a pillow, saying, "I didn't sleep much at all. I can't believe I have to go to work in three hours."

"Not today," he said. "The building's sealed. Nobody's going there today."

Relieved, she went back to bed. She slept deeply for the next three hours.

And then she woke with a grief she hadn't expected and decided she needed to do something about it.

CHAPTER
SIX

Belmont University sat at the end of one of the major streets that made up Music Row. Belmont Mansion loomed in all its antebellum glory as the frontal piece of the campus on Wedgewood Avenue, along with a matching administration building with a circular drive. Parker passed those buildings where she'd studied Music Business. The school would have been out of her price range had her mother not been a professor in the English Department. That gave Parker free tuition and a great education. She turned onto the street that would take her to the dorms. The campus commons couldn't be seen from the street because the buildings were all turned inward, providing a perimeter for the campus.

Brenna, being a freshman, had most likely lived in one of two dorms — Wright or Maddox. Parker imagined that word of the murder had spread like wildfire among the girls, so she took her chances and went into Maddox Hall. She crossed the lobby to the front desk. A girl sat at a computer with her chin propped on her hands, her Facebook screen up. She looked up when Parker approached her.

"Can I help you?"

Parker leaned in and softened her voice. "Yes, I work at Colgate Studios."

The girl perked up. "Where Brenna was murdered."

"Yes," Parker said. "Did you know her?"

The girl swept her bangs behind her ears, but they fell back into her face. "I saw her sometimes, but I never really talked to her. I didn't have any classes with her. Do they know who did it yet?"

"Not yet. I'd really like to talk to some of her friends. Her roommate, maybe. Tell her how sorry I am."

"Yeah, sure. I'll call her."

"Thanks." Parker knew the roommate would have to come down to get her. Security prevented visitors from going up without a resident to escort them. She went to one of the couches in the lobby. A TV was blaring *America's Next Top Model*. A girl on a loveseat nearby was watching. Parker tried to focus on the search for the next poor girl to starve herself invisible, but her mind kept wandering back to Brenna's roommate. What would Parker say to the girl? Her stomach tumbled, and that sick feeling returned.

She heard the elevator open down the hall and looked in that direction. A girl with black spiked hair and a nose ring emerged. Mascara was smeared beneath her eyes, and her nose was red, as though she'd cried all night. She wore a bulky sweater with too-long sleeves that she bunched in her fists.

"Hi, are you the one from Colgate?" the girl asked as she approached Parker.

Parker introduced herself. "I worked with Brenna."

The girl glanced toward the desk. "Yeah, she told me on the phone. I'm Marta. Brenna told me about you. She really liked you. You're the songwriter, right?"

Parker was surprised that Brenna would have shared that about her. "Yeah, and also the receptionist. She was at my desk when ... when it happened."

Marta's face crumpled. "What was she *doing* there? She worked afternoons, not nights."

"I had the same question. Were you two good friends or just roommates?"

"We didn't even know each other when we came here last fall," Marta said, hugging herself. "But we became good friends. We were going to room together again next fall, in Hillsboro."

Hillsboro was one of the nicer campus apartments. Upperclassmen got first pick, but younger students participated in a lottery to determine who could live there. At least, that was how they'd done it when Parker went there. And since she couldn't afford Hillsboro, she'd worked as an RA and lived in the dorms.

"You want to come up? You might as well. Everybody else has."

"Yeah, if it's okay." They started to the elevator. "What do you mean, everybody else has?"

"I mean the cops. They were here, looking around. I thought they were gonna make me move out. It was like a crime scene. I sat out in the hall with the other girls on my floor, waiting for them to finish. They took a lot of her stuff. Her computer, her notebooks, her journal."

They reached a door with a dry erase board on the outside, with the names *Brenna* and *Marta* drawn in curvy block letters and colored in with hot pink. It was filled with messages left from other students.

> *Brenna, we'll miss you so much.*
> *Brenna, we had so much fun hanging out with you. I don't know what to do now.*
> *Brenna, my heart is breaking. I'm waiting for you to walk in and say it isn't true.*
> *Brenna, you're a bright angel in heaven right now.*

Marta looked past the messages and unlocked the door. Parker followed her in and looked around. "Wow, this is a blast from the past."

Marta closed the door and wiped her nose on a Kleenex wadded in her fist. "You went here?"

"Yeah. Graduated four years ago. Lived here the whole time." There were pictures of Brenna everywhere. Her bed, lofted to five feet off the ground, was unmade, and beneath it sat two desks, side by side.

"My brother's a homicide detective, probably one of the ones you spoke to last night. He'll do his best to find the person responsible."

"I hope so," Marta said. "We hung with some of the same people. I'm scared now. It could have been anybody."

Parker bent to study the picture on Brenna's nightstand of her with her famous parents. "Is Brenna an only child?"

"No, she has a brother. That's him, there."

Marta pointed toward a framed photo. Brenna's brother sat on some steps, elbows on his knees. He had shoulder-length brown hair and brooding eyes.

"Were they close?"

"Not particularly. They're half-brother and sister. Didn't grow up together."

Parker noticed another framed print — Brenna's boyfriend. "Chase, right? What's his last name?"

"McElraney. You should have seen him last night when he found out. It was awful. He was freaking out. He heard it on the news and put his fist through his wall. I went over there as soon as I heard. I thought he was about to kill himself."

"Where does he live?"

"Over in Bruin Hills."

Parker nodded. Those were the mid-level campus apartments. "Seen him this morning?"

"No. I hope he got some sleep."

"Do you know if they had been getting along?"

"Pretty much. They had their ups and downs. But he's a really nice guy, and he loves her a lot." Marta sat down on Brenna's desk chair. "I feel really guilty about this. She wouldn't have gone to Colgate to study if I hadn't been rehearsing my songs in here."

Parker remembered the sounds that had reverberated through the dorm when she was here. A drummer next door who'd practiced night and day. A roommate who was a vocal performance major, who'd sung every waking moment. A saxophone player across the hall. At ten o'clock, they were all supposed to quit rehearsing so people could sleep. But most students didn't have the luxury of waiting until ten o'clock to begin studying.

"I had to perform in vocal seminar today. So I've been rehearsing and rehearsing. I should have found another place to practice."

"Where was Chase?"

"He had a class last night. She said his roommate and his girlfriend were there, so Brenna had to find somewhere else."

"What was she studying for?"

"Music Theory."

"Tough class." Parker remembered it well. It was the class that so many freshmen flunked. As musically oriented as she was, Parker had barely squeaked by. "I'd like to go see Chase. Could you tell me his apartment number?"

"I'll take you there. I need to get out, and I was planning to go check on him." She checked the clock. "My parents are on their way here from Indiana. They're all freaked out, thinking somebody's killing students. But they won't be here for a while. Just let me brush my teeth."

While she waited, Parker scanned the other side of the room, looking for anything Gibson might have missed. Beneath Marta's loft bed was a futon. Parker looked beneath it and found some fallen popcorn and wadded paper that no one had retrieved. Glancing back at the bathroom, she picked up and unwadded the paper. It was nothing. Just some download instructions from a computer help screen. She tossed it into the empty waste basket, realizing that the cops had probably emptied it.

Brenna's bed had an apple-green comforter, with pink and purple pillows scattered across it. She didn't seem to have any Greek accessories. She must not have rushed, which wasn't uncommon among the music students at Belmont. Sororities and fraternities held little appeal for them. They'd rather be in bands.

She stepped onto the ladder to Brenna's bed to get a closer look. Brenna had an alarm clock that apparently shared the bed with her, along with a phone charger, her contact case, and a few other items. A small lamp was clipped to her headboard.

Parker remembered lofting her own bed like this her first semester. It seemed like a good idea at the time, but she wound up hating it. There was no way to have a table that high to put your stuff on. No one could sit on the bed without climbing up. You couldn't even slide out of bed to go to the bathroom in the middle of the night; you had to climb down the ladder, then back up. Second-semester freshmen rarely repeated the set-up.

She stepped back down and went to Brenna's desk, opened the top drawer. A bunch of pens, some paperclips, Post-it notes ... Gibson had probably taken anything of interest.

Parker closed the drawer quietly as she heard the water cut off. Marta came out of the bathroom, her face washed and hair spiked a little more intentionally. She grabbed her cell phone and a purse made of frayed denim. "Okay, I'm ready," she said. "Let's go see Chase."

CHAPTER SEVEN

Chase came to the door, his eyes swollen, his nose glassy. His apartment was dark, the shades drawn. "Parker," he said.

She'd only met him a couple of times and was surprised he remembered her name. She hugged him. "I'm so sorry for what's happened."

He seemed to be trying to fight his tears. Stepping back, he invited them into the filthy apartment, typical of a college male. He kicked away the laundry that had spilled out of the basket on the floor, and moved the not-yet-folded towels on the couch to give them room to sit.

At least he did his own laundry. That was something. Her brothers never had when they were in college. They'd always carted their dirty clothes home for their mother to wash.

Marta seemed at home in Chase's apartment, as if she'd been here many times before. She sat on the floor, leaning back against the wall. "Did you get any sleep last night?" Marta asked him.

He dropped into an easy chair, rubbing at his eyes. "No. Police were here for a couple hours. They searched the house. I think they thought I did it or something. But I would never hurt her. Ever."

Parker's gaze drifted around the room, and landed on the hole he'd punched in the wall. He saw her looking at it and showed her his swollen hand. "I punched through the wall last night when I heard. I was sitting here studying and the news was on. I heard it and . . . I just went nuts." His eyes were wet as he locked in on Parker. "They wouldn't tell me much. What happened? Did they shoot from their car or was someone at the window?"

"I don't know."

"Yes, you do. You work there."

"But I wasn't there when it happened."

He wouldn't give up. "The guy who found her. Are you sure he wasn't the one?"

She thought of the grandfatherly Ron Jasper, who'd probably gone into cardiac arrest at the sight of her body. "I'm sure. I've known him for years. He would never do something like that."

Chase's cell phone began to ring, and he picked it up and switched off the ringer without checking the caller ID. He set it back on the table. Parker glanced at the readout but couldn't read the name.

"So the others in the studios. They're always full. Anybody could have been there."

"But it wasn't anyone in the building. The bullets came through the window from outside, and no one came in afterward, or they'd have shown up on the security tape." She stopped, wondering if she'd said too much. She had to quit disclosing what her brother had told her.

Chase wasn't satisfied. "There must have been witnesses. Someone saw *something*."

"I don't know. Maybe someone did."

He stared her down as though she were hiding something. "Can't you ask your brother?"

"I did ask him. He can't tell me everything."

He got up and paced across the cheap carpet, rubbing the back of his neck with his good hand. His short black hair had a cowlick in the back. "She shouldn't have even been there. What was she doing? She could have studied anywhere."

Someone knocked on the door, and shoving his hands into his front pockets, he went to it, peered out through the peephole. Whoever it was didn't interest him, so he didn't answer.

His phone vibrated again, but he ignored that, too. Parker watched as it crawled slowly across the coffee table. "Did Brenna have any angry ex-boyfriends?" she asked.

She saw something pass across his face — almost a wince, so quick and so slight that she almost thought she imagined it. "I don't think so. But ... there were those phone calls."

Marta straightened from her slump. "What phone calls?"

"I don't know ... we'd be together and she'd get up and go into another room. I'd hear her fighting with someone. When I asked who it was she'd say it was her dad, but I didn't believe her. I thought it was some other guy."

The hair on Parker's neck began to rise. Now they were getting somewhere.

"She didn't have another guy," Marta said. "She was in love with you."

"Did you tell the police about those calls?" Parker asked.

"Sure. They badgered me into remembering every detail. Every bite we'd eaten together. Every word we'd said in the last two weeks. I told them everything I could think of."

"They'll get the phone records," Parker said. "They'll figure out who she was talking to."

"Are you sure? Because I've read about witnesses giving information to the police and they don't use it. She had millions of phone calls. How will they sort out which ones they were?"

She knew it was a tall order. "Did you give them times of the calls?"

He nodded. "I remembered the ones in the last couple of days."

"Good. I'll remind Gibson to follow up on that. But what makes you think she was lying about it being her dad?"

"Because why would she go into another room? Why would she not want me to hear? She was never shy about complaining about her parents."

No college kid was. "Have you talked to them?"

"Yeah, her dad called this morning. I've never heard him sound so ... weak. Had all these questions. Same ones the cops asked." He stared at the floor. His white face looked dry, aged, in the dimly lit apartment. "Don't you think it's odd that some girl who was paid to be working would give up her shift to an unpaid intern?"

"Not really. There's not a lot that has to be done at night." The responsibilities at the front desk were minimal at night. Cat probably had confidence that Brenna could handle it. How could she have known the danger that awaited? Like Parker, Cat was probably feeling a sick kind of relief that it hadn't been her.

Chase stopped mid-pace and turned back to her. "Don't you find that odd?"

"What?"

"That the woman ... Cat, was it? That she would leave like that. It's suspicious, don't you think? Like she was setting Brenna up."

"No. She's my friend. I know her — "

"Is everybody your friend? Do you know what they're thinking? What they're feeling? Do you know everything they do?"

She suddenly felt defensive. "Of course not."

"Then how do you know?"

Her face was hot, and she looked at Marta. The girl looked up at her, apology crinkling her forehead. "Chill, okay, Chase? She didn't do anything."

He swallowed, then stared at Parker as if certain that she had, indeed, done something. She drew in a long, shaky breath. Time to leave. She slid her sweaty palms down her thighs. "It's okay. I understand you're upset, Chase." Her throat was tight. "I don't blame you."

His voice was hoarse as he said, "I just ... want to know who did this." He rubbed his mouth with his swollen hand. "Just ... want them to feel the pain that she felt." He closed that swollen hand into a fist, baring his teeth as he winced with the pain. "Want them to bleed like she bled."

Though his words were violent, his desperate expression and the soft whisper of his voice framed them as grief rather than vengeance.

The phone vibrated again, crawling.

"I'd better go." Parker looked at Marta, saw that her face was wet. "Do you want me to take you back to your dorm?"

Marta looked up at Chase. "Want me to stay or go?"

He shrugged, unable to speak. Marta looked at Parker, her eyes suggesting that she feared leaving him alone. "I'll stay."

"Okay."

Parker wished there were something she could do to comfort Chase. "I'm really so very sorry."

He just stood there.

She opened the door to leave. Two weepy girls and another guy were climbing the stairs. She felt as if she should block their way to prevent them from bothering Chase — but who was she to decide who could see him? They pushed past her and went inside. She stood on the stairs, listening to the limpid sounds of loss, as they spoke to Chase. Finally, she descended the stairs and went back to her car. Wind swept across the parking lot, chilling her soul.

CHAPTER EIGHT

Gibson woke after a couple hours' sleep, showered, and drank the brew Parker's Mr. Coffee made at seven o'clock every morning. It was too weak for his taste, but it gave the punch he needed to wake up.

On the way to work, he thought of Tiffany Teniere and Nathan Evans, mourning their child. He hated the part of his job that forced him to plow through grief and get in the faces of people in shock.

How would he feel if someone he loved were suddenly gone? Parker could have been taken out of his life just last night; it could have as easily been her as Brenna. LesPaul, though he was sometimes a pain, would leave a gaping hole in Gibson's life. His mother's loss would devastate him. Even the death of his father, Pete, with all his alcoholic flaws, would wipe him out.

His parents had never recovered from their divorce, though it had happened a decade ago. When their dad left their mother for a younger woman who sang in his band, his mother had sunk into a deep depression that lasted about a month. Then she pulled herself out of it and poured her energy into getting her PhD in English. Pete's new marriage lasted all of six months. When he came back seeking a reunion with Lynn, she had only one demand — that he stop drinking.

That was the one demand he couldn't meet. So there they were, stuck in love and no longer married, good friends but not lovers, dependent on each other while living independently. What some called unforgiveness, Gibson and his siblings called tough love. His mother's one weapon for saving Pete from himself was depriving him of herself.

He got to the precinct and headed inside, straight for the coffee. He passed Rayzo's desk; his partner looked decidedly more calm and rested than Gibson felt.

"Hey, where you been?"

That chafed him. "Up all night searching garbage bins and interviewing witnesses," he snapped. "I got two hours' sleep. Where have *you* been?"

Rayzo didn't seem to think he owed him an answer. "You get the security tape?"

He poured some cream powder into his coffee, then dumped in three spoons of sugar. Then he pulled the disk out of his coat pocket and tossed it onto Rayzo's desk. "It doesn't show anybody coming in or out around the time of the shooting. Just shows Brenna sitting at the computer minding her own business, when the bullets came flying."

The phone rang on Rayzo's desk. "Rayzo here."

Gibson headed to his own desk. He heard Rayzo grunting into the phone, muttering something unintelligible. When he hung up, he called out, "Chief wants to see us. He wants us to bring everything we've got on the Colgate case."

Gibson set his coffee down. "What for?"

"Got me."

Rayzo grabbed the disk Gibson had just given him and the little notebook with all his notes from last night. "Grab those pictures you printed out and anything else you got."

Gibson just stared at him. "All of it? Every last thing?"

"You heard me."

Gibson scrambled to get all his stuff together. If he'd known he was going to have to make a presentation he wouldn't have taken the time to sleep. The chief tied Gibson's stomach in knots. He was impatient and brusque—like Rayzo, only with more power—and he hated explanations and excuses. Maybe he thought the case should have been solved on the spot, like the other three Gibson had worked on. But those had been easier. There had been witnesses and motives and trace evidence lying out for anyone to see. All they'd had to do was question people who knew the decedents, and they'd had those cases solved.

Didn't the chief know that this one was tougher? A drive-by shooting with no witnesses?

He gathered all his notes and pictures and followed Rayzo upstairs. Chief Sims wasn't ready to see them, so Rayzo took a seat on an old couch with creaky springs that looked like something the chief might have dug out of one of those dumpsters Gibson swam through last night. The chief had furnished the entire police headquarters with second-hand furniture, much of it from garage sales. The city council loved him for it.

Dog tired, Gibson kept standing anyway, wanting to appear energetic and on top of the situation. But fatigue sent toxins into his shoulders and neck, aching through the muscles of his back. Night before last he'd been awake all night because his roommate was having a screaming fight with his hysterical girlfriend. He'd had no idea then that he'd get so little sleep the next night, too.

Finally, the chief's door opened. Chief Sims was a short, skinny guy with facial hair that looked like peach fuzz, but he had a deep bass voice that made up for his small stature. A radio voice, Gibson thought. If police chiefing failed, he could always be a DJ.

"Get in here, guys," the chief boomed. "Let me see what you've got on the Brenna Evans murder." He went back around his desk and plopped into his chair. Something about Sims's huge chair intimidated Gibson, and those knots constricted more tightly around his stomach.

Rayzo laid out everything they had while Gibson sat like an idiot.

The chief leaned back in his chair, arms behind his head. "Look, guys, no need to beat around the bush. I'm taking you off the case."

"What?" Rayzo asked. "Why?"

"Because of you, James."

Gibson felt the blood draining from his face. He'd known it. The moment he'd passed the detective exam and been assigned to Homicide, he'd known it was just a matter of time before he botched something and ruined this chance.

"Conflict of interest," Sims said. "Your sister works at Colgate, James. I think you have a stake in this. Makes it hard to see things objectively."

Relief trickled through him. So it wasn't his performance. He hadn't done anything wrong.

At the same time, defensiveness crept in. "I understand your concerns, sir. But the fact that the victim was at my sister's desk makes me even more anxious to solve the crime. I also have an advantage — I know a lot of the people who were there."

Chief Sims propped his elbows on the desk, rested his face in his hands. "Yes, you work on the side as a studio musician, don't you?"

Gibson looked at Rayzo and swallowed, wondering if that would upset the chief. There was no policy against it, yet he knew the chief expected total devotion to his work. "Yes, sir," he said in a weak voice. "But not that much now that I'm in Homicide."

"Son, the fact that you know the people you're investigating might cause you to overlook a crucial piece of evidence."

Gibson wasn't going to give up so easily. The knots tightened, but he forced himself to fight for it. "Sir, my sister is a storehouse of knowledge about this case. I already know what it would take other detectives weeks to find out. The key players are my friends."

"One of those key players could be the killer. And so could your sister."

Gibson's swallowed. "My sister is not a killer. She wasn't even there. She was playing a concert in front of a roomful of teenagers."

"I don't care where she was. I'm taking you off the case." The chief jerked off his glasses. "End of discussion. Let me have your notes."

Rayzo, who probably didn't care whether he was assigned to this murder or the next one, finally straightened. "Chief, we did a lot of legwork last night. We've interviewed a lot of people, taken a lot of pictures. We were on the scene minutes after it happened."

"If you did your job properly, then Carter and Stone should be able to take it without missing a beat."

"Carter and Stone?" Rayzo said with distaste. "Not those lightweights, Chief. This is a tough case. I have the most experience. If anybody in this department can solve it, it's me — you know that."

The chief groaned. He rocked back in his chair and flipped through the pictures in the notebook. He read through the notes on the security tape, scanning everything quickly.

Gibson had heard that Sims was practically a genius. Never forgot anything, and speed-read five newspapers every morning. He watched the chief's eyes move across their evidence. Finally, he sat back and looked up at them. "You're right, this is a tough one." He closed the notebook and rubbed his eyes with his thumb and forefinger. "All right, tell you what. I'll give you some time to find this killer. But if it looks like your closeness to the principals is inhibiting the investigation or jeopardizing prosecution, then I'm putting on the brakes." He stacked everything back up, slid it across his desk.

Rayzo got up. "Thanks, Joe. You won't regret it."

"Make sure of that. And steer clear of the press. We'll let Fred do all the talking."

Fred was the public relations officer for the department. He'd been a news anchor before he was a cop. He knew how to tell the press nothing and make them feel like they had something.

"Considering who the girl's parents are, there'll be a lot of reporters trying to drag this out. No leaks, no gossip. Careful what you say, even to witnesses."

As they walked out of the office, Gibson let out a sigh of relief. "Thanks, Rayzo. I appreciate you going to bat for me."

"Not for you," Rayzo said. "I want this case because it's high profile. I'm lookin' to be a hero."

Gibson grinned. There was nothing Rayzo hated worse than television cameras.

"So now we do the grunt work," Rayzo said. "Call the phone company and get the records for Brenna's cell phone. Find out who she was talking to during the times her boyfriend said she was getting those secret calls. Find out *everybody* she talked to last night. Then go interview the friends you haven't already seen. See what they have to say about Brenna and her relationship with Chase McElraney. Or anybody else."

"What will you do?"

"I'm gonna check out the other businesses on Music Square East and see who was coming and going last night. Somebody might have seen something." He patted Gibson's aching shoulders. "Don't worry, kid. We'll catch this guy before you know it. I feel it in my bones."

CHAPTER NINE

On her way home, Parker drove by Colgate Studios to get a look at the building in daylight. The road was roped off and blocked. Three media vans were parked there. Crime-scene investigators came and went.

The windows had been boarded up, probably at George's initiative, since the studio contained so much expensive equipment that looters would love to get their hands on. The glass in the building was high-grade security glass, meant to keep thieves from smashing it out and breaking in. But it clearly wasn't bulletproof.

She drove past. Stopping would invite reporters who might recognize her now. In their hurry to report her death last night, they'd probably found her MySpace page and studied her picture. Just as quickly, they'd probably forgotten her name.

She drove around the block to a favorite Starbucks. The drive-thru had half a dozen cars, so she parked and went inside. She ordered her coffee, then sat down at one of the tables to wait, chin on her hand.

A man with stark, fake blue eyes looked at her as he fixed his coffee. Was he staring at her because of her recent celebrity? She decided to get up and wait for her coffee at the counter. The drive-thru traffic had slowed the baristas down considerably.

"Excuse me. Are you Parker James?" The man had a charming British accent.

She turned around. "Yes."

"I'm Nigel Hughes. I thought I recognized you." He was still stirring his coffee. "You're the songwriter who writes for Serene, aren't you?"

Since he didn't refer to her as the previously dead girl, her defenses lowered. "I am."

"Grand. So nice to meet you. I work for the *New York Times*. I must say, you're much more attractive in real life than in your publicity pictures."

She didn't know whether to be flattered or defensive. "*New York Times*?" Then he *was* interested in her because of the murder.

"I wonder if you might sit down with me for a bit."

"I'm sorry. I don't really have any comments about the murder."

The girl at the counter called out her order. Parker took it across the room, pried off the top, and grabbed a couple of sugars.

"I actually have all I need about the murder for now. I had the good fortune to get an interview with one of the detectives this morning."

She wondered if it had been Gibson.

"When I'm working on a story, I often like to work on side stories as well. Kill several birds with one stone, you see. And when I was looking at your website last night, I grew interested in your songwriting. I thought perhaps I could do a story on you, as well. It would be excellent publicity."

Parker looked at him more closely. She did need PR, and depending on when the article came out, it could do her a lot of good. "I could talk to you for a few minutes," she said, stirring her coffee. "But I really can't talk about the murder."

"Excellent," he said and waved his hand toward an empty table. She sat, took off her coat, and sipped her coffee. When he was seated, he looked into her eyes. His eye color didn't look quite as fake as it had before. Maybe he'd been born with stunning blue eyes.

"Were you close to the girl who was killed?"

She set her jaw. "I told you, I don't want to talk to you about the murder."

"Yes, you did. Very sorry. I simply wanted to offer my condolences. Terrible thing, it was."

Parker looked down at her coffee.

"So how long have you been writing for Serene?"

She brought her eyes back to him over her cup. "Since the beginning. We've known each other since we were kids."

"She's always recorded your songs, then?"

"No, she started out doing covers. You know, recording songs that other artists had made popular. But she decided she liked my songs better. She started recording them, and some of them became hits."

"Christian hits."

"At first. But 'Trying' hit the secular charts."

"Secular charts. Is that what you call *Billboard*'s rankings?"

She smiled. "I guess people outside of the Christian market don't call it that."

"You have an interesting way of looking at things, you Christians."

She smiled. "Can I take that to mean you're not a believer?"

"Oh, I wouldn't say that. I believe in many things. Just not Jesus Christ."

"Funny that you'd call him Christ if you don't believe."

"Why is that?"

"Because *Christ* means 'the Messiah.' If you think he's the Messiah, then why don't you believe?"

He grinned. "I didn't say I think he's the Messiah. I was merely calling him what you do."

She gave him a smile that she hoped was winsome. "I call him Lord."

He matched her smile. "As I said, you Christians have a funny way of looking at things." He shifted in his seat. "So tell me, how has Serene taken her fame?"

"Very well."

"Rumblings are that Jeff Standard is trying to sign her."

Boy, this guy had done his homework. How had he gone from reporting on the murder at Colgate to snooping into Serene's record deals?

"I can't talk about that."

"Then you confirm it?"

He was good. "No, I don't confirm it. I simply don't feel comfortable talking about Serene's career with a stranger."

"And here I thought we were friends."

"You Brits have a funny way of looking at things."

He laughed. "Touché. You're very clever, you are." He glanced toward the counter. "Can I buy you a scone? A muffin?"

She shook her head. "No, I'm good."

"You're not on one of those starvation kicks like so many of the girls in the entertainment field, are you?"

She wanted to ask him if she looked like she was starving, but she knew his answer might crush her ego. "No, I eat when I'm hungry."

"Unlike your friend, Serene."

She frowned. "What?"

"Oh, come now. I've seen the girl in concert. She's practically skeletal, she is. Anorexic, isn't she?"

That was enough. Parker pulled her coat back on and got to her feet. "I'm sorry, I have to go."

He looked wounded. "Did I offend you? I'm very, very sorry if I did."

"I have things to do." She took her coffee and started for the door.

"May I talk with you again? Dinner, perhaps? Not for an interview, but just two people enjoying one another's company? I don't know many people here, after all."

Was he asking her for a date? "No, I don't think so." She pushed through the door, leaving him standing there.

As she got into her car, she looked back. He was still at the glass, hands in pockets, watching her. Either he was captivated with her, or he saw her as a source of information.

She would Google him when she got home, and see who this Nigel Hughes really was.

Google confirmed that Nigel Hughes was a staff writer for the *New York Times*. Parker looked at some of his stories over the last few months. He seemed to be fascinated with celebrity scandals. His column appeared in the Entertainment Section.

He'd been one of the first reporters to dig up compromising photographs of one of the hottest Disney teen stars last year, and when Paris Hilton and Lindsey Lohan were suffering the indignities of their DUI scandals, he'd written about it extensively.

The fact that he was interested in Serene's eating habits worried her. Why would he even care about a star in the Christian arena? One song on the *Billboard* charts wasn't enough to warrant such scrutiny, was it?

If it was, maybe Serene could get her act together before he uncovered too much.

Resolving not to talk to him again, she went to the *American Idol* website to see if they'd posted any information yet about this summer's auditions. Two years in a row, she'd stood in line with thousands of people and hadn't made the cut, even past the producers who screened the singers. She had never even seen Randy, Paula, and Simon in person. She was neither bad enough to get on camera, nor good enough to go to Hollywood. It would have discouraged her, if not for all the fabulous singers she'd seen turned away.

Her latest idea for a shortcut to fame was through Christian music festivals that drew thousands to hear the most popular Christian bands play. Some of them had contests for new singer/songwriters. She'd submitted demos to all of them.

No word from any of them yet.

She was also considering other reality shows than *American*

Idol. She'd written off *Survivor* because she didn't think she could ever do anything athletic without losing an arm or a leg. So she'd applied to be on *Big Brother,* hoping that being trapped in a house with a bunch of others for six weeks might give her some notoriety. They always needed a guitar-playing Christian to mock, didn't they? She hadn't gotten a reply from her application or the video she'd sent in, though.

So lately, she'd thought of trying to get on a decorating show. She'd applied for *Trading Spaces* and convinced her mother to trade houses for a weekend to decorate a room in each other's home. If she could just have a camera crew here for the weekend, she would paint like a screaming banshee and sing her original songs while she did it. She'd get a decorated living room to boot.

But none of them had responded. There were fifteen emails from people who'd heard she was dead, then subsequently found out it was all a mistake. They gushed as though she'd been their best friend. Though she saw the irony in their emailing instead of calling, she was glad they hadn't added their voices to her growing voice mailbox.

Besides the condolence/praise emails, she had a dozen e-cards she didn't want to take the time to open. She wondered if DaySpring Cards had come up with a *So Glad You're Not Dead* card, but she didn't want to take the time to find out. She hit the delete key on each of them.

Familiar anxiety swirled up in her stomach, starting a bitter churning. She realized she hadn't eaten lunch, so she went to the pantry and pulled out a bag of caramel rice cakes she'd bought on one of her health kicks. The idea was that one or two would assuage her hunger when she was trying to lose a few pounds. Instead, she binged on them and ate the whole bag. Unlike Serene, she didn't purge. No, she preferred to let her calories go straight to her thighs.

Her father had aptly named her. Parker was the name of a guitar that was handcrafted and unusually shaped. What could be more fitting? Not her jeans, that was for sure.

Who did she think she was kidding? She wasn't skinny enough to be a star.

Now that she'd finished the bag of rice cakes and the email, she still felt uneasy. Sick, almost. Her anxiety was pushing toward panic. There was only one remedy for that.

She went to her bedroom and got her Bible, which sat on her nightstand, on top of her workbook on James. Crawling onto her unmade bed, she opened the Bible to where the ribbon marked her place and began to read. As always, when she got into God's Word, she felt sucked in, totally absorbed, fascinated by the living words that had such application to her life.

Time passed before she knew it, and just as she'd hoped, the churning in her stomach stopped. The anxiety level went down. She didn't feel like she was going to explode.

She heard a door and looked out the window. Gibson's car sat in the driveway. She slid off the bed and met him in the front room. "Did you solve the case?"

She'd never seen her brother look quite so tired. "Not yet."

"I saw Chase this morning, and Brenna's roommate Marta."

He opened the fridge and shot a look back at her. "You need to stay out of this, Parker. I'm serious. You don't have any business interrogating witnesses."

"I didn't. I just wanted to tell them how sorry I am."

He closed the refrigerator door. "You ought to go to the grocery store."

The nerve. "I wasn't planning for company. I have rice cakes." She grabbed the bag off her computer table. There were mostly only crumbs left, but she tossed it to him. "I'll make you a sandwich. I have bread and some ham."

"How old is it?"

She grunted. "Would I offer you something spoiled?"

"I don't know. I get you and Tom mixed up." Tom was his lazy, inconsiderate, womanizing roommate.

"Yeah, I see how that could happen."

So Gibson and his roommate hadn't yet reconciled. Which meant Gibson would be staying awhile.

"So how did Chase seem?" Gibson asked. "I have to go talk to him again today."

"Sad. Upset."

"Did you see his hand?"

"Yeah. He put it through the wall when he heard about her murder."

He shook his head. "Something's not right about that."

She got the ham out of the fridge and checked the expiration date, just to make sure. "What do you mean?"

"Well, her roommate said Brenna was studying at Colgate Studios last night because she — Marta — was rehearsing in her room."

"Right."

"And she said Brenna didn't go to Chase's because he was in class."

"Yeah," she said, looking for the mayonnaise in the refrigerator door shelf.

"He had that swollen hand when he went to class that night."

She found the jar and looked back at him. "Are you sure?"

He nodded. "And that was before the murder. I talked to his professor to verify his story, and he'd noticed it."

Parker sucked in a breath. "But why would he lie about that?"

"Why do you think?"

No, that couldn't be right. She didn't see murder in Chase's eyes. "Gibson, don't waste time pursuing him. He's a nice guy."

"Parker, most killers don't *act* like killers. He's also a liar. You should stay away from him."

That churning in her stomach began again. "Maybe there's some other explanation. Maybe it has nothing to do with the killing. Did he have gun powder residue on his hands?" Her eyes widened. "Or in his car. Did you check his car?"

Gibson rolled his eyes. "I should've never let you help me study for that exam."

"You didn't *let* me. You begged me."

"But I didn't expect you to memorize the textbook. Yes, we checked all those things. No gunpowder residue."

"Well, there you go."

"He still lied. That's suspicious. I'm telling you, something stinks."

She opened the mayo and sniffed the contents. She put the sandwich together on a plate, then shoved it across the counter. "He didn't kill her," she said. "He's so distraught he can't even think straight."

"I mean it, Parker. Whether you've exonerated the guy in your mind or not, don't go near him again. You're going to make me lose my job."

She thought of taking the sandwich back. "Me? How?"

"You're intimately involved in the case, which gives me a conflict of interest, according to the chief."

"So did he take it away from you?"

"No, he gave me a few days. He'll renege on that if he finds out my little sister is going around trying to solve the stupid case for me."

"I'm not trying to solve the case. You don't have to worry."

She saw the despondent slump of Gibson's shoulders as he dropped to the couch, his plate on his lap. He bit off a third of the sandwich, as if he hadn't eaten in days. Maybe she should make another one.

He picked up the remote and turned on the television. Fox News came on with a report about a tamed alligator somewhere in Florida. "Look at this," he said. "Maybe I'll get some pointers for dealing with my roommate."

"You should move out."

"Can't. The lease is in my name."

"Then lay down the law. Tell him his girlfriend can't live there. Make *him* move out. It's ridiculous that you can't sleep in your own place."

"You talk tough, Parker. But you'd do what I'm doing. I'll deal with it as soon as I have time to think. Subject closed."

"A little defensive, aren't we?" Parker muttered. "Okay, how about a new subject? Confidentially, Serene had some news last night. Apparently, Jeff Standard is considering buying out her contract. He wants to cross her over."

She had his attention now. "Are you kidding me? That's great!"

"Not so great," she said. "They want her to tone down all the songs on her new album."

"The songs you wrote."

"That's right."

"And what does 'tone down' mean?"

"Just what you think it means. Take out the Christianity and make them love songs. She's all gung ho about giving Standard what he wants, lock, stock, and barrel. The musical tracks won't have to be changed. Just the lyrics and vocals."

"No hill for a climber. "

She sighed. "I don't know. It goes against my grain to make my songs superficial." She went back to the kitchen to make him another sandwich. "I want them to make people think of God, not some fictitious boyfriend out there in *Billboard* land."

"Are you crazy? What good is it to have all these great songs if nobody ever gets to hear them? You could make so much money, Parker. Your songs are great. This could be your ticket."

She stared at him over the counter. "You think I should do it?"

"It's a no-brainer, Sis. Why *wouldn't* you do it? You could buy a bigger place."

"So I'd have a room for you?"

He ignored the barb. "You could travel. You've never even been out of the country."

"Yes, I have. I went to Mexico on a mission trip."

He got up and came back to the counter separating the kitchen from the living room. "Parker, you can't say no to this. It's not like you're going to hit it big performing. Songwriting is your gift."

That stung, and Parker tried not to wince.

"Take this time off and hammer out those lyrics. It'll open all sorts of doors for you. I can see the charts now. Serene won't just have the number-one spot. She'll have five or six spots. And people will hear about Parker James, the songwriter. You'll be in huge demand. Other artists will start begging you to write for them. Big ones. This is your chance, Parker. Do it."

She went back to making another sandwich.

"Parker, look at me," Gibson said.

She looked up grudgingly, aware that her face was burning.

"I know you're trying to honor God. That's important. But God doesn't only call us to do things in Christian arenas. I'm not a Christian cop. I'm a cop who's a Christian. I don't just solve Christian murders."

She grinned. "Okay, I get your point."

"I'm just saying, no matter how big and famous you get, you don't have to write anything you don't want to write. You can let your Christian influence shine in your life and all you do. And the songs you *perform* can still be Christian songs."

She swallowed the urge to ask him why she'd perform at all if, in his opinion, she wasn't going to hit it big. But she didn't like sounding bitter. "But if I give her the songs, the original lyrics that I thought God gave me will be dead. I can't perform them. Who would want them if Serene's made the other ones famous? Those songs started out as acts of worship, Gibson."

"Hey, would God open doors that he doesn't want you to go through?"

"Maybe it's not God opening the door."

"And maybe it is. Just consider it, okay? Don't slam the door shut without at least peeking through."

She didn't want to talk about it anymore, so to shut Gibson up, she promised to give it more thought.

But later, when her phone began to ring, she didn't even check the caller ID. She decided to ignore it. It was probably Serene, and she didn't have an answer for her yet.

CHAPTER TEN

The funeral was on Saturday at Two Rivers Baptist Church, which was packed to the gills with celebrity mourners. Parker and her brothers, who'd gotten there early, found a seat in the middle of the sanctuary. Gibson had come to get a look at the mourners, thinking the killer might show up, but LesPaul, her younger brother, came because he knew Brenna. LesPaul was one of Colgate's most in-demand studio musicians, as well as one of their house engineers.

LesPaul took the end of the row and spent most of his time on his feet, shaking hands of people he knew well from spending hours with them in the studios. Parker knew a lot of them, too, but she sat quietly, not feeling social at a time like this.

Her eyes scanned the heads in front of her, and she caught the eye of Nigel Hughes, the *New York Times* reporter. He played the role of mourner on the tenth row, but he sat sideways on his pew, taking inventory of the Christian leaders in attendance who might wind up as stars in his upcoming articles. He smiled and offered her a wave.

Parker waved back, then quickly looked away.

When the Evans family was led in, she saw Tiffany Teniere, looking as forlorn and heartbroken as a mother could look. She leaned on her husband, who seemed to support her weight as they slowly walked in. His face looked like granite, gray and hard, unreadable. Behind them trailed an entourage of family members — some who looked devastated, some who didn't. Funerals were funny things, she thought. People laughed and shook hands at them, told stories and laughed, and enjoyed seeing people they hadn't seen in years. But that buoyancy was never a barometer of their grief.

The funeral was long, complete with a compilation of videos of Brenna growing up. Had the parents chosen this, or had some well-meaning friend put it together? Whoever did it, Parker wondered whether it might shift the family's mourning into overdrive. It seemed to Parker that it might be horribly painful for the parents and friends, even if it was a precious tribute to the murdered girl.

As the pastor spoke, friends eulogized, and stars sang, she felt no celebration of Brenna's life — just a heavy, overwhelming sadness at the way she had died, a sense of despair that heaven couldn't assuage.

As the pastor wrapped up his sermon with Revelation 22, a piano riff began to play. Startled, she realized that it was her phone ringing. She'd forgotten to turn it off. She tried to find her phone at the bottom of her purse. Amid all the junk she kept there — hand lotion, a tape recorder, her appointment book, a small notebook to jot her song ideas in — the phone hid itself.

"Turn it off!" LesPaul whispered harshly.

The piano riff continued. Ta-dada-da-da, Ta-dada-da-da, like some burlesque orchestra backing up Gypsy Rose Lee. By the time she found the phone, people were turning to look. She couldn't remember how to switch the ringer off, so she answered and whispered, "I can't talk right now."

"You're not gonna believe this!" The voice was Serene's. "Jeff Standard is doing it for sure. This afternoon I'm signing the contract. He bought me out of my previous contracts and I'm on my way to my dreams coming true!"

"I'll call you back," Parker whispered.

"No, don't hang up. I need your commitment now. Will you rewrite the songs or not?"

On the phone, Serene's voice packed the punch that it had in a stadium full of twenty thousand people. Parker knew that everyone within several feet of her could hear the conversation. "Not now," she whispered through her teeth, and clicked the phone off.

Blood rushed to her face. Her skin was flaming. She hoped Brenna's family hadn't been distracted by the sound. Quickly she turned off the ringer and dropped the phone back into her purse.

When the service broke up, LesPaul leaned into Parker. "Way to go, Parks. Nice ringtone. Everyone liked it."

She glanced around. "Maybe nobody knows it's me."

"Oh, no, they don't know. Your answering the phone didn't tip anybody off."

She wanted to cry.

"It wasn't that bad, Sis," Gibson said as LesPaul scurried off to talk to more friends. "Forget it. Are you going to the graveside service?"

"Yeah, you want a ride?"

"No, I'd rather go in my own car, so I can hang back and watch."

Relieved, she headed out to her car and closed herself in. As she waited for the procession to line up, she called Serene back.

"You hung up on me!" her friend said as soon as she answered.

"I had to. I was at Brenna's funeral."

"Don't you know you're supposed to turn the ringer off?"

"When someone answers the phone and says, 'I can't talk right now,' you're not supposed to start talking."

"It's an emergency," Serene said. "This is the best thing that's ever happened to me. You're my best friend and I wanted to tell you. Are you in with me or not?"

Parker pulled into the procession of Hummers and Beamers, feeling insecure about her Bug. "I don't know. I need to call you back. I'm going to the gravesite."

"No, don't call me back. Tell me now! I need to get into the studio today."

"You can't. It's still sealed by the police."

"Then I'll find another place to record. Work with me here, Parker."

She felt cornered. "Did you try telling Jeff Standard why you went into Christian music in the first place? Did you remind him that it's those songs about Christ that have gotten you where you are?"

"Parker, let's not do this again."

"Okay, let's not." She hung up, then held the button until the phone powered down. Tossing it onto her passenger seat, she whispered, "That should take care of that."

Up ahead, the hearse turned into the graveyard. She slowed as car after car turned in behind it. She followed them down the winding road leading to a tent.

She got out of her car and stepped across the moist earth, walking between graves and headstones toward the tent. She paused as the pallbearers got the casket out of the hearse. Her gaze landed on Brenna's mother. Tiffany was beautiful in a nip-and-tuck, ageless kind of way. Parker wondered how old she was. Normally, Tiffany could hold her own with most of the twenty-something stars with whom she competed. But today her eyes looked glassy and distant, her swollen eyelids heavy. She'd been sedated after hearing about the murder, Gibson had said. She still looked sedated today.

"Hello again, Parker."

The whispered greeting turned Parker around. Nigel Hughes. "You know," she said, "it's in really bad taste to show up at a teenaged girl's funeral looking for dirt."

"Why do you suppose I'm looking for dirt?"

"Because that's what you do. See, I do my homework, too."

"Ah, you've read some of my articles."

"And I don't want to see any more." She started to walk away.

"Your brother's working on the case, isn't he?"

"I told you, I'm not talking to reporters about the murder."

"No, no, I quite understand. That's perfectly fine. But I would imagine it's occurred to them how strange it was that Nathan Evans's daughter would be working at Colgate Studios. Makes one a bit suspicious, doesn't it?"

Parker's attention was snagged. "Suspicious of what?"

"One would simply wonder if Brenna had been sent. You know, to spy."

She grunted. "You're amazing. You take a girl's death and try to manipulate it into one of your hack stories. I have nothing to say."

"Well, it isn't outside the realm of possibility, now, is it? Word is that your boss didn't even know Brenna was Nathan Evans's daughter. Why do you suppose she would have kept that little tidbit of information private?"

"Maybe she wanted to make it on her own."

He breathed a laugh. "Come now. Filing and reception work is hardly *making* it. Nothing against what you do, love, but it would hardly be a draw for a young woman wanting to climb the proverbial ladder, now would it?"

"She was eighteen. She probably didn't even know yet what she wanted to be when she grew up."

"Ah, you could be right. But Nathan Evans is known to be a ruthless man."

Parker walked away, not looking back. She was sure he'd find someone else to pump for information. And they would, no doubt, give it to him.

Already, the seeds he'd planted in her mind began to sprout. She tried to remember everything she knew about Evans Music. The record company was successful, though lately they'd been having problems. One of their unmarried big-ticket Christian artists, Alena Moore, had wound up pregnant, which put a hold on her career in Christian music. Now *there* was a story Nigel Hughes could sink his teeth into. Rumor was that Nathan Evans had taken a huge loss because of it. He'd had a ton of money invested in her promotion.

Now he couldn't get any of the Christian stores to carry her most recent album. And because the songs were so blatantly Christian, they wouldn't cross over to the secular airwaves.

Parker had prayed for the young artist whose mistake had changed the course of her life. She couldn't help respecting her for the courageous decision to have the baby. Life was more precious to Alena than her career, apparently.

But Nathan was left holding the bag for an aborted career.

What would he have to gain by sending his daughter to work for the studios? Brenna might have picked up rumors of secrets about competing record companies — but then, no official deals were made at Colgate. Then again, the lounge at Colgate was often filled with artists and their people hanging out, talking, sharing industry scuttlebutt. Parker supposed if one were looking for secrets, they might find some at Colgate.

At the tent, Parker looked around the crowd, wondering if the killer had come. Some of the faces she recognized, some she didn't. LesPaul could have named half of them.

As Brenna's family filed in to take the chairs under the tent, a man entered with them — about Parker's age, hands in his pockets under a tailored suit coat. He paused as he waited for the parents and grandparents to be seated. As he waited, his eyes met Parker's.

He was about five-ten, with long brown hair pulled back in a ponytail. He had the same jaw line and eyes as Nathan Evans.

He took a seat on the end of the front row. Her brother, Parker realized. Yes, he was the one in the picture in Brenna's dorm.

When the funeral was over, she waited on the outskirts of the crowd, hoping to get close enough to Brenna's parents to express her condolences. But it was impossible. There were too many people around them. She gave up and headed back to her car.

"Hey, Parker."

It was Brenna's boyfriend, Chase. He looked as bad as he had Thursday when she'd first met him. Gibson's warning about Chase's lies flashed through her mind. But a little compassion wouldn't hurt anything. She hugged him. "You okay?"

"No, not really." He seemed to stiffen under the sympathy. "My girl was murdered. I'll never be okay again." Tears welled in his eyes, and he rubbed his mouth. He made an effort to talk. "Her mom's begging us to get all her friends to come back to their house. Says having us around makes her feel better. There'll be food and stuff. You can come, if you want."

This would give her the chance to offer her condolences. Brenna's parents might have questions she could answer. Brenna had been killed at Parker's desk. She hadn't really been Brenna's friend, but she should have been. "Okay, I guess I can go for a little while."

As she got into her car, Gibson approached. "What did Chase say to you?" he asked in a low voice.

"He invited me to the Evans house."

"I asked you to stay away from him."

"It's not *his* house, it's theirs. I just want to tell them I'm sorry for their loss."

"Then take me with you. Maybe I'll learn something about the case."

Parker shook her head. "I can't do that! They know you're one of the detectives on the case. They didn't invite you." She looked back at the family as they got into a limousine. "Look, I won't stay long. I'll let you know if I find out anything."

He sighed. "All right, but be careful."

"Do you think the killer was here?"

He shrugged and looked back at Chase, walking to his car. "Could be."

"Anybody you're going to follow up on?"

"You go do your thing, and I'll do mine."

He didn't have to be snooty about it.

CHAPTER ELEVEN

The house that Brenna grew up in was among the mansions in Franklin, Tennessee, a well-to-do suburb of Nashville. Parker guessed it was about 10,000 square feet. She couldn't imagine how anyone could fill every room in a house this size. Feeling awkward, she pulled into the line of cars parked along the circular driveway and waited until she saw Marta and some of Brenna's friends getting out of their cars.

She slipped out and greeted Marta. "Chase asked me to come. Do you think it's all right?"

Marta looked rougher than she'd looked a couple of days ago when Parker had met her at the dorms. "You worked with her, so they'll want you here. They made us promise to come. Heads up, though — her mother's on something."

"On something? You mean, drugs?"

"Yeah. They must have tranquilized her for the funeral. Maybe that's what we all need."

Parker's heart swelled for the broken mother. She turned back down the driveway and saw Chase walking toward the door. His nose was red and shiny; he'd probably been crying on the way over. What a day for him ... for all who'd loved this girl.

Parker followed Marta up the front steps. Stepping into the opulent mansion, she had the sense of stepping into greatness.

Brenna's mother was sitting in a throne-like chair in the parlor. For over a decade, she had been the top-selling Christian star in the US. Now, pushing fifty, her numbers had dropped, but Parker suspected that at least some of the opulence in this home had come from her income. She had her sunglasses on, no doubt to hide the grief in her eyes. She spoke with a slur and fawned over Brenna's friends as they leaned down to hug her. She seemed a little like Anna Nicole Smith in the days following her son's death.

When it was Parker's turn to greet her, she took the woman's hand in both of hers — brimming with sweet, comforting words. Instead, she got stuck on whether to call her Mrs. Evans or Ms. Teniere. She decided to skip her name, altogether.

"I worked with Brenna at Colgate Studies," she said softly. "I thought she was a wonderful person." She mentally kicked herself; that sounded so lame. And frankly, Parker didn't know whether Brenna was a wonderful person or a terrible person. She'd never taken the time to find out. "I'm so sorry about what happened."

"What's your name, honey?" Tiffany's hoarse voice had a drag to it, as if her tongue moved seconds behind her thoughts.

"Oh, I'm sorry. I'm Parker James."

"Parker James," Tiffany slurred. "The songwriter."

Pride flooded her chest. "That's right."

"You wrote all the songs for Serene what's-her-name."

"Serene Stevens."

"That's right. You're a good writer, sweetie."

"Thank you. I worked with Brenna at Colgate."

"I remember her talking about you." She stroked the hair out of Parker's eyes. Parker wondered if Brenna really had spoken of her. She doubted it.

The crowd behind Parker pushed closer, so Parker stepped out of the way.

The thought that Tiffany Teniere knew who she was thrilled her.

Then she slapped herself down. What was she doing, thinking of herself at a time like this? This wasn't a networking opportunity.

She looked around for Marta and saw her on the back sun porch with Chase, among Brenna's friends. She felt out of place, but something about this situation compelled her to stay. People here knew things. They knew of Brenna's enemies, her fights, her admirers. Maybe the gossip would reveal some clues to lead them to the killer. She stepped out onto the porch.

Across the pool stood a gazebo. Nathan Evans sat there with some record executives that Parker recognized but couldn't name. Nathan didn't seem to be grieving the same way as his wife. Instead, he looked angry. His lips were tight and his teeth bared as he bit out words. She wished she could hear the conversation.

After a few minutes, Tiffany came out to the sun porch. "Would any of you like to see Brenna's room?" She took Chase's arm. "Chase, sweetie, let me lean on you and I'll give you all a tour. I want you to see what a special and talented person my baby girl is ... was." As she corrected herself, Tiffany swayed. Parker wondered if she was about to faint.

"You sure you're up to this?" Chase asked her.

Tiffany seemed to rally. "Of course." Her voice was weak, nothing like the sound on her CDs. "I need to get away from all the well-wishers who didn't even know her. Wouldn't know her if she spat in their faces. Don't even know why they're here, except to see and be seen. Blood-sucking leeches."

Parker felt a rush of guilt, but Tiffany reached out a hand to her. "Come on, kids, let's go upstairs."

Feeling like a fraud, Parker took her hand and let Tiffany lead her up the grand staircase, down the wide hallway floored with rich mahogany.

They went past several beautifully decorated bedrooms and a big study with Brenna's portrait on the wall. Parker wanted to pause at each room and see how the upper class lived, but Tiffany kept walking.

Finally, they stepped into Brenna's bedroom suite. Why would the girl have chosen to live in a cramped dorm on campus when she had a home like this? The room had the look of a penthouse in a five-star hotel. Parker was afraid to touch the furniture.

Tiffany went to Brenna's bed and sat down. She grabbed a satin pillow and stroked it gently. Chase lost it — he covered his face and leaned against the wall. Marta and some of the other girls surrounded him, hugging him, trying to comfort him. Feeling like an intruder, Parker backed into the hallway.

She should leave, right now. She had no business here.

She heard footsteps on the stairs and saw Nathan Evans coming up with the three men she'd seen outside. Two of them she knew to be promoters. The third one was the guy with the ponytail, the one she had guessed to be Brenna's brother. His eyes met hers again, calm and familiar as if he knew her, as they went into the study and closed the door.

Quietly, she headed back to the staircase. As she passed the study, she heard angry voices and paused. "This didn't just happen by accident," she heard someone say. "This was deliberate and it's aimed at me."

"Let's not get carried away," someone returned. "It could have been a case of mistaken identify."

"You don't gun *my* daughter down by accident. It wasn't a mistake."

The voices grew more muffled and she stepped closer. She couldn't hear the words anymore, but the heated exchange sounded angry, bitter.

Maybe she should stay, after all. She might hear more. But she couldn't lurk outside this door. She went back to Brenna's room and, taking a deep breath, stepped back inside. Tiffany sat on the bed, leaning back against Brenna's ornate headboard, her vacant eyes locked on another portrait on Brenna's dresser.

"I told him," she muttered. "He has so many enemies. They finally got even."

Parker's heart slammed through her chest. She waited for someone closer to the family to ask what she meant, but no one did. So *she* did. "Enemies? What enemies?"

Tiffany looked at her as though seeing her for the first time. "My husband's enemies. She was his little girl. The thing that would hurt him most."

Parker had the strangest feeling that the identity of Brenna's killer might roll right off Tiffany's tongue. "You sound like you know who did it."

Tiffany seemed to snap out of it then. "Who knows? Dozens of people over all these years ..."

"But ... was there someone recently? Someone who made threats?"

"Not outright. Not that I know of." Tiffany's eyes fixed on some distant, unseen memory. "I don't feel well. I have to go lie down."

Parker swallowed, wishing she could get more out of her. "But if you could think of a name to give the police, they could arrest him."

Tiffany got off of the bed and locked into Parker's gaze. "It could have been anyone. It could even have been you."

All eyes turned to her, inquisitive, accusing.

Horrified, Parker brought her hand to her chest. "It wasn't," she whispered. "You don't think I — "

"Of course not, sweetie." Tiffany touched Parker's face. "Thank you for coming. Give my apologies." Then she wandered down the hall and vanished into another room.

Brenna's friends were quiet as they went back downstairs. Parker didn't have the stomach for any more snooping. As the others headed back to the sunroom, Parker stepped out the front door, glad for fresh air. She hurried out to her car and pulled out of the line of parked cars. Trembling, she powered on her cell phone and dialed Gibson's number.

He was quick to answer. "Hey, Sis. Whatcha got?"

"I was just at the Evanses' house," she said, "and I heard this weird conversation. Her father was talking to these guys. Promoters, I think. Nathan told them that he didn't think Brenna's death was random, that someone killed her purposely because of him."

Gibson was quiet for a moment. "What else did you hear?"

She related her conversation with Tiffany.

"I don't like this," Gibson said. "That she suggested the murderer could've been you. Brenna's friends will be talking. That'll get all over town."

"She didn't mean anything by it."

"Doesn't matter. It'll take on a life of its own."

"Well, should I be concerned? Is someone going to show up and handcuff me?"

"No. You have an alibi and no motive . . . and a brother working on the case. But Parker, you've *got* to stay away from the investigation. Don't go near those people anymore." He paused, clearly waiting for her to agree. "Parker, do you hear me?"

"Yes, I hear you."

"This is not sister-brother stuff, Parker. This is police business. Your getting more involved could cost me the case, and maybe even my job. And worse, it could enable the killer to get away with it. You got that?"

"Yes, I've got it. Well, one good thing. If Tiffany and Nathan are right, the killer didn't intend to kill me. I'll feel safer."

"Good," he said. "So go home and work on your songs. And call Serene. She's been calling everybody in the family, trying to reach you. She has good news. She's about to hit the big time."

Good news was relative. But Parker would have to talk to Serene. It wasn't fair to put her friend off any longer.

CHAPTER TWELVE

Serene's "Double Minds" photo shoot took place the next day at the Parthenon in Centennial Park, close to Parker's house. It was a popular park where people jogged or walked their dogs, where nearby college students studied on blankets on the grass. The building was modeled after the Greek original in Athens, and it was a common place for Nashville stars to be photographed.

Parker found the photo crew on the front steps. The location was clichéd, if you asked her. She'd suggested to Serene that she try someplace different, but Serene was in a hurry to get the cover of her album done. Sometimes Parker wondered if she was the only creative person on Serene's team.

She strolled toward them, her fake Uggs squishing in the damp earth. A small crowd had formed a perimeter around Serene as she posed with wind blowing her long blonde hair — courtesy of a couple of fans provided by the photographer. Her band members stood off to the side, unshaven and artistically disheveled. Daniel Walker, the youth minister she'd been playing for the night of Brenna's murder, was clean-shaven, but someone had moussed and tousled his hair, as if that would complete his transition from minister to guitarist. They should have left him alone, she thought. His look needed no help.

Serene's manager stood behind the photographer, checking every picture digitally as it was made. Parker swept her hair behind her ears and stood back with the spectators. She met Daniel's eyes, and he winked at her. She smiled, maybe for the first time in days.

She remembered what he'd told the youth group about her, that she had left her concert early to keep from getting the glory and applause. He had a picture of her in his mind that wasn't quite accurate, but somehow, she wanted to live up to it.

The photographer finished with the band, and they came down the steps, leaving Serene for her solo shots. Parker knew it would be Serene's face that shone on the cover. The shots of the band would be reduced to a thumbnail shot on the liner notes. Still, she was glad Daniel would get some credit. His youth group would love it.

Daniel came toward her. "Hey, Parker." He hugged her. "Are you okay? I've been praying for you."

That warmth flushed through her again. "Yeah, it's been a rough few days."

The other band members mingled with the crowd, but Daniel took her hand and pulled her closer to the camera crew and away from the spectators.

"You did great the other night," he said. "I've been wanting to tell you."

"Thanks. Sorry I left you holding the bag."

"No, I love how you did that."

Guilt surged through her again. "Daniel, about the reason I left —"

Serene called out to her then. "Parker, I'm so glad you're here! We're almost finished. Don't go away!"

"I won't," she called back. She turned back to Daniel, saw him checking his watch.

"Wow, it's late. I have to get back to the church. We have a staff meeting."

Parker admired Daniel's devotion to his church. His music was a side business, something that supplemented his income while he went about the work of God. He was also a ripping guitar player, and Serene was lucky to have him.

Her explanation about the other night could wait. He packed his guitar. "So are you going to rewrite the songs so we can get back in the studio?" he asked.

Parker glanced back at Serene. "We're talking about it today."

He zipped the case and slung it on his back. "I understand your hesitation, but you don't want anybody else butchering up your songs, do you? You let these guys get hold of them, they'll sound third grade. Besides, I have a feeling Serene's about to make you an offer you can't refuse."

Parker's eyebrows came up. "Oh, yeah? What?"

"I can't say. I'm just the hired help."

The photographer finally shouted out, "That's a wrap!" Serene bounced down the steps to examine the digital images. "Parker, come see. Do I look too washed out? Did the camera make me look fat?"

Parker said good-bye to Daniel and watched as the shots came and went, Serene banishing some of them to the computer trash bin. To Parker, they were all good. Serene was a natural. But you couldn't put *Parker* on the steps of the Parthenon and make her look like a star. Her shoulder-length red hair was too short to blow in just that way, and she'd look ridiculous if she wore the costumy, flowing dress that Serene had on. Serene's star quality shone in every picture. She supposed that was why her friend was famous. That ... and because she could sing. Boy, could she sing. Serene's voice was what had pulled her from life's ghetto. It was her currency, her hope. Parker had recognized that when Serene was only thirteen.

Satisfied with the shots, Serene turned back to Parker. "We're going to Fido to get a bite. We'll meet you over there."

Parker stood there a moment as Serene signed autographs, then she turned and squished back to her car. As she was getting in, her cell phone rang. She glanced at the readout. It was George Colgate, her boss.

She clicked the phone on. "Don't tell me we're opening today."

"No, the building's still sealed. I need your help. We've got to shuffle around these session times. We can't have people immigrating to other studios. Can you get your brother to tell you how long before we can get back in? I'm losing tons of money every day that we're closed. And see if he'll give you your appointment book."

"I think he's logged it as evidence. He's even got my laptop, because it was on my desk."

"Come *on*! What are we gonna do? If we can't open, we at least need our schedule so we can move things around. Use your influence, Parker."

"I'll ask him if he can at least give me a copy. But even if he doesn't, I can call some of the labels this afternoon and try to shuffle things around. Since we can't make up the days we missed, maybe we could farm some of the groups out to other studios."

"Yeah, and take a huge loss. I'd rather just encourage them to record when the studios are available — like early morning hours."

Mornings weren't popular with vocalists, because their voices weren't at peak performance level. Most musicians preferred to record in the afternoons and evenings, and some would work all night.

"The hours from, say, five a.m. to noon would be open," Parker said, "if we could get anyone to come then. It won't be easy, but mixing and editing could be done then."

"It doesn't pay to have a girl murdered in your lobby. Why did we hire Nathan Evans's daughter anyway, for Pete's sake?"

"You hired her, George. And remember, she worked for free. She was a nice girl and a good worker."

"Just goes to show you, you ought to check people out, even interns. Are you sure they weren't after me? Or you?"

"Nobody's sure of anything yet, but I don't think so."

"I've decided to hire an off-duty cop for security."

"Great idea," she said. "It'll make me feel a lot better."

"Then it's done," he said. "I don't want any more shootouts at the OK Corral."

As Parker drove home, she wondered if her own death would have been such an inconvenience to the people who knew her.

CHAPTER THIRTEEN

Fido was a trendy little café on 21st Avenue, where Vandies — what the locals called the Vanderbilt students — worked at their computers as if they kept office hours there. Occasionally, someone with marginal fame would come into the place and start an acoustic jam session in the corner — creating a flurry of excitement. Parker noticed that same charge in the air as Serene pranced in — still in the dress in which she'd been photographed — and took a table near the window where passersby could get a glimpse.

Because she wasn't famous and had no excuse *not* to stand in line, Parker waited at the counter for over ten minutes to order coffee and muffins for everyone in the group. She paid for it even though she couldn't afford it, hoping that someone at the table would reimburse her. But that wasn't how it usually worked.

Carefully, she carried the coffee to the table on its tray. Serene had saved a seat for her, so she slipped into the booth beside her.

"So Jeff Standard is coming to see me tomorrow, Parker," Serene said as she took her coffee off the tray. "And you're not going to believe this. He didn't just buy out my contract. He's buying the whole label."

Parker shot her a look. "NT Records is a Christian label. All their artists are evangelicals. Why would he do that if he wants to ditch Christ?"

"He doesn't want to ditch Christ," Butch said, unwrapping a Tootsie Pop. "He's allowing all the other artists to keep recording and producing what they've always done. But he wants to take a different approach with Serene."

Parker looked at Serene. She had no doubt that her friend was a Christian. The two of them had been fourteen when they'd answered an altar call at a Dawson McAllister concert. If not for that, Serene might have committed suicide before she'd even been old enough to date. Her faith had sustained her for years and had provided a vehicle for her gift of song. "Serene, are you sure this is all okay with you? Spiritually, I mean?"

"I'm not going to abandon my faith now," Serene said, "but don't you think I can reach more people if I sell more records? I mean, think about it. Right now I'm playing to crowds of two to five thousand people. If Jeff keeps his promise to get us into bigger arenas, I could be playing for ten, fifteen, twenty thousand people at a pop."

"Twenty thousand?" Parker asked. "Isn't that a little high?"

"Maybe right now," Serene said. "But once he promotes me and gets me secular radio airplay, the sky is the limit. All I have to do is take his advice."

"Advice to ditch Christ," Parker repeated.

"Would you stop saying that?"

Parker sighed. "What's different about you if you conform to what everybody else is doing?"

"My *voice* is different," Serene said. "And I don't live my life the way everyone else does. They would see that I'm not like the brat pack, getting high every night. That's not my thing. I would let them know that Christianity works."

"But you already have crossed over to the *Billboard* pop charts. You were number one last month, *with* a Christ message."

"That was one time. People think it was a fluke."

"It was enough to get Jeff Standard's attention."

"Yeah, it was, and we've got to take advantage of the opportunity. Look, once I get going, I can do whatever I want. He knows I'm going to bring my Christian fan base with me, but if I can get a whole bunch of new people to like my songs — "

They were *her* songs, Parker thought. *She* had written them. They had *her* soul, *her* heart. She wasn't fond of being a surrogate mother.

Butch took out his Tootsie Pop and pointed with it. "Parker, I've been thinking about your career, and the reason you can't get a record deal."

Now there was a topic she'd rather not discuss. She crossed her hands in front of her face, wishing for an escape.

"The reason is that you haven't yet proven national demand for your product."

"How can I prove national demand without a record contract?"

A slow grin came to his lips, and he looked at Serene across the table. "Tell her, Serene."

Serene swallowed. "Honey, what you've got to do is build up a national fan base. You've got to establish some name recognition."

"Like that's ever going to happen," Parker said.

"It *can* happen. We've got a plan."

Parker braced herself. Serene's plans usually required a lot of effort from Parker. "I'm listening."

"Jeff has already booked some huge venues for our upcoming tour, besides the usual venues — the bigger churches and small coliseums we already had booked across the south. If you could piggyback off my tour, people would begin to recognize your name."

Parker wasn't following. "What do you mean by 'piggyback'?"

Serene leaned close and fixed her eyes on hers. "Parker, if you'll rewrite these songs for me, and do it quick so we can record the vocals and still get the record out on time, I'll let you do three of your own songs during my costume change on the tour."

Parker almost choked on her coffee. "You mean I could perform? On stage?"

"Yes." Serene's eyes were dancing. "We'd have a special segment of my concert, where I'd introduce you as my friend and songwriter. Your band could step in while mine takes a break. Three songs, then I come back in a different fabulous outfit, and take over again. The crowd will go wild, and you'll sell a zillion CDs."

"But I don't even have a CD ready to sell."

"You have time to get one done. You could press enough to sell on the tour."

Parker's eyes narrowed. "And you think Jeff Standard would go for that?"

"I talked to him about it yesterday. He had no problem with it. He said it was a lot more interesting than instrumental or video while I change."

"Well, what if he doesn't like me?"

"What's not to like?" Serene asked.

Parker couldn't believe she would be so naïve. "Well, my Christian message, for one thing. If he wants the Christianity taken out of *your* songs, he sure won't like mine."

"He wants it taken out of my new album. But he's smart enough to realize that the people coming to my shows now are Christians. He's not asking me to go back and redo my whole backlist. My audience comes for my Christian hits, so of course I'll be singing them. He's just planning to put me in bigger venues, hoping that the cross-over songs will draw a bigger crowd with new fans. I want to do this for you, Parker, because I think people should be introduced to your talent. You helped jump-start my career with your songs, and I want to return the favor."

Parker felt the warmth of those words, but she knew they were empty if she couldn't deliver. Serene had a voice that could pack stadiums. Parker didn't.

"Do you think I could pull it off?"

"Parker, you have a great voice, and a really unique sound. I wouldn't chance it if I didn't think so."

"Neither would I," Butch interjected.

Parker couldn't believe the producer would even consider this. "Really, Butch?"

"I do. What's more, Jeff Standard does."

She almost choked. "Are you serious?"

"We played him a demo tape of your song 'Inscribed,' and he liked it. He really appreciates your sound, and he said having you sing three songs to break up the concert was clever."

Parker stared at her friend. "Why didn't you tell me this earlier?"

"It just happened. I'm telling you now. You only have a few songs left to record, don't you?"

"Yes, but I don't know when I can get a studio again."

"Can you get it ready in time or not?" Butch asked. "We've been working on the tour for a year. It's only three months away. You could do it without a CD to sell, but if I were you, I wouldn't want to miss the opportunity."

"We're going to be busting our bustles as it is to get *my* album out," Serene said. "You don't need as much of a print run. Just enough that you can sell them on the tour yourself. I know it's a backward way to get a record deal, but when the labels hear that you're a part of my show and that your CDs are selling like crazy, somebody is going to want to sign you."

A thrill at the possibility rose up inside her. "But how will I pay for the tour? I'd have to pay a band. People aren't going to do this for free. They can't just leave their jobs and hit the road."

Serene grunted. "Parker, you can work it out! This is your big break. Don't you understand?"

It was almost too good to be true. Parker gave her a long look. "Are you sure you're not just promising me the world so I'll rewrite the songs?"

"No way, Parker," Serene said. "We're going to keep our promises. I want to take you with me. You deserve it. You're the one who makes the magic."

God was who made the magic, Parker thought. He was the one who woke her up in the middle of the night with song ideas. He was the one who put Lola in her head. But maybe it was all part of his grand plan. Maybe he really did want to exalt Serene this way so that she could influence people by her example. Was it possible that quieting down her message would give her a bigger field of influence? Could it really work that way?

She saw Serene's glance at the muffin Parker had bought her. She licked her lips, then forced her eyes away. She wasn't going to eat it.

So much for that, Parker thought. She wondered how Serene's anorexia would play if she got more famous. Would the press learn of it — or guess at it — and use it to mock her faith? Or was it such common problem that no one would notice?

Hardly, since a *New York Times* reporter was onto it.

"Okay, Parker, I need an answer," Serene said. "Come on, girl. Tell us what you're thinking."

The opportunity to play in Serene's venues made Parker's stomach flutter. If that could really happen, her dreams could come true. She wouldn't need *American Idol* or any cheesy reality show.

She'd have a ton to do between now and then. The thought of clearing all those hurdles almost shut her down. But she could do it. Her family could help.

A slow smile spread across her face. "All right, I'll do it."

Butch slapped the table. "Can you have the songs ready by tomorrow?"

"I'll try. It's not like flipping a switch. Not if they're good."

They seemed to understand that, but as Parker walked out to her car, she knew she'd been a little disingenuous. Though it sometimes happened that God gave her an idea that "flipped" her switch, she never waited for a muse to strike or for any special revelation to fall over her. She was a storyteller who wrote for a living.

She went home and sat in her backyard, where she often got ideas. She'd decorated it after watching HGTV do one just like it. She'd done an excellent job, if she did say so herself. It looked like an English garden with a sweet little swing and a hammock, and the smell of jasmine and rose vines climbing over the fence.

She heard the sound of children's laughter. Her next-door neighbor's little boy screamed over the fence. She saw his head bouncing up, blond hair flying as he plummeted down to his trampoline. Some people liked living out in the country with lots of land, but Parker liked neighborhoods. She liked knowing people were close by, and she liked the sounds and smells of families cooking out or chasing their dogs. Even though she didn't know most of her neighbors, it was good to know that if someone saw her house in flames, they'd care. Or if they saw some crazy killer stalking her house, they'd call the police. Even living alone — for the most part — she felt a part of things in this neighborhood.

On her patio table, she spread out the song sheets to "Double Minds," her favorite of the songs Serene had chosen for this album. Butch had scratched through the "offensive" lines that she needed to change. Without those lines, it sounded to Parker like a love song. In fact, that was what it had been. A love song to Christ.

Her own father considered her talents wasted on her Creator, since he wasn't big on faith. Pete James was a wannabe rock star. But the music business had almost done him in. For years they had tried to get him to stop drinking, and he'd made a valiant effort — for short periods. He paid lip service to Christianity, but in her heart, Parker couldn't believe that he really understood what had been done for him on the cross. Christ had died to set him free, but her father was still in bondage. He was a double-minded man — professing one thing while his life showed something vastly different.

She looked down at the songs, sick that she had to rewrite the lyrics she'd been so happy with. After she did, they'd be like all the other songs that played on the radio every day — songs that had no eternal value, songs that people hummed for a few days, or maybe a month, and then forgot.

The phone inside rang, so she went back inside and reached for it. "Hello?"

There was a long pause, then a man's low voice. "Her death was about you, Parker."

Parker caught her breath. "What? Who is this?"

"It was about you," the voice said again. "But don't worry. I'm protecting you."

The phone clicked off, the dial tone humming in her ear. She dropped it as fire flashed in her cheeks. Her heart hammered as she forced herself to pick it up again. Shaking, she dialed Gibson's cell number. As she waited for it to ring, she hurried to every door and window, making sure they were locked.

Gibson's voicemail clicked on. "You've reached Detective Gibson James of the Nashville Police Department ..."

She waited, jittering, as the greeting finished. When it beeped, she almost yelled her message. "Gibson, some guy who didn't give his name just called me and told me that Brenna's murder was about me. I'm scared. Please call me back."

She wondered if Gibson could trace the call. What had the man said again? That Brenna's death was about Parker. He'd said it twice, and then he'd said he was protecting her. What did that mean? Was someone trying to kill her, after all?

She ran back to her bedroom, grabbed a duffel bag, and began packing it. She was getting out of here, fast. There was no way she was going to stay here another night alone, even if Gibson wound up on her couch. No, she would go home and stay with her mother.

She grabbed the music and ran out, locking the door behind her. She threw it all into the backseat. As she backed her car out of the driveway, she looked up and down the street, wondering if someone was watching her, planning to shoot her through the car window.

She drove way too fast as she made her way through town to her mother's house, praying that her mom would be home so she wouldn't be alone.

CHAPTER FOURTEEN

Parker's mother lived in a sprawling ranch-style house on fifteen acres, not the kind of place you would just happen upon. Driving up the driveway, Parker felt a sense of security, as though no killer could find her here. She'd checked her rearview mirror all the way, looking for any sign that someone had followed her down the maze of roads that led to her childhood home. But she'd seen no one.

Still, the location of her mother's home wasn't a secret in Nashville. With so many family members in the music business — her brother LesPaul working as a musician and recording engineer, her father a guitar player who had once garnered some respect, and her brother Gibson, the cop, working part-time as a studio musician — almost anyone could have known the address. Besides, Lynn had weekly Bible studies that filled her house with gossiping young women.

The thought that someone could find her here dropped like lead in her mind.

Her death was about you. The words rang through her head and made her heart race as she turned her car off near her mother's house and rushed in through the open garage.

She burst inside. "Mom?"

"Back here, honey!" her mother called. "Grading papers."

Parker locked the door and bolted it. "Mom, you shouldn't leave the door unlocked like that — "

Her mother came into the kitchen, wearing a pair of jeans and a T-shirt that said, *Fifty is the New Thirty.* "Everything all right?"

"The garage," Parker cried, pressing the button to close it. "You can't leave it open like that. Anything could happen."

Her mother's look of dread made Parker feel even worse. "What happened, honey?"

"I got this phone call." She headed for the other doors to make sure they were locked. "He told me that Brenna's death was about me."

"Oh, dear God, help us." Lynn grabbed the phone from the wall and dialed. "You have to tell Gibson."

"I left a message, but he hasn't returned it." Even as she spoke, her phone rang. She took it out of her pocket and answered. "Gibson?"

"Speakerphone," her mother whispered.

Parker put it on speaker.

"I saw you called. What's up?" Gibson said.

Clearly, he hadn't listened to her message, so she told him about the call. "He said that he would protect me, or something like that. That I didn't need to worry."

"He said that?" Lynn asked. "Gibson, what does that mean?"

"I don't know, Mom. But I'll work on it."

Lynn took the phone out of Parker's hand. "Can't you get phone records and see who called her?"

"I'll get right on it. Meanwhile, stay at Mom's, Parker."

"So where are *you* going to stay tonight?" Lynn asked weakly.

"Guess I'll go home and negotiate a surrender of my apartment."

Lynn touched her chest. "Don't get in a fight with Tom. If he gets too belligerent, just come here. But for heaven's sake. Do me a favor and call me before you come in. I don't want to wonder if you're a prowler."

"Do you think we're safe here, Gibson?" Parker asked.

"I think so. Mom? Better load that gun I gave you."

They hung up, and Lynn drew Parker into a hug. "You did the right thing coming here." She combed her fingers through her hair. "So now, let's see. Where is that gun?"

Parker followed her mom to her bedroom closet and watched as she searched under blankets and boxes and Bible study notebooks lined up on the top shelf — James, Romans, 1 Corinthians, 1 Kings, Isaiah. Finally, she pulled out a case. "Here it is."

Parker's stomach tightened as Lynn took the Taurus .45 caliber revolver out of its box and laid it on the bed. "I hate guns," she said.

Lynn nodded. "Me too."

"Is it loaded?"

"I don't know. I'm not sure how to tell." Lynn stared down at it. "I should have taken that shooting class Gibson wanted me to take."

"So are there bullets anywhere?"

"Somewhere, probably." Lynn went back into the closet and stood on a suitcase as she tried to see. "Here are some. But I don't have a clue how to put them in."

Her mother picked up the pistol, pointing it carefully toward the window. "It's a revolver, so we have to stick the bullets into that rolling chamber thingy, like in Clint Eastwood."

This was absurd. "If we try to load it and we make a mistake, the gun will be more of a danger to us than to the killer."

"We could throw it at his head," Lynn said, beginning to laugh.

Parker caught her mother's smile. "Not funny."

"Yes, it is. Kind of." Laughter overtook them both. "At least we can scare him with it. Make him *think* it's loaded." Lynn scrunched her forehead and gave Parker a pleading look. "Want to sleep with me?"

Parker knew she wouldn't be sleeping much. "Can't. I need to work on my songs. First I have to go out and get my stuff out of the car. Want to cover me while I do?"

Lynn took the empty gun and turned her back to her, aiming outward like a soldier escorting a dignitary through enemy fire. "Let's go."

"Don't get carried away, Mom."

Her mother was a scream. She had a way of lightening the heaviest of moments and making her children forget their fears.

After her mother went to bed, Parker went into the music room her mother had created when Parker was a kid. She'd sound-proofed it with white floor-to-ceiling curtains all the way around the room. It held a grand piano and several of her brothers' guitars lined up on stands around the room. She warmed up with a praise chorus she hadn't written — "Agnus Dei," singing the "Alleluia" with all her spirit. *Worthy is the Lamb . . .*

Christ *was* worthy. Worthy to receive praise through her songs.

He'd given her this opportunity to get her songs heard, this chance to be on a stage in front of thousands of people, singing the songs that she was able to keep for herself. The ones that weren't drained by some musical sieve that dripped the Spirit out of them, leaving them with only dried-out thoughts that meant nothing much to anyone.

Just do it, she told herself. *Sit down and write the stupid lyrics, and let Serene record them. It's her big break, too. Think what she can do for the Lord if she's there, in the midst of all that music industry madness.*

But madness wasn't what Serene needed.

Parker heard the door and sprang to her feet. The gun . . . her mother had the gun. Then she heard the familiar sound of her brother LesPaul dropping his keys into a bowl on the kitchen counter.

"Les, is that you?"

Her younger brother peered around the doorway. "Hey, Parks. What're you doing here?"

She told him about the phone call. He stiffened and went to

the window to peer out. Apparently satisfied that there was no one there, he came into the music room, eating peanuts, and plopped down onto a couch. "So what're you working on?"

"Just doing a little surgery on some of my songs."

"Yeah, I heard about that. Gibson told me."

She sat down on the piano stool. "So what do you think? Am I making a big mistake?"

He popped a nut into his mouth. "Are you insane?"

She sighed. "Maybe."

"The sooner you rewrite the lyrics, the sooner you can finish the songs on your own album."

"I'll need a band."

"Well, I work cheap."

She grinned. "You'd go on the tour with me?"

"Sure. Gibson, too, if he can take off work. Maybe we could sign on as Serene's roadies, to help pay our way. And then there's Dad. He would love to be a part of this."

Just what she needed. "I can't take Dad on tour. That would be a disaster."

"He's a good guitar player, Parker. And it would do him good."

She leaned toward her brother. "Read my lips. I cannot take Dad on this tour."

"Whatever. I understand. I'm just saying." He got up and started for the door. "I'm going to bed. Long day."

She watched her brother head for his room. Then she turned back to the piano. *Just do it*, she told herself again. Write a stupid poem. Words ... they're just words. Get them down, and then you can make them brilliant.

She clicked her pen and started to write replacement words that fit where "Lord" and "Christ" and "Father" used to go. Her heart wasn't in it. But she had plenty of skill, and she needed every bit of it as she took her songs apart and put them back together.

CHAPTER FIFTEEN

It was two a.m. when Gibson came in. He called from his cell phone first, warning Parker that he was coming so she wouldn't panic when she heard him, then came in looking more exhausted than she'd ever seen him. "I got the phone record. The call you got was from a pay phone at the BP convenience store on 12th Avenue South."

"Great. So we have no idea who it was?"

"I went by there to see if they had security cameras that might have caught the guy. They didn't have a camera near the pay phone, but I was able to see the tape of the store the few minutes before and after the call. There was a guy. He had long dark hair, but a Volunteers baseball cap hid his face. Probably five-ten, 175 pounds."

"That describes half the men I know."

"Yeah, me too. He was in a light-colored four-door sedan. The image was black and white and a little blurry, but could have been a Corolla or Civic or one of those little cars. We can't say for sure if he's the one who made the call, but from the tape, it looks like his were the only headlights lighting up the store around the time the call was made."

"I want to see."

He opened his binder and showed her a picture. The angle showed only the top of his head. The picture was black and white, and she couldn't see his face. In the first photo, he was buying a pack of cigarettes and a drink. In the next, he was heading out.

"You recognize him?"

"Not at all." She studied his clothes. Jeans, clean white sneakers. No visible tattoos. No distinguishing characteristics at all. He didn't look like either a killer *or* a protector.

"Did he buy gas? Give a credit card?"

"Nope. Paid cash. No gas."

"Then we're right back where we started."

"Not necessarily. I'll keep these pictures, just in case something comes up."

"Meanwhile ..."

"Meanwhile, you let me know if you hear from him again. Since he said he would protect you, it's possible he's not the killer, but that he knows who is. Or he *thinks* he knows."

"And he knows whoever it was, was after me."

He turned to his notes in the binder. "He said it was *about* you. Not that you were the target."

"He also sounded crazy. You know. Making himself my protector."

"Did Mom get out her revolver?"

"Uh ... yeah. But I wouldn't count on her skill. We could both use some instruction. If we ever figure out how to load it, we're liable to shoot our own feet off. But it's okay. You're home now."

"Yeah, but just for tonight. I evicted Tom. Told him he had twenty-four hours to get out."

"Girlfriend going with him?"

Gibson managed to laugh. "If she doesn't I'll arrest her for trespassing."

"Way to go. I didn't think you had it in you."

"I finally got tired enough. Your couch isn't all that comfortable."

"Yeah, sorry about that." She got up and punched him on the arm. "I have to get back to rewriting my songs."

"So you committed. When do we start recording?"

The "we" made her smile. She knew she could count on him. "You tell me. When are you unsealing the studios?"

"We need a few more days, and then we'll get the crime-scene clean-up crew in."

"The longer you force us to stay closed, the longer it'll be before I can get studio time."

"Doing the best I can, Sis. Trying to solve a murder here."

She didn't have to be reminded.

CHAPTER
SIXTEEN

When the police department unsealed the studios a few days later, Parker met George Colgate there to assess what needed to be done before they opened back up for business. She and her boss stood in the lobby, surveying the plywood that boarded the windows. The company contracted to clean up crime scenes had gotten Brenna's blood out of the carpet and off the walls. Parker was glad of that — still, she didn't think she could sit at her desk as if nothing had changed.

George seemed uneasy, too. "Call Jarailly Glass and see if you can get that pane replaced ASAP. It's the strongest, most secure kind they have. They probably have our original order on file. If they have something bullet-proof, go with that."

She looked at the window, trying to imagine the angle of the bullets from a car driving by. At least with the plywood no one could see through it to shoot her. They'd have to come inside.

Somehow, that didn't ease her tension.

George seemed to read her thoughts. "Hey, if you want to reorient your desk so you're not sitting right there ... where she sat ... we can move it right now."

Her eyes grew misty. "Yeah, okay. Let's do that."

They each got on one side of the heavy desk. "Where do you want to put it?" George asked.

She looked at the wall where the window was. Not there. She'd never rest knowing her back was to the glass. There was only one other place, catty-corner to where it was before. It would have to do for now. "Right there, I guess. We can move it back when we get everything ... back to normal."

"If you want."

"Where's my chair?"

"They must have taken it."

Of course. Brenna had fallen with it. It probably had blood ...

"I'll get you the one in my office." A couple of minutes later, he rolled his executive desk chair to her desk.

"Where are you going to sit?" she asked. "You are gonna be here when we open tomorrow, aren't you?"

"Yes. I'll bring the chair from my study at home until I can get a new one. The security guard will be here at eight a.m."

She swallowed. Maybe the guard's presence would calm her tripping heart.

"You gonna be all right, Parker?"

She wanted to say yes, but that would be a lie. "I'll survive," she said.

She hoped it was true.

The next morning, Serene and her people showed up at eight — an unheard-of hour for musicians, who rarely went to bed before dawn. But there was much left to do on Serene's records, so they'd taken any and all hours they could get. Parker went into the studio with them and listened as Serene belted out the new lyrics in her unique, powerful voice. The new verses weren't half bad, she had to admit. If she wanted a career in secular songwriting, she could probably have one. She could be like Dianne Warren, who had her own star in the Hollywood Walk of Fame. She'd read that her music catalogue was worth over a billion dollars. Or Dolly Parton, who'd written three thousand songs, recorded by countless artists.

Maybe making a few compromises wouldn't be so bad. Wasn't God opening these doors for her? For the first time, she allowed the excitement about the tour to take hold. She had so much to do, but the things she'd dreamed of were finally coming true.

All she had to do was pull it off.

First, she had to line up the rest of her band. Though she'd be taking the stage during Serene's concert, using Serene's band's equipment and setup, she would need her own musicians. And her budget was so limited that she had to give more thought to taking along her dad.

When she expressed her reservations about her father to Serene, her friend urged her to include him.

"Hey, your dad beats mine hands down. I'd take Pete James on the road with me any day."

Pete was a great musician, and a loving father. He just had that overwhelming flaw that sabotaged everything he touched. Give him the world and all its opportunities, and before you knew it, he'd ruin it with alcohol and run everything good into the ground. Pete always harbored that hope that the next opportunity would be the thing worth staying sober for. The next big break. The next job. The next wife.

Parker had long ago stopped believing that she or her brothers could rescue him. And her mother certainly couldn't. She'd tried.

The ringing phone drew Parker back to her desk. She found Daniel Walker, Serene's guitar player, surveying the boarded window. She smiled and waved as she answered the phone. It was a reporter fishing for a statement from George. She took a message, then hung up and looked at Daniel. "I didn't think you guys were rerecording the musical tracks."

He shook his head. "We aren't. I just came by to hear the new lyrics." He rubbed his chin and glanced at the wall where her desk used to be. "This is all so ... tragic.

She looked at the floor. "I know."

He shook his head. "There's something not right about Brenna Evans working here in the first place."

She narrowed her eyes. "Do you know the family?"

He nodded. "I was in Tiffany's tour band about eight years ago, when I was twenty-two. Nathan Evans is shrewd, and Brenna was his little princess. She was only ten then, so I didn't recognize her when she started working here. Have you considered that she might have been here spying for her dad?"

Parker didn't want to tell him a reporter had suggested the same thing. "I don't know. That's a stretch. It's more likely she just wanted to get to know all the musicians who record here. Maybe she was star-struck."

"Trust me, she knew plenty of musicians."

She didn't like where he was going with this. Why did people keep trying to blame the victim? Brenna had been shot, and that was that. It wasn't her fault. Even if Parker had correctly interpreted what she'd overhead Nathan Evans saying, Brenna was an innocent victim.

Daniel leaned on her desk, his gaze locking with hers. He had thick black lashes that framed dark brown eyes. They were clear and deep ... wise, somehow. "I know I sound cold. I just don't trust that family."

"I think we need to cut them some slack. They're going through a rough time."

"You're right. It's just ... history. Listen, you be careful, okay? I've been worried about you."

Something about that concern, coming from a man who wasn't her father or brother, melted her irritation. She could do a lot worse than having Daniel Walker care about her.

CHAPTER
SEVENTEEN

On her lunch break, Parker went to the police station, hoping to find Gibson in. He was on the telephone, taking notes, his desk littered with papers and pictures, drink cans and empty coffee cups. Rayzo was eating a hamburger at his desk. He had a mustard stain on his shirt. She gave him a wave and dropped into the chair at Gibson's desk.

Gibson acknowledged her with an uplifted finger telling her to wait, then finally got off the phone. "What's up, Parks?"

She leaned toward him. "I didn't want to call you from work because I didn't want to start more rumors if anybody else overheard. But Daniel Walker just told me something I think I should pass on to you."

"Serene's guitar player?"

"That's right."

She related what he had told her about the Evans family and the possibility that Brenna had been spying for her dad. "I feel bad even saying it," she said in a low voice. "But it's the second time I've heard it. But even if she was a spy, it wouldn't explain why she was killed."

"It might." He shifted through his notes. "You did hear Nathan Evans saying somebody meant it for him?"

"Yeah, but what could that mean? That one of his enemies came after his daughter for some reason, right? Not that *she* did anything wrong."

He rubbed his eyes and flipped back through his notes.

"But that doesn't explain my phone call," Parker said. "If the killer was trying to get at Evans, why did the caller say it was about me?"

Gibson shook his head. "It's possible it's a prank, that some kid decided it would be fun to scare the living daylights out of you. Your number's in the phone book, so it would be easy for them to do."

"At night from a pay phone at a convenience store? Besides, it wasn't a kid." She looked down at her hands, wishing she could know for sure. "And it seems like they would have threatened me instead of promising to protect me, if it was a prank."

"Parker, don't worry. I'm not discounting that call. I'm taking everything we've found into consideration."

"Are you making any headway?"

He looked from side to side, and met Rayzo's eyes. "Some, yes. But I can't talk to you about it right now."

Realizing her being there might cause problems for him, she slid her chair back. "Guess I'd better get back to work."

"How does Serene like the songs?"

"She loves them. Looks like we've got a tour to prepare for."

"Yeah, let's hope we can solve this case so I can put in for the time off."

CHAPTER EIGHTEEN

Parker couldn't help being jumpy for most of the day as people came and went from the studios. Each time the front door opened, her heart leapt. The off-duty cop moonlighting as a security guard was two inches shorter than Parker's five-eight — not the bouncer type. The fact that he carried a gun gave him a little more credibility, though. She hoped it was enough.

She spent the day on the phone with the labels, scrolling through her computer calendars, trying to find space for the artists who'd been booked in the studio during the lost days. The delay had ruined deadlines and cost people money. She hoped some of them would finally go to one of the lesser studios around town. Their sound boards might not have all the bells and whistles that were the pride of Colgate Studios — and they might not be drug- and alcohol-free — but they were adequate for the needs of some of these artists.

Her own hopes of finding studio time were quickly vaporizing. What was she going to do? Her main purpose for working here was to get free studio time. Now, when she needed it most, there weren't any available except from seven to ten a.m. She had to be at work at eight, so that wouldn't work.

When Serene's group finally broke for lunch, her friend came out and leaned on the upper ledge of Parker's desk. "Going to the concert tonight?"

Parker had forgotten about the free concert at the Ryman Auditorium tonight to raise money for an inner-city ministry. "I don't know, Serene," she said. "I've got to work on my songs. And I don't know how I'm ever going to get any studio time. I'm starting to lose hope that I can get this done in time for the tour."

"Don't lose hope," Serene said. "We'll work it out."

She looked up. "We?"

"Yeah. We got a lot done today. I'm about to finish up in the studio. I have extra time booked. If this keeps up, I can give it to you."

"But I can't pay for it," she said. "That's why I work here, remember?"

"You have a right to the time. If I have it booked and then I pull out, surely it's okay if you take it."

Parker looked at the long list of artists waiting to get into the studios. It wouldn't be right to take early evening hours when there were paying clients waiting to use them. "I'll have to think about it," she said.

"Don't think too hard, Parker. This is business. I won't cancel the time until we've finished mixing, and that could be a while yet."

Parker stood up to stretch. It was after five. Cat was in the back doing some filing, waiting to relieve Parker on the night shift. "I can't believe this day is finally over. Want to get something to eat?"

"I'm not hungry, but I'll go with you," Serene said.

Parker doubted that Serene truly wasn't hungry. She had to be — she was starving to death. Maybe Parker could coerce her into eating, once they got there.

Parker got her laptop and purse, then headed out to the car and unlocked the door for Serene. As she got into the driver's side, she realized how small Serene looked sitting in the round pod of the VW. She seemed to be shrinking away. Parker felt huge next to her.

"Hook your belt," Parker told her. Serene did. "So, how are the songs going?"

"They're beautiful," Serene said. "We finished recording 'Double Minds,' and as soon as it's mixed, we're going to press some singles and release it to the radio stations."

Parker's stomach churned as she thought about the true meaning of that song. Now it was anything but what she had originally planned. "Have you been thinking about the video?"

"Not really, and it'll be on a crash schedule," Serene said. "Any ideas?"

Parker thought about it. "Originally, when I conceived the song, I thought of a crowd of people with spirits moving in and out of them, pulling them to the right path when their flesh took them somewhere else."

"The song doesn't mean that anymore," Serene said. "The video is supposed to be about me wanting to leave the man I love, but the other side of me can't do it."

"Yeah, I know. Two sides of you battling the same problem with different solutions."

"I guess it's basically the same. We could computer generate the ghostly parts. Maybe show me fantasizing about whether to throw him out or let him stay."

The more Serene went on, the more excitement thickened her voice. Parker didn't even want to make suggestions. The video was going to be about Serene and some guy. She'd probably spend all her time making pouty poses and letting the fan blow her hair. Real deep stuff.

When Parker started up the car, she plugged in her iPhone. "Want to hear the title song for my CD?"

"Something new?" Serene asked.

"Relatively new," Parker said with a smile. "I've held it back for myself."

"No fair!"

"Oh, yeah, it's fair. I've given you my best. This one's mine. It's called 'Ambient.'"

Serene listened to the demo, rapt, as Parker's song filled the small car. Neither of them spoke as the song played. She drove, softly singing along with her own voice.

When the song came to an end, Serene looked at her. "Okay, I seriously hate you."

Parker grinned. "Why?"

"Because I could have gone platinum with that song."

Parker laughed. "Maybe I will, instead."

Serene sighed. "It's beautiful. Vintage Parker. It'll make you a star."

"You think so?"

"You're playing it on the tour, aren't you? Because you have to. It's your best yet."

"Of course," Parker said, "if I can get it recorded."

"Play it again."

Her three favorite words. Parker obliged, and Serene listened quietly. When it was over, Parker realized she was driving aimlessly. "Where do you want to eat?"

"Doesn't matter. I told you, I'm not hungry."

"Have you eaten today at all? Did you eat yesterday?"

Serene had to think about it for a moment. What a shame. Eating was not something Parker had to think about.

"I had half a piece of cantaloupe this morning," Serene said. "But I'd love a drink."

Parker decided to just pick up a salad and eat it later. She turned into McDonald's. "Too many cars in the drive-thru. Let's go in."

"Okay," Serene said, "but I don't feel like dealing with any fans right now."

It wasn't as though Serene had paparazzi chasing her whenever she left the house. Nashville was pretty jaded where celebrities were concerned — and Christian celebs garnered even less attention. But people did recognize her, and she got stares almost everywhere she went.

Parker got her salad and drink, and as Serene ordered, Parker went to stand by the glass exit door. She looked out into the parking lot. *Lord, I don't know what to do for her. Help her before it's too late.*

Absently, she scanned the cars — until she saw a man with long brown hair sitting in a white Corolla. He seemed to be staring right at her, through sunglasses. Her heart went into overdrive, and she stepped back from the glass.

Calm down, she told herself. Just because the guy who called her *might* have had long brown hair and *might* have a small, light-colored sedan, didn't mean that *this* guy was watching her.

Serene came out, sipping on her drink. "Ready?"

Parker pushed open the glass door and started across the parking lot. Glancing back at the man, she saw that he was looking down now, as though reading. She got in and started her VW, and glanced over again. "Do you know that guy over there?"

Serene glanced toward the other car. "Nope."

"He was staring at me a few minutes ago."

"You sure?"

Parker realized that he could have been watching for Serene. She was the beauty, the talent, the celebrity. Still . . . "No, I guess not."

As they pulled out, he kept looking down. She pulled into traffic, then glanced in her rearview mirror. He was pulling out of his space.

She turned off the main street and navigated her way through a neighborhood. The man didn't turn after her. Relieved, she made her way through the back streets, back to Colgate. She dropped Serene off and watched as she went in, saying another prayer for her shrinking friend. Parker wanted to see her succeed and be happy, but she feared that Serene's dreams were, once again, taking her somewhere destructive.

As a child, Serene's seven-year-old dreams had been about having different parents — a mother who wasn't being gnawed to death by cancer, a father who knew how to smile, siblings who could hunker with her under the bed when things got loud and out of control, who would keep her from being so alone in her fear. When her mother died not long after her eighth birthday, Serene's dream world grew more intense. They were dreams of going to heaven and meeting her new, improved mother, with color in her face and energy to run and swing and play. She longed to be there ... prayed to be there ... *plotted* to be there.

When Serene was eleven, she swallowed a bottle of her dad's sleeping pills and woke up days later, woefully alive. The doctors concluded that she was headed down the wrong path — a path to drugs and destruction. They suggested that her father send her to a camp for troubled youth. The hope of going there had given Serene — then called Sal — a new dream of escape from the oppression in her home. But her father had quashed it, as he did everything else in her life. No way he could stand to be without his little Sal, he told the doctors. He would steer her back to the right path. And steer he did.

When she returned to school, there were rumors about her attempted suicide, started by neighbors who cared enough about her plight to gossip, but not enough to do anything more. The kids in her class treated her as though they would absorb her darkness if they got too close.

But Parker wasn't put off by it. One afternoon, not long after Serene's return to school, Parker crossed the imaginary line that she saw around Serene, and approached her lonely table at lunch. "Did you take the pills to get high, or to kill yourself?" she asked.

Sal looked at her, shocked that anyone would ask outright what others only whispered about.

"Don't worry, Sal," Parker said, sitting down. "I won't tell anybody. I can keep secrets."

The girl considered Parker for a moment. In her eyes, Parker saw her running through what she knew about her. She hoped she remembered that Parker wasn't mean.

Finally, trust and resolution glimmered in her eyes. "I was trying to kill myself." She said it almost defiantly, as though she expected Parker to gasp and choke, then run to tell the teacher.

Parker didn't move or change her expression. "Why'd you want to do that?"

Sal looked down at her hands. There were scars on her palms, burn marks in the shape of a grill rack. "No reason."

Parker studied her for a long moment, then she looked away, hoping it provided a measure of mercy to the distant girl. She dug into her lunch sack and pulled out a zip-locked sandwich, an orange, a baggie with a cut-up apple, a bag of Cheez-Its, and a small Tupperware dish. "This is embarrassing. My mom thinks I have to eat five fruits or vegetables a day, so she crams them into my lunch bag. The sandwich is peanut butter and bananas, which I like. But I only want half of it, because after I eat part of the apple and orange, I'm full." She pulled the sandwich out and thrust half of it at Serene. "Here's your half. I think my mother secretly packs extra for friends."

Sal seemed moved that Parker would consider her a friend. She pushed aside the bag of Cheetos she'd gotten from the vending machine and ate the sandwich. Later, when they spoke of that day, Serene told her that lunch had spawned dreams that her mother was alive, that she'd packed a balanced lunch — the kind that would make Mrs. Branch, their health teacher, smile. Dreams in which her mother stood in the kitchen in her pajamas in the morning, slicing up bananas while she reminded her to brush her teeth.

Dreams that would never be fulfilled.

From that day on, she and Parker had been best friends. Her desire to head for heaven anytime soon had diminished. Apparently, she chose to head there the long way now, through slow, brittle starvation that masqueraded as her ticket to beauty and fame. That call to suicide was insidious, offering freedom, then trapping its victim in bondage.

Sal had legally changed her name to Serene when she broke free of her father and her deadly home, but she still saw the world from behind the bars of her eating disorder. Parker had tried for many years to pray her free … just as she'd done with her own father. But a person had to want freedom more than bondage before God would grant it. Prayers of the double-minded often went unanswered.

CHAPTER NINETEEN

The call from Marta, Brenna's roommate, came that evening as Parker drove to her mother's. "Parker, I need to talk to you."

Surprised to hear from the girl, Parker said, "Well, sure. What about?"

"About Brenna. Can I meet you somewhere?"

Fatigue clawed at her bones. She didn't really want to make a pit stop for a chat with the grieving roommate, especially after Gibson had warned her to stay away from Brenna's friends. "What about Brenna?"

"I have some information about her murder."

Parker caught her breath. "Shouldn't you be calling the police instead of me?"

"Your brother's working on the case, right?"

"Yes. I could call him. He could meet you."

"I'll meet with him as long as you're there. I just want this kept quiet. I'm afraid if word gets out I went to the police, I'll be next. I'm really nervous."

Parker had no idea why the girl would trust her when she hardly knew her. "Okay. Where do you want to meet?"

"Can you come to the downtown library? There's a writer's

room on the second floor. I'll be in there. Just ask someone where that room is. It's quiet and private, and we can talk there. Can you be there in half an hour?"

"Okay. I'll try to catch Gibson and get him there."

She pulled into a parking lot and called her brother. He agreed to meet her there. Half an hour later, she met him on the front steps of the Nashville Library, and they went upstairs and found the writer's room.

Parker pushed the door open. Marta was sitting at the end of a small conference table, her laptop in front of her. Her hair wasn't quite as spiked today. It lay down on her head like any other short haircut, the black a stark contrast to her pale face.

Marta got to her feet as they came in. Parker hugged her.

"Thanks for coming." Marta's hands were trembling.

They all sat. "Parker said you had information on the murder," Gibson said.

"Yes." She closed her laptop and swallowed hard. "But I need your promise that you'll keep my name out of it."

Gibson leaned up on the table, a frown cutting his forehead. "I'll do my best."

"No, I need a promise. I'm not telling you any of this unless you swear."

"Marta, if you have information that would lead us to Brenna's killer," he said, "then you need to tell us. I'll leave your name out of it as long as I can."

"Why can't you promise?"

"Because sometimes I have to lay things out on the table in order to get search and arrest warrants. But if your information leads to an arrest, then you won't have to be afraid."

"I'm just afraid that it'll get out and then he won't get arrested. Or someone will bail him out and he'll come after me."

Parker's chest tightened. Did Marta know who the killer was?

"Marta, do you feel safer knowing he's going to get away with it?" Gibson asked.

She covered her face then and groaned. "No." She looked at Parker over her fingertips. "Can I trust him?"

"Of course. Gibson won't let you down."

"Okay." She sighed and kept her hands clasped in front of her face. "I was at Chase's house today, just hanging out with him. He's still acting all upset about Brenna, crying all the time ..."

"Acting?" Parker asked.

"Yeah, acting. See, I thought it was real. I felt so sorry for him. I thought we were in the same boat, still in shock. I was in his kitchen, and I was going to make him some soup. He said he had some Campbell's, but I couldn't find it. Some people in Bruin Hills keep stuff on top of their cabinets since they don't have much cabinet space, so I got a chair and looked up there." She stopped and cleared her throat. "I saw a gun."

Parker stared at her.

"What kind of gun?" Gibson asked.

"A rifle. I'm not real familiar with them." Parker and Gibson exchanged looks.

"Could have been a hunting rifle," Gibson said. "Lots of guys have them."

"It was just weird that it was up there, like Chase was trying to hide it or something."

Parker leaned on the table. "Did you ask him about it?"

"No! It freaked me out. I didn't want to let him know I saw. I got out of there as fast as I could. I told him I'd go buy some soup and come back. That's when I called you."

Gibson's frown told Parker he was taking this seriously. He took out his notebook and began writing. "You did the right thing," he said.

"Does that mean he killed her?" Marta asked. "I don't want to believe that."

"Not necessarily. He has a roommate, doesn't he?"

"Sort of. Mike moved in with his girlfriend a couple of weeks ago. He kept the apartment so his parents wouldn't know, but I don't think he's even been there since then."

Parker frowned. "Didn't you say the reason Brenna couldn't study at Chase's that night was that Chase's roommate and girlfriend were there?"

Marta wiped her tears. "Yeah, that's what Brenna said. But apparently that wasn't true. Chase told me later that things weren't so good between him and Brenna. That they had a fight that day. That's the real reason she didn't want to study over there."

"What about the hole in his wall?" Parker asked. "You told me he did that when he found out about Brenna. How did you know that?"

"He told me. But people in his class are saying he already had a sprained hand earlier that night."

"Had he ever been violent with her?" Gibson asked.

She shrugged. "She never talked about physical violence, but he has a temper. I've seen him yell and cuss at her before. Throw his arms around, like he was going to hit her."

As Gibson questioned her a little more, Parker's mind drifted back to the guy she'd been so certain was demonstrating authentic signs of grief. Was he really a killer? Was it all an act? Maybe Gibson had been right — Chase wasn't to be trusted.

"So what are you going to do?" Marta asked as they stood.

"We'll have to search his place again. It's very important that you don't tip him off."

"Don't worry. I haven't told anybody. I called you as soon as it happened. I'll have to tell him why I didn't come back with the soup."

"Tell him something came up."

"Okay. He thinks I'm flaky, anyway."

Parker offered to walk her out to her car, but Marta insisted on staying behind and leaving alone, in case anyone she knew spotted her. As Parker returned to her car, she thought of that young man who'd seemed to be experiencing such sincere grief. Was he capable of murder? If he was, then she was a terrible judge of character.

As she got behind the wheel, she prayed a silent prayer for Marta's safety, and for Gibson's speed in getting a search warrant before Chase moved the gun.

CHAPTER TWENTY

Gibson and Rayzo surprised Chase at his apartment. He denied owning a gun of any kind. When they showed him their search warrant, he waited on the steps outside his second-floor apartment while they went in to search it. The tiny two-bedroom campus apartment had only a front room that would barely hold a couch and chair, and two tiny bedrooms with standard college-issued furniture. Twin beds, a desk, a small closet. The kitchen was barely big enough for two people to stand in, yet somehow he'd squeezed in a small table and two chairs.

There was an eight-inch gap between the top of the cabinets and the ceiling. Gibson moved the chair from the table to the counter and stood on it.

"There it is." Gibson took his camera out of his pocket and took a picture. "It's a 6mm. Same caliber as the murder weapon."

"Let's take him in for questioning while ballistics checks to see if it's the one," Rayzo said.

As Rayzo secured the gun, Gibson stepped out into the stairwell. Chase was still sitting on the steps. He looked up. "I told you there was nothing there. I didn't kill my girlfriend. I loved her."

"We need to take you to the department for questioning."

Chase's eyebrows drew together. "Should I call my parents?"

The question seemed innocent — naïve — reminding Gibson that Chase was still a teenager who hadn't considered whether he needed a lawyer. Then again, lots of eighteen-year-olds were killers. Maybe Chase was just extra slick. "There'll be time to call them later."

"But why can't you question me here? I've been cooperative."

"We'll talk about it at the station."

Chase stood and took a step down, then looked back at his apartment. "Shouldn't we wait until your partner comes out so I can lock my door?"

"He'll lock up for you. Come on, pal."

Chase looked confused as he followed him out to the police car.

The gun's serial number had been scratched off, so its ownership couldn't be traced. But it wasn't registered to Chase. The DA reviewed the evidence and instructed Gibson and Rayzo to arrest him for possession of an illegal firearm. That would hold him until they had enough evidence to charge him with murder.

Gibson did the honors.

Parker took the news of Chase's arrest as a reprieve from the fear in which she'd been living. Though she couldn't shrug away the sadness that she'd had him so wrong, she did relish the idea of going home and sleeping through the night without worrying that someone was coming for her. Her little house felt safer.

So Brenna's death had been about a scorned boyfriend's wrath. What was the world coming to, that a man could claim to love someone, then end her life because he couldn't have her? The thought made her sick, and her fatigue made work seem impossible. She needed to lie in bed and watch mindless TV until she fell asleep. She needed to think about nothing for a while.

But time was running out, and she had a CD to record. When space became available in the studio, she would have to be ready.

She met deadlines just fine when she was writing for Serene. Why couldn't she do it for herself?

So she went into her music room and tried to focus, intent on making some progress on finishing the songs for her own album tonight.

The phone shrilled at one a.m., startling Parker out of the nap she'd taken at her keyboard. She hadn't meant to fall asleep. She had just laid her head on her folded arms for a few minutes.

The phone rang again, and fear shivered through her. Praying it wasn't her anonymous caller, she searched for the phone under sheet music and print-outs of lyrics. Finally, she found it. "Hello?"

Her mother's voice sounded raspy, as if she'd been crying. "Parker?"

"What is it, Mom?"

"It's your father. I got a call that he was at the Gold Rush and that he's not himself. They want me to come and get him."

"Not himself" were code words for "drunk." Her mother could never bring herself to call it what it was — at least, not to her children. It was as if she still harbored hope that they wouldn't know if she didn't tell them.

"I don't know where that is. Do you?" her mom asked.

"On Elliston, across from Exit/In."

"I guess it's urgent. I don't want him to get arrested. I called Gibson, but he's not answering. LesPaul's in a session."

"I'll go with you."

"Good. I'm almost to your house now."

Parker hurried to the bathroom and brushed her teeth and hair. She heard her mother's car turning into her driveway as soon as she finished. She locked the door behind her and got into her mom's car. Her mother wasn't wearing makeup, as she usually did. "So what are we going to do with him once we find him?" Parker asked.

"I don't know. It depends on how bad it is."

"You should let him have it. Demand that he go back to rehab."

"How many rehabs will it take?" Lynn asked.

Parker knew the question was rhetorical.

She helped her mother find the small bar where live bands performed nightly. The parking lot was full of cars, and they could hear the music blaring even in their car.

"Well," Lynn said as she pulled into a spot. "Here goes nothing."

Parker followed her mother in and looked through the smoky crowd. Pete James stood near the stage, staggering as he argued with two bouncers, his arms flailing. It looked as if a fight was about to erupt. "There he is," she said over the noise. "We better hurry."

Lynn shot through the crowd, crossing the glutted dance floor, and made her way to her ex-husband. "Pete!" she shouted.

Pete's arms came down, and he turned and saw her. His face lit up. "The love of my life." He fell into her arms. "Ladeeez and genelmen, the love of my life."

Parker had to hand it to her mother. She didn't push him away or humiliate him in any way. She just held him for a moment, whispering something in his ear. He looked up then, and spotted Parker.

"My li'l girl. My precious Parker. She's not dead, y'all. It was a false alarm. She's right here."

That old familiar humiliation burned in Parker's cheeks. She was grateful that the band was still playing, so no one could hear. "Dad, we need to go. We came to get you."

He still clung to her mother, his weight almost pulling her down. Looking down at Lynn, he said, "You're beautiful, ya know that, baby? My beautiful little wife."

"Come on, darlin'," Lynn cajoled. "Let's get out of here."

He came without protest, steadying himself on her shoulder. Parker followed, refusing to make eye contact with anyone. As they reached the door, one of the bartenders stopped her.

"Sorry I had to call," he said. "He was harassing the musicians, demanding that they let him play with them. Crazy old guy."

Parker didn't like hearing her father referred to like that. "He's not crazy or old. And he's a better musician than those guys."

"Even drunk?"

"Even drunk." She pushed through the crowd of people at the door and caught up to her parents.

Lynn was coaxing him into her car.

"Where are you taking him?" Parker asked, getting into the back seat.

"Home."

He fell into the car and leaned his head back on the seat. "Whose home?" he said. "Mine or ours?"

Her father's yearning always put a lump in Parker's throat. After all these years, she still yearned for her parents to be back together, her family to be intact. Her mother had never given up on him entirely, even when he'd traded her in for a younger wife.

"I'm taking you to your house." Lynn got in and reached across him to buckle his seatbelt.

He caught her arm and nuzzled her face. "I'm sorry, Lynn. Sorry for ever'thing."

"I know you are."

"Sorry to you, too, Parks."

"It's okay, Dad."

"No, not okay. They used to know me. I used to matter."

"You still matter, Dad."

He put his big hand over his face, fingers splayed, and began to cry. "I'm such a loser."

"Stop that!" Lynn said. "You're not a loser, Pete." She started the car, pulled through the parking lot. "You're a child of the Most High God. You just don't realize it. You keep eating out of the garbage bin when you could be at the banquet."

He wiped the tears off his face. "Tha's why I love you. You always say things like that."

He was quiet for a moment as they drove through town, and Parker thought he'd finally drifted into an alcoholic sleep. How would they wake him to get him into his house? But after a moment, he spoke again.

"Don't take me to my place, Lynn. I wanna go home."

Lynn was quiet.

"Please, Lynn."

Parker almost hoped that her mother would say yes. But she was too strong for that.

"Sweetie, you know the deal. You get sober, stay sober, and we'll talk."

"But I can't do it without you."

Parker looked at her mother in the rearview mirror, saw the emotional struggle in her eyes. Tears glistened. "We've been all through this, darlin'."

"But it'll be different this time."

No, it wouldn't. It would never be different. Not until Pete surrendered his addictions, and let God do his work of deliverance in his heart and mind. Parker sat quietly, remembering all the times in her childhood when her mother had thrown them into the car in their pajamas and set out to find her drunken father. She had been rescuing him for years.

But her rescue missions had their limits.

"You'll be okay at your apartment, darlin'," she said in a tender voice. "I'll take you there and make sure you get in all right."

"Can I see you tomorrow?"

"If you're sober, come on by."

He was quiet then, and Parker wondered if he was trying to work out in his mind a plan for being sober. Could an inebriated mind really do that? Was there really any way apart from a work of God?

By the time they got to his house, Pete was snoring. Parker and her mother roused him enough to walk him into his apartment. Not for the first time she considered the blessing that it was on the first floor instead of the third. She looked around at the sad, sparse furnishings — a couch in the living room, a bed in the other room. Whatever good things he'd ever had, he'd sold for alcohol. He lived like a fifty-two-year-old frat boy.

Parker helped him off with his coat; then they sat him down on his bed. He fell back on the pillow, and Parker lifted his booted feet to the bed. She pulled off his boots, straightened his socks, then stepped back as Lynn covered him with a blanket. He was out cold — snoring like a chainsaw — before they could even say goodnight.

Parker stood back and watched her mother press a kiss on his cheek. Then she, too, kissed him. "Night, Dad," she whispered.

Her mother hurried out of the room, and when she stepped from the bedroom, Parker saw her rummaging through his cabinets. "What are you looking for?"

"Some aspirin. He's going to need them tomorrow." She found some and shook out two, then filled up a glass of water. She went back into the bedroom and set them on the crate he used as a nightstand.

They were both quiet as they got back into the car. They were halfway to Parker's house when she asked, "Mom, why didn't you let him come home?"

"Because he wouldn't leave. He'd dig back in."

"Into the house?"

"No. Into my heart." Her voice caught, and Parker saw her swallow. "I don't like leaving him alone like that. But my enabling him will lead to his death ... mine, too. If he wants home badly enough, then he'll get sober and stay sober."

"Do you think it's even possible?"

"Isaiah 50, verse 2 says, 'Is My hand so short that it cannot ransom? Or have I no power to deliver?' Of course God has that power. People are delivered all the time. Pete has made life very hard for himself. He'll have to pull out extra strength and courage to overcome all this. He'll have to repent, and as John the Baptist said, 'Perform deeds in keeping with repentance.'"

Parker knew the Bible — her mother had seen to that — but she wished she could pull passages out of the air like her mother did. Some people read the Bible. Her mother savored it ... digested it.

"Do you pray for your father?"

The question convicted her. "Sometimes. Not enough, probably."

"Do," her mom said in a tone that held no accusation. "I need all the praying help I can get. Your father is a heavy burden. Remember when Jesus was healing people, and the friends of the paralytic lowered him through the roof? We have to carry your dad to Christ, because he's paralyzed, too. We have to get him before Jesus as much as we can."

"Sorry, Mom. I'll pray more. I promise."

As an oncoming headlight lit her mother's face, Parker saw the deep sorrow in her eyes. "God's going to deliver him from this someday," she whispered. "How could he not, with all the prayers I've prayed?"

As they pulled into Parker's driveway, she wished for something that would comfort her mother. But it wasn't Parker's comfort she needed. Parker leaned over and kissed her cheek.

Her mom returned it. "You lock up, now."

"I will. But don't worry. Brenna's killer is in jail." She got out of the car and headed through the carport, her mother's headlights illuminating her door. She dug her keys out of her purse — just as her shoes crunched over something on the step.

Her eyes flew up.

The glass on the upper part of her door had been shattered.

Someone had broken into her house.

CHAPTER TWENTY-ONE

Lynn sat in her car, engine idling, her headlights illuminating Parker as she fumbled for her keys. She wouldn't leave until her daughter was safe inside.

She saw Parker jump, saw her back down the steps. Something was wrong. Lynn opened her car door and leaned out. "Honey?"

Parker ran toward her. "Someone broke in!" Her words came out as whispered hysteria. "Get back in the car!"

Lynn closed the door as Parker slid into the passenger side. With trembling hands, she locked the doors.

Parker was gasping for breath. "Let's go. They could still be here."

Lynn backed out. "Call Gibson!"

Parker was already dialing her phone.

As she drove away, Lynn looked back. All the lights in the house were off. If someone was there, they were hiding in the dark.

She listened as Parker told Gibson about the glass in the door. Lynn could hear his voice.

"Keep driving," he said. "Just circle the block until somebody gets there. Don't go inside."

Gibson arrived at the same time as the three squad cars, and

Lynn pulled back into the driveway. Lynn and Parker waited in the car as the police went through her house. The temperature had warmed, and the car felt muggy. "You can't stay here again," Lynn told Parker. "You know that, don't you?"

Parker slammed her hands on the dashboard. "The killer is supposed to be locked up. *Who is doing this?*"

Lynn didn't want to talk about murderers and weapons. Her son was in the house. Why hadn't he come back out?

Just as her imagination took flight, she saw light spill out the doorway. Gibson stepped out, and Lynn breathed easier. Parker opened her car door.

"There's no one there now," he said. "But somebody's definitely been here. Come have a look."

Heart pounding, Lynn followed Parker in.

Dread burned in Parker's chest as she stepped over the threshold. More glass crunched under her feet. Though nothing seemed to be out of place, her house felt violated. "What did they take?"

"I can't tell that they took anything."

Parker stepped into her music room and took quick inventory of her equipment. Her computer and keyboard were intact. She came back and checked her stereo equipment. Everything was there.

"Was this here before?" Gibson's question turned her toward the coffee table.

There, in the center of the table, lay some hand-written song sheets for "Double Minds." The word STOLEN was scrawled across the music in huge, red capital letters.

"No. That wasn't there." She leaned down to pick it up.

Gibson caught her hand. "Don't touch it. It might have prints."

"Gibson, what's going on?" Her volume was shrill, but she couldn't lower it. "Who would break in to leave something like this? Why wouldn't they just mail it?"

"I'd guess they were trying to make a strong statement."

"But what does it mean?"

"I don't know, but we'll find out."

Her mother spoke up. "Could this have anything to do with the murder?"

"I don't see how," Gibson said. "Chase McElraney is in jail."

The room began to spin, and Parker touched the counter to steady herself.

Her mother muttered, "Help us, God," and took Parker's hand, as though she were a child poised to stray in front of a car.

"Parker," Gibson said, "I don't think you should stay here until we get to the bottom of this. Whoever did this is toying with you. It's a head game. And that's probably all it is. If you'd been home, I doubt that they'd have tried to get in."

"I *was* here until Mom called. And my car's out in the carport! How did they know I wasn't here?"

Lynn straightened, as if she were taking over. "Parker, go pack your things. You're moving in with me for a while."

Parker didn't argue.

She went to the back of the house, grabbed a suitcase, and packed it, wanting to get out of here as soon as she could. Had she slept here for the last time?

CHAPTER
TWENTY-TWO

Parker couldn't sleep that night. She sat up in her childhood bed, staring at the moonlight blotching her wall. Leave it to her to have such a bizarre break-in. Breaking in to *leave* something. No one would believe it.

She'd have to add it to her annals, along with being pronounced dead on local television. Maybe someday she'd write a ballad about the whole crazy thing.

Someone was clearly messing with her head. "Double Minds" hadn't been stolen. Serene was recording it, and Parker had licensed it to her fair and square.

But someone was sending her a message. She just didn't know what that message was. The phone call she'd gotten played in her mind again.

The murder was about you. But don't worry, I'm protecting you.

Chase sat in jail right now for the murder of the girl whose death he seemed to genuinely be grieving. Yet the murder weapon in his apartment was clear evidence, wasn't it?

Giving up on sleep, she slid out of bed and got her MacBook, which Gibson had released from evidence when they'd unsealed Colgate. She took it into her mother's living room. If her mind refused to rest, then she could put it to work writing the liner notes for her album.

A key in the door brought her off the couch, almost toppling her computer.

It was just LesPaul, keeping his late hours. She caught her breath and told herself she needed to get a grip. At this rate she'd have a coronary before she was thirty.

He came in, tossed his keys on the table. "I have great news. Studio E at Colgate is going to be available tomorrow night from midnight to seven a.m."

She frowned. "Crater has E booked."

"Nope," he said. "I'm the engineer. We've finished mixing, so we don't need it. You want it?"

"Yes." Other groups would want that time, if they knew it was available. But that was why she worked there, after all. "Can you be there?"

"Of course. Gibson, too," LesPaul said. "I already checked."

"So that's guitar and bass. We can use the computer drum machine. That sounds pretty real, right?"

"Sometimes it sounds better than the real thing. But if I'm engineering, it could get tricky with me playing guitar. We'd lose precious time because I'll have to get Gibson to watch the board while I lay down my tracks seperately. I think you need to ask Dad to play so we can avoid that step."

Parker sighed. "I don't want to deal with Dad when I'm in a hurry."

"That's exactly *when* you need him," LesPaul said. "You won't have as many takes with Dad. He gets it right the first time. His music is always good. Besides, he could use a break. It would mean a lot to him."

Wearily, she dropped back to the couch. "I went with Mom to get him at the Gold Rush tonight. He was harassing the band to let him play with them."

"He used to know those guys. He filled in for their guitar player when he was out with a broken arm."

"Doesn't matter. They didn't want him to play with them this time. The bartender called Mom to come get him."

He shrugged. "He'll be ashamed in the morning. Shame sometimes keeps him sober for a few days. Maybe having the chance to play on your album will stretch that out even longer."

"When are you going to learn, Les? We can't save him. He hasn't made up his mind yet to give up his first love."

"Mom?"

"No, Jack Daniels."

Her brother seemed so young, sometimes ... so idealistic. No matter how many years went by, he kept waiting for a different outcome. He sat down and pulled off his shoes. "Just think about it, Parker. He needs a break. And you need a free guitar player."

What choice did she have? There was little chance she could book a decent musician with only twenty-four hours' notice. Knowing that she wouldn't sleep at all tomorrow night, and realizing that her brain was too weary to do her any good tonight, she went back to bed and recited the Twenty-third Psalm until she drifted into a shallow sleep.

If Parker had had a good record deal and plenty of money with which to record her album, she would have hired a top-notch producer who could direct the whole process and deliver a sound that would sell. But without a record deal, she'd had to create a tiny little independent label of her own, which she called LHM, an acronym for "Lord, help me." LHM had little money and no employees. It would have to make do with family and favors.

When she finally admitted to herself that she had no choice but to ask her father, she waited for things at Colgate to settle down, then she called him, hoping he wasn't too hung-over. He sounded groggy as he answered the phone.

"Dad? How are you feeling?"

He cleared his throat. "Fine. I'm great, Parker. How are you?"

Did he even remember last night? "I thought you might be a little hung over."

He paused. "A little." At least his speech wasn't slurred, which meant that he hadn't tried to fight the hangover with more booze. "Listen, I'm really sorry about last night." His voice was deep, gravelly. "It's a miserable thing to wake up and remember that your daughter and wife had to drag you out of a bar." His voice broke, and he cleared his throat again. "I'm really sorry, Parker."

His apology covered a host of sins. But tomorrow he'd probably have to make another one. "It's okay, Dad. There's help available if you'll take it."

"Sweetheart, I've been to umpteen rehabs. I know what to do. I just need to do it."

"I heard about a Christian ministry where you can go for free, and stay for a year, or even longer."

"I'm not going away for a year." His tone had finality, and she knew her pleas had fallen on deaf ears. They'd been through this so many times before. "Is that why you called?"

"No. Dad, I need a guitar player on my album. We have a studio tonight between midnight and seven a.m. Can you come?"

His soft chuckle made her smile. "Can I come? Does the eagle fly? Of course I can come. We'll knock 'em dead."

"No alcohol," she said. "We're recording at Colgate."

"Can I smoke if I do it outside?"

"If you're not afraid of bullets flying out of nowhere."

"I'll take my chances."

He always did. "We're going to rehearse at Mom's at seven."

"I'll be there."

She was hanging up when she saw Daniel Walker standing in the hallway, a Coke in his hand. She smiled. "You guys on a break?"

"A short one. Hey, are you looking for a guitar player for your album?"

"Not anymore. My dad's gonna do it."

"So you'll have Gibson on bass, your dad on lead guitar ... who's playing rhythm guitar if LesPaul's working the sound board?"

"We'll just let Dad do both parts."

He pushed off from the wall and came to lean on her desk. "That'll take twice as long. How about if I come help out? I already know most of your songs."

That was true. He'd played with her when she'd performed for his youth group. "But you're working all day. We're talking midnight to dawn."

"Hey, I do youth lock-ins. Just make a pot of coffee and I can handle it."

She breathed a laugh. "Wow. That would be great."

"Okay," he said. "I figure I'll get out of here around six or so. So you're rehearsing before you get into the studio?"

She hated to ask more of him. "My mother's at seven. But you don't have to come ..."

"I'll be there."

The thought of having someone of Daniel's caliber in the studio thrilled her. He wouldn't be able to play for her on the tour, but LesPaul could do that. Maybe they could pull this off, after all.

CHAPTER
TWENTY-THREE

Parker went back to her mother's after work. She'd heard from Gibson. The fingerprints he'd collected from the song sheets didn't match any they had in the database, meaning that the mysterious delivery person had never been printed before. Since it was impossible to tell whether the prowler had meant to find her at home, Parker planned to stay at her mother's, trying to put her fears out of her mind so she could focus on recording. With her trusty laptop and the music room at her mother's house, she was able to apply the finishing touches to her songs before going into the studio.

Her brothers, her dad, and Daniel showed up at her mother's house around seven, and they rehearsed there until time to leave for the studio. Her dad seemed mercifully sober, though she knew he'd probably had *some* alcohol that day or his hands would be shaking too badly to play.

The problem would be her voice. The guys were young enough and her dad was wild enough to stay up till the wee hours and jam until daylight, but in the middle of the night, her voice was likely to be tired and hoarse. She sipped what seemed like gallons of tea with lemon, hoping when the time came to record vocals, her throat wouldn't sound fatigued. Everything hinged on the sound of her CD.

Parker had spent so much time already trying to get a record deal. She'd used every contact she had and called in every favor she was owed, but so far, to no avail. Her best hope now was to get a pressing and distribution deal. That wasn't ideal by any means; it wouldn't pay many of her costs. It also wouldn't get her on the radio or in the stores. DJs didn't play songs they didn't know about, and stores didn't stock CDs by unknowns from indie labels. So much rode on their turning out a stellar product. If her record sounded amateur, none of their hard work would matter. It would take the Holy Spirit empowering them to get it right in the time allotted.

When they got into the studio, Parker got her Bible and brought them all into a circle on the carpeted studio floor. She opened it to the Psalms.

"Uh, what are we doing?" Pete asked.

"Just a little Bible study, to get us focused," she said.

Pete looked from one of his sons to the other. "Do we have time for this?"

"Yes," she answered for them. "This song we're about to record is meant to glorify God. I want to be sure that this whole session honors him."

She could smell the scent of alcohol on his breath. He must have found a way to take a swig somewhere between her mother's house and here. She glanced at Daniel, embarrassed. But he had pulled a Bible out of his guitar case.

That warmed her. Her father wouldn't respond to the quick Bible reading, but what really mattered was that *God* responded, that he was pleased with it and that he filled her with his Spirit at a time when she sorely needed it. The song was praise to him, after all. At least Daniel got it.

She read the Psalm, then began to sing "Ambient" a cappella. The men in her life seemed riveted as they saw that the source of the song was the Psalm she'd just read. But even as she sang, Parker knew that her voice wasn't going to carry the day. The melody would help, but it would be the lyrics that had the power.

When she finished singing, she closed her eyes and prayed that God would give her the power, the strength, and the voice to carry out this praise to him. Instead of saying Amen, she just sat in the silence for a moment.

Her dad's chuckle broke the quiet. "I've played with people who practiced transcendental meditation before they recorded. One crazy cat forced us to do yoga. Some dropped acid or smoked weed. Leave it to my eccentric girl to start with the Bible and prayer."

It wasn't eccentricity, but her dad wouldn't understand.

They moved into high gear. It was pure grace that the studio that was available was divided into booths that separated Daniel, Pete, and Gibson in isolated rooms. Parker played piano in the main booth. That way, the sounds didn't bleed into each other on the tracks, making it easier and faster to mix. If they'd had one of the lesser studios, they would have had to record each instrument one at a time. They used the computer drum machine since they didn't have a drummer, but it sounded like the real thing.

When they'd finished laying down the musical tracks, she got ready to do the vocals. She put the headphones over her ears and closed her eyes as the track began to play. Gently, she sang the song that she hoped people would sing in churches for years to come, lifting up the name of Jesus and praising his power. When she finished, she kept her eyes closed as the music played to the end. Finally, she opened her eyes and looked through the glass into the control booth. Daniel was smiling. He lifted his hands and began to applaud.

"I think we may have gotten that on the first take," LesPaul said into the microphone.

"No way." She doubted that was even possible, until he played it back. Then she agreed that she probably couldn't improve on it. They could move on to another song. She was in the zone, and now she was confident they'd be able to pull it off in the time they were allotted.

God was blessing the album. What else did they need?

CHAPTER
TWENTY-FOUR

Morning came too soon. They'd gotten down the tracks for three more of Parker's songs — something other artists might consider miraculous. Counting the songs she'd already mixed before the tour opportunity came up, she had seven recorded. She needed to record three more, and the three they'd just recorded still had to be mixed. They were still so far from finishing. Spent, she came out of the studio at seven a.m. as a producer showed up to take the room over. Pete and LesPaul, and even Daniel, were able to go home and get a few hours' sleep. But Gibson had to go back to work. She hoped he wasn't too tired to figure out who her weird delivery prowler was. Yesterday's efforts had gotten him nowhere.

Not sure she'd make it through the day, Parker went to Starbucks and got two coffees and a banana nut muffin. She ate the muffin in the car, not caring about the crumbs going all over her shirt and seat. As she drove back to the studios, she wished she had time to go home to shower and change clothes. But it was too late now. George expected her there at eight, and Andy, who'd worked the desk since midnight, was ready to leave. She had no choice.

She got to Colgate on time. As she set her laptop and coffee down and dropped into the chair behind her desk, she prayed the phone wouldn't ring much today. If things were quiet, she could work on her album cover. She flipped through the snapshots in her computer files and found a few artsy shots her mother had taken. She would use PhotoShop software to zoom in and put it in negative, then add bright colors and stock elements until it looked somewhat professional.

If she had six more weeks and a lot more money, she could do a drop-dead job. But the tour provided a brutal deadline, and time was running out.

She dropped her head to her desk. What had she been thinking? She couldn't get this all done. It was impossible!

"Hey, you okay?"

She pulled her head up, hair stringing into her eyes. George Colgate leaned against her desk. She hadn't realized he was in the building.

"You look terrible. Are you sick?"

"No, I was here all night. Crater finished early, so I took his midnight to seven a.m. slot in Studio E." She sat up straighter. "I'm fine, though. Just need a little more coffee."

He looked tired, too. "I would have thought you'd be afraid to be here in the middle of the night."

"My brother the cop was with me."

"Oh, yeah. Gibson's good to have around." He went to the part of the window that hadn't been shot through, and peered out. "I sure wish the glass guys would get out here today. We need to replace this pane as soon as possible."

"They said the insurance adjuster had to sign off on it first. I'll call them again." She was also waiting for them to replace the glass at her house, too. Gibson had boarded up the broken window in the meantime.

George rubbed his eyes, leaving them red. "Poor Nathan Evans. Knowing it was Brenna's boyfriend must have really knocked them for a loop. I don't know how they'll recover. Tiffany's got a new album coming out. They were already promoting it when Brenna died. Word was they were racing to get it out before Serene's new one releases. Street date's next week."

Parker thought of Tiffany Teniere's condition the day of the funeral. Grieving like that, she wouldn't be touring anytime soon.

After George ambled back to his office, Parker did an Internet search on Tiffany Teniere. The hoopla at her website, much like Serene's, made her out to be a super-spiritual person who happened to be sexy at the same time. No cleavage in her pictures, but poses and smiles and seductive looks that would make young men salivate, even though she was old enough to be their mother.

Parker looked back over the record charts. The Christian Top 20 had had Tiffany in the top ten for the last few years, but it had been a long time since she'd hit number one. Serene had knocked her off every time she had a new release. With the failure of Alena Moore's album and Tiffany's decline, Nathan Evans's bank account had undoubtedly diminished quite a bit in the last couple of years.

Evans's angry words the day of the funeral played through Parker's mind, tangling with Tiffany's slurred declaration that Nathan's enemies had used Brenna to get at him. What had he done to deserve that?

And of course, if Chase was the killer, then both of Brenna's parents were wrong.

But how were Parker's prowler and the song sheets and the man on the phone connected to Chase? Since he was in jail, he couldn't have been the one who broke into her house. According to Gibson, ever since his arrest, he'd been claiming he'd been framed. Maybe his claims were true.

She had a sudden desire to talk to Chase. If only she could see him face to face, ask him some hard questions. Yes, Gibson had warned her not to get involved. But Chase couldn't hurt her from a jail cell.

She looked for the number for the county jail. Maybe they would let her visit him. Maybe that would help Gibson get to the bottom of this case sooner, before someone else lost their life.

CHAPTER
TWENTY-FIVE

Parker had never visited anyone in the slammer, and she was nervous as she pulled into the parking lot of the Davidson County Detention Center. Men in orange suits loitered near the door, smoking. She recognized the uniforms — these were the men who picked up trash along the highways. As she got out and locked her car, she wondered how these prisoners had earned this amount of freedom. Had they been rehabbed into law-abiding citizens, or should she fear them as she walked through?

She went in and made her way through the crowd of waiting visitors to the booth at the far corner. A woman wearing glasses with half-inch-thick lenses seemed to be the gate-keeper.

"Hi." Parker leaned on the counter and offered an overbright smile.

The woman didn't match her feigned perkiness. "What can I do for you?"

"I'm Parker James. I'm here to visit Chase McElraney."

"You on his list?"

"Yes. I called yesterday and they said they would ask him to put me on it. This morning I was told that he did."

"I need your ID."

Parker realized that her hands were trembling as she pulled her driver's license out of her wallet. She handed it to the woman, glad she had no way of knowing that Parker barely knew Chase.

The woman read it and typed something into her computer, then thrust the card back. "Wait over there."

Almost surprised that it was that easy, Parker found an empty chair among the waiting visitors. A dozen children were in the place, some preschoolers, dodging people as they came and went. Women barked complaints at them as if they were little adults. She wondered if the children were there to see their fathers. What must it be like to visit your child this way?

Several seats down, she saw a couple that looked as uncomfortable here as she did. The woman, about forty-five, wore black slacks and a lavender pastel sweater. Her hair was pulled back in a sleek ponytail, and though she had on makeup, it was smudged by the tears in her eyes. The man next to her looked the same age. He wore jeans and a golf shirt, and he held the woman's hand and whispered softly to her.

Parker tore her eyes away, crossed her legs and wiggled her foot, trying to distract herself from the nervous tension stiffening her muscles. Were they going to search her before she went in? Should she put her purse in the car? No, it was all right. Many others, including those who looked as if they'd been here many times before, had purses with them.

What would she say to Chase? She dug through her purse for the piece of paper she had jotted notes on.

"Excuse me."

Parker looked up. The nicely dressed woman stood over her. "Yes?"

"I heard you say you were here to see my son."

Chase's parents. Parker stood. "Yes. I work for Colgate Studios. I met him a few days ago. I just wanted to talk to him today, but ... I didn't realize you were here. They said he only gets twenty minutes. I don't want to cut into your time."

His father stood and put his arm around his wife. "I know he wants to talk to you. He called last night and told us. We'll see him after you do."

"All right. Thanks. I won't take long, I promise."

Chase's father's eyes were soft, moist. "I know they're only holding him for the gun thing," he said, "but it feels like they're going to charge him with murder. He didn't do any of this. He's never given us any trouble." His voice broke, and he rubbed his face to hide his trembling mouth. "Your brother's a detective, right? Please tell him this is all a big mistake."

Nodding, she sat back down, wondering why they hadn't warned him not to talk to her without an attorney. Since they hadn't — what did that mean? That they thought Chase could convince her to influence Gibson? Clearly, they didn't know the ropes yet. How sad that they'd been thrust into the justice system without any warning.

She felt bad about taking any of their visitation time. Since they didn't live close by, they would have to travel some distance each way to visit him twice a week. She would hurry, leaving them as much time as possible.

A child came running out of an open door. "Your turn," she yelled, and her sister got up and raced inside. She heard the child cry, "Daddy!"

Hoping she didn't look too conspicuous, Parker stepped over to the open door and peered in. She saw a row of windows with people sitting at them, visiting prisoners in orange jumpsuits on telephones, on the other side of the glass. No wonder purses were allowed. There was no way to pass anything to the prisoners through a system like this. She felt bad for the children who couldn't even get hugs.

She went back to her seat and jittered for fifteen minutes more until the group in the visitation room came out. Her name was called, startling her. She dropped her bag. Her cell phone, lip gloss, and two pens rolled out. She knelt and grabbed them up like a kid with something to hide. Throwing everything back in, she slipped the straps over her shoulder and followed the group into the room.

A new group of jumpsuited men were taking their places at the windows. She spotted Chase and gave him an awkward wave. He pointed to an empty space, and she went to it. Sitting down on the metal stool in front of him, she picked up the phone. He punched in a few numbers, and then she heard his voice.

"Thanks for coming."

She gave him a half-smile. "Thanks for putting me on the list. I didn't know if you would. I know your parents are waiting, so I won't take long. I just wanted to ask you a few questions."

"Anything," he said. "Anything I can do to prove that I'm not guilty." He leaned forward, his face close to the dirty glass. "Parker, I know your brother's working on this case. I hope you believe me — I didn't know that gun was in my apartment. I don't even *own* a gun."

"Then where did it come from?"

"I don't know. It's like I told your brother. Someone put it there. The real killer, apparently. Whoever it was is setting me up. Making the police think I'm the one who killed Brenna. But I wouldn't do that. I loved her." The emotion squaring his lower lip seemed real.

"Chase, some weird things have been happening. Someone broke into my house the other night and left something. Song sheets, with a word written across it."

"What was the word?"

It was part of a police investigation, so she decided not to tell him. "It doesn't matter. The point is, my house was broken into. And before that I got this freaky anonymous phone call ..." She didn't know why she was telling him this. Shaking her head, she tried to steer her thoughts back to her questions.

"Chase, why did you tell me you put your hand through the wall *after* you found out about the murder?"

He paused a moment. "I knew how it would sound to say I did it earlier because of my fight with her. They would think I'm violent. That I could hurt her."

Her hand was slick against the phone. "Tell me about that fight."

He sighed, and for a moment she thought he wouldn't. "I shouldn't be going into this with you, but I really want you to believe me." He leaned forward again, the knuckles of his free hand touching the bottom of the glass. "Earlier that day I was talking to her on the phone, and I felt like she was being secretive again. I accused her of cheating on me, and when she wouldn't tell me what was going on, I lost it and slammed my fist through the sheetrock. But she wasn't even there when I did it — we were on the phone." He studied her face. "I need you to believe that, Parker."

She glanced at the man in the booth next to him. He had a tattoo of Pegasus on his jaw. "What I believe doesn't matter. I'm just trying to work through all this in my mind. There's a lot at stake for me, because if you didn't kill Brenna, then somebody else did — maybe the same person who came into my house."

"Check out her father."

"Her father? You think he killed his own daughter?"

"No. But I think he was into some things that were pretty corrupt. Maybe somebody got mad at him and killed Brenna to get even."

Again, the light was back on Nathan Evans. "What kind of corruption are we talking about?"

"He was always doing dirty stuff. Brenna told me about some of his publicity stunts, tricks to get his artists name recognition. He had a little payola going on, too, to get his artists airplay. He had a lot of the radio people in his pocket."

"But he's in the *Christian* music industry."

"It's still business, Parker. Brenna told me over and over that money is the bottom line."

"And what about Tiffany?"

"I know she loved Brenna. You saw her at the funeral. She was a mess."

"But what about her career? The grapevine says she was failing and that she and Nathan were trying to rally to recoup some of their loss."

"Nathan would have done anything to boost Tiffany's career, and trust me, he's not above using Brenna's death to do it."

"Using it in what way?"

"As a sympathy card. To make people buy Tiffany's records. Trust me, he'll have her out there onstage talking about her grief way before she's ready. The sad thing is, she'll probably mean every word of it, but he'll exploit it."

"Sounds like you don't think much of Nathan Evans."

"I don't. He had this weird hold over Brenna. She would do anything for him. They were really close. Whenever I reacted to the stuff she told me about him, she would get mad at me. She thought he was smart, not corrupt."

Parker just looked at him for a moment. "Chase, what is the real reason that Brenna was at Colgate Studios? It wasn't for her career. She wasn't trying to make it on her own. That's not the place to do it."

He shrugged. "I thought she was there to meet guys in the music business. It ticked me off."

She stared at him a moment, imagining him driving by and seeing her through the window, talking to a musician. Could it have ticked him off enough to get revenge?

He seemed to read her thoughts. "Not ticked off enough to kill her, Parker. Ticked off enough to put my hand through my wall." His eyes looked honest, and her gut told her he was telling the truth. But she had more questions. "Do you think Brenna could have been at Colgate to spy on our artists?"

Chase stiffened. "Don't make this something *she* did. She was the *victim*."

"But she could have done it for her father."

"She didn't do anything wrong, except show up in the wrong place at the wrong time."

She saw the conflicted emotions pass over his face. If he had been the one to kill her, would he be defending her now?

He rubbed at a spot on the table in front of him. "The gun ... it must have been registered to *somebody*. Can't they find out who?"

"Even if I knew, Chase, I couldn't talk about it."

"Look, I don't blame them for locking me up if that's the gun that killed Brenna. Of course, they would think I did it. But if it's the murder weapon, then they should be looking at everyone who's had access to my apartment since the murder. I gave your brother a list of all my friends who've come and gone. Whoever killed Brenna wanted to get the heat off themselves and put it on me, the most obvious suspect. I'm taking the fall for something some lowlife did to my girl." His voice broke off, and his mouth quivered. He shielded it with the phone. "Parker, I want you to promise me that you'll do everything you can to see that your brother looks into those people. I'm telling you, one of them is the killer."

Parker realized she believed him. "I'll do the best I can."

CHAPTER
TWENTY-SIX

Calling Gibson probably wasn't a good idea right now. He'd go ballistic when he heard that Parker had visited his number-one suspect. Still, Chase had a point — she wanted to make sure Gibson had interviewed the friends who had access to Chase's apartment.

When she called and told him what she'd just done, he let out a yell. "Parker, what did I tell you?"

"I know, Gibson. But I was thinking that — "

"No, don't think! It could get you killed. I know how to do my job. I don't need my little sister solving my cases."

"Okay, I hear you! I just want to know if you interviewed the people on his list."

"We found the murder weapon in his apartment. He'd put his fist through a wall that day, when he fought with her. He lied about it."

"So that's a no? You didn't talk to them."

"We interviewed a ton of his friends before we found the gun."

"And none since?"

He groaned. "I'll talk to them, okay? You're enough to drive a person crazy."

She'd been told that before.

She thumbed the End button and dropped the phone on the passenger seat. She needed to get back to Colgate. Cat was sitting in for her, but that meant Parker would have to work later tonight.

She turned on the radio, hoping to put her mind on autopilot for a while. Bebo Norman's voice pulled her under its spell, and she found herself humming along. Finally, the DJ came back on. "And now, here's Tiffany Teniere with her new hit, 'Altar Ego.' Email us and tell us how you like it. This is John and Sherry Rivers, at K-Love."

Tiffany's new song, already? She turned up the radio. The intro sounded familiar, and as Tiffany crooned out the opening verse, Parker's lungs shut down.

She pulled off the road, almost hitting a pedestrian as she turned into a parking lot.

Staring at the radio with her mouth hanging open, she listened to the lyrics and melody of "Altar Ego." It sounded familiar ... way too familiar. It was almost identical to "Double Minds," the song *Parker* had written!

A few key things had been changed — the chorus was slightly different, the bridge totally new, and the words "double minds" had been changed to "two minds." But the message of the song, the tune, and most of the lyrics were still unmistakably Parker's.

"Unbelievable!" She slammed her hand on the steering wheel. This would derail the release of Serene's album.

Grabbing her phone, she navigated her way to the iTunes screen and checked to see if Tiffany's song was available for download. What had they called it?

Oh, yes. "Altar Ego." She hit Buy, hoping she had a strong-enough signal. The song quickly appeared in her music library. She played it again.

Yes, it was unmistakable. This was no coincidence. She tapped back to the phone screen and called Serene. Her voicemail came on. "Serene, call me as soon as you get this. I just heard Tiffany Teniere's new song and it's ripped off from 'Double Minds.' Somehow she got our song and put it out before you could. Call me!"

She hung up, found Butch in her contact list and punched his number.

"This is Butch."

"Butch, you've got to hear something!" Her words rushed out like water through a breach. She plugged her iPhone into her car stereo and began to play the song.

After the first few bars, Butch was yelling. "Those low-down, sneaky, conniving . . ."

"But how did they get it?"

"Brenna!" Butch said.

Of course.

She heard things crashing at Butch's end. "It'll sabotage Serene's album!" he yelled. "They knew that. It's what they wanted, to get her off the number-one spot."

"But how could they not know that we'd recognize it? It's so blatant."

"This really puts us in a mess, Parker," Butch said through his teeth. "We can't release Serene's song now or the fans are going to think *she* stole it from Tiffany. I'm calling David, my entertainment attorney. Can you meet with him today?"

"As soon as you get an appointment," she said. "Call me back and let me know." She cut off her phone and listened to the song again, wishing she could believe it was all just a grim coincidence. But it wasn't possible — there were too many similarities for this to have happened purely by accident.

Her mind slammed back to the break-in at her house. Song sheets for "Double Minds," with the word *Stolen* written across it. Her prowler knew about the theft!

Had Brenna managed to copy the master of Serene's recording, before she redid it with the new lyrics?

Not likely. Butch would never have left it lying around. And Brenna didn't have enough clout to go in and out of studios during sessions. And the rooms were soundproof. She wouldn't have even had the opportunity to hear the song.

Then it hit her. It could have been much simpler than that. Parker had her own demo recordings on her laptop computer. They were lined up and labeled in her iTunes program. Brenna could have easily downloaded them onto an iPod when she was at Parker's computer. There were so many times that Parker had left her laptop on her desk when she'd run an errand or gone to lunch.

And if Brenna had heard Serene's musicians mentioning the titles of the songs on her album, Brenna and her father could have chosen those to sabotage Serene's album.

She pulled back out into traffic, tears blurring her eyes. She had felt so badly for the girl who'd been murdered right there on the floor in front of Parker's desk. She'd had no idea that Brenna was stabbing her in the back, that she'd been at Colgate simply to find a way inside Parker's computer.

What other of Parker's songs were on Tiffany's new album?

She sat in the parking lot at Colgate and looked up Tiffany on iTunes again. This time, she downloaded the whole album to her iPhone. She waited, heart pounding, as each song downloaded. Then she checked each one. There weren't any other stolen songs. But "Altar Ego" was the only release they needed to sabotage Serene and keep her album from coming out on time. Now they would have to ditch that song and record something else. Parker would be expected to replace it.

She listened to "Altar Ego" again, eyes closed. They'd kept the original message, unlike Serene's new version, which had no mention of Christ. Tiffany, who had clearly stolen it *before* it was rewritten, *was* spreading the message of Christ. What irony.

The phone rang, and Serene's face lit up her screen. She clicked it on. "You heard?"

Serene was hysterical. "Butch just told me what happened. This is a hoax, right? Some kind of joke?"

"No, Serene, I think Brenna stole the song out from under me. We've solved the mystery of why she was at Colgate."

"Did you leave a disk of my rough cut lying around?"

"I didn't *have* your masters. Either she got into your studio while you guys were on a break, or she stole my demo version off my laptop."

"Parker, this puts me in serious trouble. I can't release that song now. If I have to find another one, I'll never get my album out on time. What'll we do?"

"Has Butch contacted a lawyer yet?"

"Yes, we're meeting at three this afternoon. You have to be there."

"I will."

"I'm not giving up this song!" Serene said. "I'm going to fight her in court if I have to. I'm going to make sure every radio station knows that she's a thief."

Parker didn't know what to say to that. As she drove home, she thought of that message about the double-minded man, unstable in all his ways ... the story her father had inspired. The message she had written in the middle of the night, hoping to impact people for Christ. Nigel Hughes would hear about this mess and write about it. What would it say to the world about Christianity?

If only she had a publisher or label who could fight for her. Instead, she'd chosen to self-publish her songs. Having a contact like Serene meant that she didn't need a publisher shopping her songs around. It had seemed like a waste of money to split the profits with a publisher if she didn't have to.

Because she didn't have time for all the paperwork required to register each of her songs, she'd hired an accountant to handle that for her. She merely wrote the songs and turned her rough, computer-cut demos over to him, and he registered them with the copyright office and ASCAP, who collected her royalties whenever the songs were played.

Now she wondered if having a publisher would have put her in a better position to fight copyright infringement. Maybe it was a police matter. Property had been stolen. Gibson would know if she needed to file a police report.

"She did *what*!" he said, when she got him on the phone.

After he'd cooled down, he said, "I've never worked a stolen intellectual property case," he said. "But I have the security tape. I'll look at the tapes for the days Brenna worked at Colgate and see if they show anything. This might be a criminal matter. But not my area, of course."

"They would have had to steal the song weeks ago for them to have gotten it on the album. But Gibson, whoever broke into my house knew."

She could almost hear his mental wheels turning. "I'll go back to the tape around the time she started working at Colgate."

"Her laptop was the same model as mine. How will you know if the one on the desk is hers or mine?"

"I'll see if we can figure it out from the tape. This really stinks, Parker. Let me know what the lawyer says."

When she got off the phone, she prayed for wisdom. This was one of those times when the wisdom of man wasn't going to cut it. This could be the end of her songwriting career. Butch might even kick her off the tour for being careless with the song.

And as far as Parker was concerned, they still didn't know for sure who killed Brenna Evans.

CHAPTER
TWENTY-SEVEN

Gibson signed Brenna's laptop out of the evidence warehouse and took it back to his desk. The security tapes had turned up nothing. Gibson found it impossible to tell whether Brenna was working at her own laptop or Parker's, since they were the same model. If there had ever been a time when she'd been found working on Parker's MacBook, she could have claimed it was hers. But clearly, she didn't have hers at work with her the night of the murder. And all she would need was her iPod to download all the songs she wanted.

Brenna's iPod was gathered with her other possessions the night of the murder, and returned to the Evans family a few days later. Thankfully, he didn't surrender the laptop. If she downloaded the songs to her iPod that night, they wouldn't have made it to her computer. But if she'd been downloading a few at a time each time she found the opportunity at Colgate, there might be some there. All Gibson needed was one of Parker's songs to prove that Brenna was the one who stole "Double Minds."

He scrolled through the hundreds of songs she had there, looking for a grouping that didn't have the usual pattern — song title, artist, album name. Parker's unproduced demos would look different.

He found a grouping of songs with only the names Track 01

through Track 12. He found his headphones and plugged them into the computer, then clicked on Track 01.

He recognized Parker's song immediately. It was one of those they'd recorded the other night. This version was a demo Parker had recorded on her computer at home. She'd played it for them before their rehearsal the other night. He clicked on the next one. Another Parker demo. One by one, he went through them, until he came to "Double Minds."

So here it was. Clear evidence that Brenna had downloaded Parker's songs. He leaned back in his chair and pulled off the headphones. "Hey Rayzo, over here."

His partner pulled his arthritic body out of his chair and came over. "Yeah?"

"Found Parker's songs on Brenna's iTunes. She couldn't have had them any other way than outright stealing them."

Rayzo leaned on his desk. "I don't even know how this works. How can you be sure?"

"See, iTunes is like a record store. You can download songs or albums and pay through your credit card. Once your card's been approved, you can have the songs in just thirty seconds or so."

"So you listen to them on the computer?"

"Yes, or you can plug into an iPod or mp3 player and download the songs to that. Then you can carry your music around and plug it into your car or a stereo, or listen with headphones right from the device."

He pointed to the stolen tracks on Brenna's iTunes. "These don't have titles, because they were rough demos — not purchased. Parker always converts the file format to iTunes format so she can listen to them on her iPhone ..."

"I thought we were talking about iPods."

"An iPhone is an iPod that's also a phone. Don't you watch TV?"

"I fast-forward through commercials."

"Doesn't matter," Gibson said. "The songs are here."

"Any other way she could have gotten them?"

"Nope. No one had copies of the songs Parker was keeping to record herself. Not even me. Brenna could have easily downloaded them to her iPod anytime Parker had her filling in for her and left her laptop there. If she got caught, she could just say her computer was the same model Parker had. People wouldn't think she was doing anything wrong."

"Parker seems too smart to leave her laptop sittin' around."

"She sometimes eats lunch back in the lounge and occasionally runs errands for Colgate — if she plans to come back, she just leaves it sitting on her desk. Just like the night of the murder."

"So how do we know your sister didn't know about this before? Maybe caught her at it?"

Gibson frowned. "Because she didn't. She just discovered it when she heard the song on the radio."

"That's what I'm saying. How do we know that ain't for show? For all we know, Parker could have given Brenna copies of the songs to impress her."

Gibson stiffened and stared at him. "Wait a minute. Are you saying you think my sister — "

"I'm just thinking like a detective, which I highly recommend if you want to stay in this department."

"No way. Parker isn't lying."

"I hate to tell you, James, but your sister has the strongest motive yet."

Gibson shot up, almost knocking over his chair. "My sister couldn't kill anyone. She doesn't even know how to load a gun."

"Maybe that's what she wants you to think."

"I don't think, I know!" He glanced around, hoping no one else heard. Lowering his voice, he said, "She has an alibi, Rayzo. She wasn't cruising Nashville shooting people through windows that night. She was on stage at a concert."

"She could have hired somebody."

"You're outta your mind!"

Rayzo pulled himself back to his feet. "Maybe we should just do what Chief wanted to do in the first place and turn this over to Carter and Stone. You got yourself a bona fide conflict of interest here."

Gibson couldn't believe his partner was becoming a traitor. "Come on, Rayzo. We're so close. We're making headway. You know my sister isn't the one. Let's just stay the course for now."

"Staying the course might mean jeopardizing a conviction. If some lawyer faces a jury and tells them we didn't investigate everyone involved because Parker James's brother was working on the case —"

"So investigate her! She's innocent. She didn't have the opportunity to commit this murder, and she doesn't have the money to hire a paid killer. Anybody who knows her will tell you she doesn't have it in her. That's just crazy. Look, do what you have to do. That's fine. I'm just telling you ahead of time what you'll find. If you want to waste your time on that, go ahead. But it won't get us any closer to closing this file."

Rayzo ambled back to his desk.

Gibson stared down at him. His jaws were beginning to hurt from clenching his molars. He couldn't let go of this case and expose his sister to suspicion. Somehow, he had to put all the pieces together.

The theft of the song chapped him almost as much as Rayzo's suspicion. He didn't like seeing his sister taken advantage of, but even worse, he detested being snowed by the family of one of his murder victims. There was something sinister going on with the Evans family, something that might have led to Brenna's murder. He rubbed his eyes as Rayzo got up again and went to the dry-erase board with the details of the case.

Rayzo had made a list of all the things they knew about the Evans family: *dishonest; corrupt; thieves; rich.*

Under Brenna, he'd listed *Secretive; Probably broke into Parker's computer.*

Under Nathan Evans he'd put, *Recently lost a lot of money after Christian star got pregnant; Tiffany's career in the tank.* Now he was writing, *Sends daughter to work at Colgate to steal Parker's songs.*

Gibson's gaze shifed to the list about Chase McElraney: *Busted hand — lied about how it happened; Jealous; Suspected Brenna of cheating.* And in all caps, he'd written, *MURDER WEAPON HIDDEN IN APARTMENT.*

Now Rayzo was making a new heading for Parker James.

Rayzo's phone rang. Gibson stared at the board as Rayzo answered, mumbling. Rubbing his jaw, he prayed for wisdom and insight into this case.

Rayzo got off the phone. "That was ballistics," he said. "The gun is definitely the murder weapon."

CHAPTER
TWENTY-EIGHT

The entertainment attorney's conference room was decorated like a nightclub, with a long table, booth seating, and a neon Budweiser sign on the wall. It was a little cheesy, if you asked Parker, but no one had. David Butler was in his fifties, yet he wore his hair moussed and spiked like a twenty-year-old rock star. His shirt was a size too small and needed to be buttoned a little higher.

Serene sat next to Parker on one side of the table, and Butch sat next to David on the other. Parker closed her eyes and listened as the attorney played the song over and over, comparing all three versions — Serene's version, Tiffany's single, and Parker's original demo. Her own voice came up, raspy and unadorned, a mere computer demo she'd made to help sell the song, not to play publicly. She looked down, unable to meet everyone's eyes.

Finally, when David had heard all three, he sat back and put his hands behind his head. "I think we've got some problems here. The songs are different. Serene, yours is about romance. It isn't a Christian song at all. The bridge is different. There are subtle differences in the melody and chorus."

Parker cleared her throat. "Tiffany's version is ninety percent what I wrote originally."

"You're right," he said. "That's why you're the one with grounds for a suit."

Parker covered her face. Just what she needed. A lawsuit on top of everything else. "I can't *afford* to sue her."

"Parker, you can't let her get away with it!" Serene stood up and stared at David. "Do you understand how much this theft has cost me? My album was almost ready. We'd mixed that song. We named the album 'Double Minds.' Now I can't even use my title song!"

"I do understand," David said. "But Parker is the one who owns the rights. She's the only one who can bring legal action. Now, you could sue *Parker* for letting the song get away — "

Parker gasped. "What?"

Serene grunted. "I couldn't do that."

"Your label may feel differently," David said.

Parker leaned her head back on the booth and tried not to cry. "I thought you were on my side."

"I am if you want me to be," David said. "But Parker, that's all the more reason you need to file suit. The label will likely sue you, so you'll have to sue Evans Music to protect yourself."

"I won't let my label sue her," Serene said. "I'd rather eat the loss."

Parker looked at her gratefully.

"It may not be up to you, Serene. It's business, after all."

Serene dropped back into her chair. "If Parker sues, would she have a chance of winning?"

The attorney looked down at his notes. "Truth is, I'm not sure we could prove unequivocally it's the same song. Do you have any proof that she took it off your computer, Parker?"

Serene and Butch turned their troubled eyes to her. "Yes. My brother found the songs on her computer."

"But can you prove how she got them? Will a jury be convinced?"

"He's still going through the security tape, trying to see when she did it."

"Let me know if he finds anything. Meanwhile, I can write a

letter to Tiffany Teniere and Nathan Evans and let them know that we're aware of what's occurred. I can at least threaten a lawsuit and give them a cease-and-desist order to make them pull the song off the radio and out of stores until this is settled."

Serene couldn't stay in her seat. She got up again and walked across the room. "I want to do some interviews and publicly tell everyone what happened. The fans need to know that Tiffany's a liar and a thief."

"I'd be careful with that," David said. "If you can't prove the song's stolen, you can't prove any of that. She could slap *you* with a defamation of character suit."

"You've got to be kidding!" Serene cried. "I'm not going to just roll over. That woman stole my song!"

"She stole *Parker's* song. As far as I'm concerned, you could still put your song out and people wouldn't even recognize it."

"Yes, they would. The melody is almost identical. They would think *I* was the one copycatting. I can't do that. What's Jeff Standard going to think?"

Parker thought of Tiffany, so sedated at the funeral over the death of her daughter. She tried to imagine having a public war with her, Serene calling a press conference and raking her over the coals. Public sympathy would naturally align with the grieving mother. The Evans family had them over a barrel.

The attorney turned off his CD player. "Parker, if you want to go forward with a lawsuit, I'll be glad to file it. If we win, it's possible that the best we can do is to get them to pay you royalties on the song, and maybe a small amount in punitive damages."

Parker closed her eyes. She didn't have the money for this, and she hated the idea of two Christians airing their dirty laundry publicly. She sighed. "Let me think about it and talk to my family. I don't know what I should do."

"Parker, it's a no-brainer," Butch said. "You have to sue. And meanwhile, we've got to come up with another song to replace 'Double Minds.'"

Parker felt as if someone was screwing an ice pick through her eyebrow. "Serene, I'll give you another song. One from my own album."

Serene was quiet. "Which one?"

"'Ambient.' I'll give you 'Ambient.'"

"'Ambient'?" Butch asked. "I haven't even heard that song. How do I know if it's good?"

"It's good," Serene said. "I'll take it."

The words stabbed. Parker had planned to use 'Ambient' as the title track of her own album, the song she knew people would be humming and singing as they walked out of the concerts, the one that would send them to the CD tables to buy Parker's album. But what choice did she have?

"Okay, it's yours." She struggled not to cry. "My band and I have already laid down some tracks." Her voice was barely audible. "You can use those if you want. That'll save you some time, if you think they're good enough."

"Okay, it's a deal." Serene looked at Butch. "We don't have time to wallow in this. We need to get back into the studio today."

"Guess so," he said.

All that studio time wasted.

Butch and Serene left her there to iron things out with the attorney and to run up a bill she couldn't afford. By the time she got back to Colgate, her spirits felt like rocks in the pit of her stomach, ready to take her down.

CHAPTER
TWENTY-NINE

Parker's mother's house smelled like roast beef and peach cobbler — comfort food designed to make Parker feel better. But Parker wasn't hungry. She sat on the back porch, swinging on the wicker swing and wondering what she was going to do. How could such grand opportunities shatter into so many pieces? She looked up at the sky. A cloud sailed by on the wind. She could smell rain.

What are you doing, Lord?

She tried to live in obedience, tried to do the things that were pleasing to God. While others were cheating and selling out, she was holding her ground. Why, then, was she the target for theft and murder?

Her mother stuck her head out the back door. "Time to eat, honey. Everybody's here."

Parker had no more appetite for company than she did for food, but her mother had gone to a lot of trouble. She went into the house and saw her dad already at the table, plucking a green bean out of a bowl and popping it into his mouth. "Hey, darlin'."

"Hey, Dad." She gave him a hug. His breath had the faint tinge of alcohol, but he was clean and seemed sober. She hadn't really wanted him here. He tended to be a distraction, and she desperately needed to focus now. But when her mother called a family meeting, she included the whole family.

Her brothers were already seated. She knew they didn't have much time, but she was grateful they had come.

After her mother led them in prayer, they began to eat. Parker only picked at her food. It wouldn't sit well next to the anxiety churning in her stomach.

"So," Lynn said. "Everyone enjoy. But what we're really here for is to decide whether Parker should get an attorney and sue."

Pete slathered some butter on his bread. "Of course she should." He looked across the table to Parker. "Sweetheart, you don't have any choice. This Tiffany woman needs to be blackballed from the whole industry. People need to know what she's done."

Parker sighed. "It's not just her, Dad. It's her husband and his company."

Gibson looked as dejected as she did. "There's a lot going on here," he said. "A lot of pieces that add up to murder, and I don't yet know how they all fit. But I think Parker's in over her head. I'm not sure it's a good idea to start agitating things now."

"Agitating things?" LesPaul asked. "Parker shouldn't have to roll over every time somebody tries to take something from her. And frankly, Parks, I'm really disappointed that you gave 'Ambient' to Serene. It's the best song you've written, and to just hand it over to her, complete with all the tracks that we laid ... well, that's just wrong. Is she even going to pay us back for the time we invested?"

Parker poked at her meat. "She'll pay our standard rate, plus you'll get credit on a major album. And she'll give us some of her studio hours so we can record."

"Yeah, if she gets finished before her studio time runs out," Les-Paul said. "And I don't think she will. I'm sending her a bill for the engineering. I don't work free, except for you."

"We're not here to talk about 'Ambient,'" Parker's mom said. "We're here to discuss what Parker needs to do about 'Double Minds,' or 'Altar Ego,' or whatever they're calling it."

Pete stopped eating and pointed his fork at Parker. "I say you hire that lawyer to file suit and take care of this before any more time passes."

That was easy for her father to say. He didn't have to deal with these people in the music industry any more. All of his bridges had been burned years ago. "I'm just not sure it's the right thing to do," Parker said.

LesPaul looked personally offended. "Why in the world wouldn't it be?"

"I'll tell you why," Gibson said. "She could spend a lot of money and still lose."

"You have *proof* that Brenna stole the songs," LesPaul said. "What else does she need? A stupid letter isn't going to stop those people."

Parker set her fork down. "They just lost their daughter."

"I understand your compassion," Pete said, "but the fact is, they do junk like this. You make enough people mad, and people come gunning for you and yours."

The room grew quiet, and Parker stared down at her plate.

Lynn was the first to speak again. "Pete, you don't think someone killed their child because they stole Parker's song."

"Not that, specifically," Pete said. "But come on. If this is how Evans does business, he's bound to have a lot of enemies."

Parker met Gibson's eyes, and she knew he was remembering what she'd overheard in the Evans house, the day of the funeral.

Lynn pushed her plate away, leaned her elbows on the table, and folded her arms. "Tell us what's going on in your head, honey."

Parker swallowed her tears and said, "I'm just thinking how it would look to people who aren't ... Christians. There's this reporter who's been snooping around. He caught me in the coffee shop and asked me a bunch of questions about the murder. And then he started asking about Serene having an eating disorder. Stuff like that. Turns out, he's a *New York Times* reporter, and he's sniffing out stories about hypocritical Christian celebrities."

"There are plenty of those," Pete said.

"I know, Dad, but there are a lot who aren't, too. I just hate to drag all this through the court and give him more dirt for his articles."

LesPaul pushed his plate away. "Parker, you can't worry about that. This is business, and if people can't understand that — "

"But it's not *just* business!" Parker cut in. "We're representatives of Christ."

"Tiffany Teniere is no representative of Christ," LesPaul said. "How can she claim to be a Christian if she steals something outright and puts it out there with her name as the songwriter?"

"Whatever she really believes, wherever her heart really is — to the world, she's a Christian. And they'd love seeing us tearing at each other's throats."

Her mom touched Parker's hand. "It's true, the Bible does tell us not to sue each other. We're told to settle it out of court, among ourselves."

"That's absurd," Pete bit out.

Parker knew her father could never understand. "I don't want to drag another Christian performer through the mud in front of the secular media. I can just see it on CNN. 'Christian artist Tiffany Teniere accused of being a liar and a thief while she grieves over her murdered child.' It's lose-lose." She picked up her napkin and wiped her mouth.

"But Serene's label might sue *you*," Gibson said. "You don't have a choice, Parker."

Tears rimmed her eyes, and she blotted the corners. "I'm just thinking, maybe I should just go to Tiffany myself and talk to her as one Christian to another."

Pete pointed his finger in her face. "Parker, don't you pull a bleeding heart on us. You're scaring me to death here."

"I'm not saying let her get away with it, Dad. I'm just saying that maybe I should lay all the cards on the table and give her the opportunity to make it right."

LesPaul was about to come out of his skin. "What are you going to say? Don't do it again, or else? Or else *what*?"

Parker didn't have an answer. Pressing the inside corners of her eyes to hold back tears, she whispered, "I haven't had enough time to pray about this."

Gibson looked at their mother. "Mom, what do you think?"

Lynn stroked Parker's hair, patted her back. "I think Parker's right. She doesn't need to decide anything until she's prayed enough to have peace about it. It says in James that if anyone lacks wisdom, he should ask of God, and he'll give it liberally if you have faith."

"Okay," LesPaul said. "So she's going to pray. Meanwhile, what do you think?"

Lynn got up to get the iced tea from the sideboard. "I think there's one more option you should pray about, Parker. You should pray about hiring a Christian mediator."

Parker looked up. "A what?"

"A mediator." She went around the table filling everyone's glasses. "I've seen it done a lot. You go to Tiffany and tell her your beef, then you ask her if she's willing to take her case before a Christian mediator and accept the verdict. It's just like a lawsuit, only it stays in the Christian family. But both sides have to agree to accept the outcome."

Parker considered. Maybe that was an option. "How would I find something like that?"

Lynn sat back down. "I'll talk to a few friends and find out."

A tiny spark of hope caught inside her. Still ...

"Even if I get credited as the songwriter and start getting royalties on it, it won't undo the mess this has made. I still don't know if Jeff Standard will keep me on the tour. He'll see this whole thing as suspicious and unprofessional, and blame me for leaving my computer out where Brenna could get the songs. He might even think I was in on this."

"Serene will tell him that wasn't your fault," Lynn said.

"But maybe it was. Maybe I was just negligent, and I deserve —"

"Stop it," Lynn said. "That's not true and you know it. The enemy is telling you lies. He'll paralyze you into missing this opportunity. You can't let him do it. I didn't raise you to be a defeatist."

Parker covered her face and battled with her tears.

Her mom set the pitcher down hard. "LesPaul, you snoop around and find out who's booked studio time they won't be using. Gibson, keep looking for evidence that can't be denied."

LesPaul smiled. "And Mom, what are you going to do?"

She straightened as if she had the most important job of all. "I am going to clean the table."

CHAPTER THIRTY

Parker sat in the music room in her mother's house, playing the piano, trying to decide what her new title song would be, and which one would replace the one she'd given Serene. She almost ignored the phone when it rang, but curiosity forced her to pull it out of her purse.

Daniel Walker's name flashed up. Her heart caught, and she slid her thumb across the screen, answering it.

"Hello?"

"Hi, Parker. I wanted to check on you after I heard about the song. We had a rehearsal of 'Ambient' tonight. I couldn't believe you gave that to Serene."

"What else could I do? It's my fault the song was stolen."

"No, it wasn't. Look, I work for Serene, but she shouldn't have taken your title song. There are others that would have worked for her."

"I knew she liked that one."

"Well, if you don't mind my saying so, you're an artist just like she is. You're the one taking the greatest loss in this deal, and you can't afford it. Besides, you've written other songs Serene has already licensed but not recorded. She could have chosen one of those."

"Too late now."

"I know." He paused for a moment. "It's just like you, Parker, to put Serene before yourself."

His glowing words reminded Parker of what he'd said that day at the youth concert, when he thought she'd left before the applause, so God would get the glory. She started to come clean, but he spoke first.

"If you're trying to decide what your title track should be," he said, "I have a few ideas."

"Yeah? I'd love to hear them."

"Well, that night when we recorded, I was really drawn to 'Inscribed.' I thought it was brilliant."

She smiled. "Really? You think it's good enough to name the album after?"

"It's every bit as good as 'Ambient.' I'm guessing Serene hasn't heard it yet."

"She hasn't."

"Then don't let her. She'll snatch it up, too."

The thought had occurred to Parker.

"Listen, Parker, I'm really sorry all this has happened to you. But remember Isaiah 43:2: 'When you pass through the waters, I will be with you; and when you pass through the rivers, they will not sweep over you. When you walk through the fire, you will not be burned. The flames will not set you ablaze.'"

The verse dripped through her like warm honey, sweet to the taste, invigorating. "Thank you, Daniel."

"Sure. Call me if you want to talk. Anytime. I keep late hours. Whenever you're ready to record, I'm there. And Parker?"

"Yes?"

"I'll be praying for you."

She hung up and sat a moment, basking in the afterglow of Daniel's concern. No one else could have called her and made her feel better tonight. He'd done so much for her in that one short call.

Now she felt up to her tasks. She would pray about the songs, and if Daniel was right, if God wanted 'Inscribed' to be her new title song, he would give her a peace about it.

After praying, she went through each of her songs that she'd decided not to include on her album. She had hoped to sell them later, especially now that Serene's songs were hitting the *Billboard* charts. Her contract with Serene gave her first option to buy Parker's songs. But any that Serene turned away could be sold to others, if Parker didn't use them herself.

But these songs just weren't good enough for her album. She played a riff on the keyboard, hesitated, then tried again.

She heard a sound, then stopped, listening.

Her mother had gone to bed long ago, and LesPaul hadn't come in yet. Was that sound the wind against the house or someone prowling around? She was sick of being afraid, sick of trying to puzzle together the pieces of this murder that had come, unwelcomed, into her life. But wasn't that how it always went? Tragedies came uninvited, and the evidence left behind was often sketchy and incomplete. God wasn't one for explaining himself.

Maybe that was it. Maybe she could write about puzzle pieces, scattered and lost. She started to play again, humming along with the lilt of the lyrics coming to her mind. "Pieces ... nothing more than pieces." Then she realized she was playing the tune for that old seventies song "Feelings."

How many songs had she written to that tune before she realized what she was doing? She banged her hand on the keyboard and dropped her forehead against the music rack.

Think. Write. Don't just sit here.

She had to get out of this room, away from the instruments and the pressure. She walked through the living room and into the dining room where her mother's Bible sat. She looked up the passage Daniel had quoted to her. Her mother had highlighted much of the chapter.

Though God was speaking of Israel in these verses, the chapter contained much about God's nature and his great love and care of those who were his. She dwelt on it, savoring it, then read the next chapter and the next. Though the prophecies were glum for Israel, she clung to what she learned about God's sovereign power. Underlying it all was the grace that was so redemptive, bringing sunshine through the ashes, promising his people that he would not forsake them forever. Then she came to Isaiah 49, from which "Inscribed" had come.

But Zion said, "The LORD has forsaken me, And the LORD has forgotten me."

Can a woman forget her nursing child, and have no compassion on the son of her womb? Even these may forget, but I will not forget you. Behold, I have inscribed you on the palms of My hands.

That was the theme God was working out in her own life, the message he wanted her to fold between the chords and lyrics of her album. A new story for Lola began to birth in her mind, coming to her in bits and pieces … chorus before verses.

Several hours later, after starting and stopping, succeeding and failing, she had the song just as she wanted it. When she was sure she had it down, she plugged her keyboard into her computer, fired up her recording software, and began to record. It was a crude demo, nothing more than a record of what she had written so that she could play it for her brothers, her father, and Daniel, and reproduce it in the studio. But she liked it, maybe even better than "Double Minds," and even better than "Ambient."

It went along with the theme set by "Inscribed," bringing cohesion to her album.

She could do this. God was with her.

Exhausted and satisfied, she closed her computer, unplugged it from the keyboard and took it with her to bed. If some thief came in during the night to steal more of her songs, they wouldn't get this one.

CHAPTER
THIRTY-ONE

Parker woke up the next morning to find her mother gone. But she had left a note on the kitchen counter with the name of a local mediator and a phone number. Parker waited until she got to work, then called the number. The company was made up of retired Christian attorneys who believed in keeping biblical principles regarding lawsuits between Christians. The one who took her call was named Howard Leland. His voice made her miss her grandpop, who'd died a few years ago.

She explained her situation.

"So what you have here is not just grounds for a lawsuit," he said, "but grounds for an arrest. To get that song, they had to break into your computer and steal the digital file of the song."

"Basically." Parker lowered her voice and glanced down Colgate's hallway to see if any stray musicians might be in earshot. "But how do you press charges against a dead girl?"

"Good point. You can't. So I agree that your approach is the best one."

"I have an approach?"

"Calling us was an approach, wasn't it?"

"I don't know. I was really just calling to see what you recommend."

"Well, Parker, what you have to decide is what you want from them. Do you want Mr. Evans and his wife to compensate you for the hours Miss Stevens spent recording 'Double Minds,' so that you can compensate her?"

"Maybe. Along with the studio time and the cost for musicians. And if I could get something back for the time I spent in the studio, though it didn't cost me anything."

"Yes, of course. Also, you're entitled to songwriter credit and royalties on that song."

"That would be good, too."

"How about punitive damages?"

Parker thought about that for a moment. "I don't want to be greedy. I just don't think it's right that they should do this without any consequences."

"No, it isn't. We abide by biblical principles, Parker. The Bible says that we're not to sue brothers and sisters in the world's court. But if businesses were allowed to get away with theft and fraud by hiding behind the veil of Christianity, then few Christians could stay in business. They'd be walked on like doormats and all of them would go bankrupt."

Howard told her he would fax her an agreement to sign, then contact Nathan Evans today and talk to him about the claims being made against them. If he could get Evans to commit to mediation, then Parker would have a chance of getting compensated for the songs.

She didn't hear back from Howard until later that morning.

"I'm sorry, Parker. We got in touch with Nathan Evans and he refused to even speak to us about it. He claims that you made the whole thing up, and he said there's no way he's going into any kind of mediation over a lie."

"Did you tell him that the police have evidence that Brenna stole the songs from me?"

"I did," Howard said. "His response was rather heated and emotional. I won't burden you with the details."

Parker let out a heavy breath. "Thank you."

"There's still a chance he'll change his mind after he's had time to think about it. But if he doesn't agree to mediation, I recommend that you go ahead with filing the lawsuit, just to let him know you're serious. That may encourage him to come to mediation."

"And if it doesn't?"

"Then you'll have to decide whether to proceed with the lawsuit."

She was getting a headache, and she massaged her temple. "The Bible tells us we should prefer to be wronged than to drag a fight like this into the public courts."

"Yes, but God set up the governmental system so that those who break the law would be punished. If a brother or sister refuses to commit to Christian mediation, and you have the possibility of being sued by Miss Stevens's label, then I think you have no choice but to sue."

She rubbed her eyes. "What if I try to talk to Tiffany?"

"Nathan wouldn't let me speak to her. I don't recommend that you talk to her with a suit pending."

Parker felt no better as she hung up the phone. She heard voices in the hallway. It sounded like some of Serene's group, moving from the studio to the lounge. She rounded her desk and went down the hall, peeked in the open door of Studio C.

Serene was sitting at the sound board talking to her engineer. Parker knocked and stepped inside. "Serene?"

Serene looked up at her, her eyes brighter than they'd been when she came in this morning. "'Ambient' is great, Parker. The tracks you laid are good. We're only having to add a couple more. I think I like it even better than 'Double Minds.'"

Parker smiled to hide the fact that she was on the verge of tears. "Good. I'm glad it worked for you."

"We need you to rewrite the lyrics, of course."

Parker hadn't even considered that. The tears waiting to ambush her finally spilled over. "I don't have ideas for new lyrics, Serene."

Serene got up then and asked her engineer to step out for a minute. She closed the door and pulled Parker into a hug. "It's all going to work out, Parker. You'll see."

"For you, maybe." Horrified that she'd lost it like this, when she was supposed to be the strong one, she wiped her tears.

Serene gave her a tissue and waited as she blew her nose. "I love the song just like it is, but Butch and Jeff Standard and all the powers that be are blaming you for the theft of 'Double Minds.'"

"Of course they are."

"And they're rumbling about a lawsuit. I'm trying my best to hold them off. They want new lyrics, and if you give them to us, maybe I can appease them."

Parker swallowed. "So if I rewrite 'Ambient' and give it to you, I'm still on the tour? They won't sue me?"

"I can't promise that. They're in terrible moods today. Phone calls have been flying. Everyone's upset. But if you do it, if we can get it recorded and they can see that it's better, they might keep you on. I'm fighting for you, Parker."

She had no choice. "All right."

"Make it a love song. I want couples everywhere to remember this as the song they fell in love to."

Tall order. She didn't know if Lola had it in her. "Listen," she said, dabbing at her tears. "Against my mediator's advice, I've decided to confront Tiffany about the theft of my song. But I might have trouble getting past Nathan Evans. Didn't you tell me once that she gets her hair and nails done in the salon you use?"

"She's there every Tuesday afternoon at two o'clock, without fail."

Parker opened the door and stepped out into the hall. "Do you think I could get close to her if I went in acting like I belonged there?"

"Probably. They do have security, but you'd have a few minutes before they called them."

Parker took a late lunch hour, drove to Green Hills Mall, and parked within sight of the front door. She sat frozen behind the wheel as Tiffany's limo brought her to the door of the salon. She watched as the star was ushered inside.

Parker wasn't fond of herself right now. Why was she just sitting here, staring through the window? She needed to fish or cut bait. Sitting here like an idiot was just wasting time. She felt the tightness of a panic attack across her chest, her lungs constricting.

Get out of the car. Go inside!

She tried to use some of the deep-breathing exercises she used when she had butterflies before performing. *Slow inhalation ... hold it ... hold it ... out, nice and slow ...* As she breathed, she watched through the glass as the massage therapist came to get Tiffany. Parker knew her because she'd met her once when she was here with Serene. She had a streak of hot pink hair, which she wore in a ponytail sticking like a horn out of one side of her head. Funny that her job was to help people relax, when her hair color inspired headaches.

She saw Tiffany get up and follow her back, presumably to the massage room.

Parker forced herself to move. She got out of the car, locked it, and looked around the parking lot. Carrying herself like someone who could actually afford an appointment here, she walked into the salon. The therapist, waiting for Tiffany to change clothes, hadn't gone into the massage room yet. Parker went right to the door and knocked on it.

"Come in."

She looked around. Satisfied that no one had noticed her, she opened the door and slipped inside. Tiffany lay face-up under the sheet on the massage table. She glanced at Parker as she came in, and a frown worked at her botoxed forehead. "You're not ..."

Parker kept her voice soft. "Miss Teniere, I'm Parker James. I need to talk to you."

Tiffany clutched the sheet to her chest and sat up. She didn't appear to be sedated anymore, but shadows dragged circles under her eyes. "Parker ... Brenna's friend."

"Yes, I want to talk to you about Brenna."

Tears rimmed Tiffany's eyes. "It's horrible what he did to her. Just because she didn't love him."

Parker frowned. "Who?"

"Chase. I thought we could trust him. I thought he really loved her."

"Miss Teniere — "

"Tiffany, honey. Call me Tiffany."

It was as if no song theft had ever taken place. Tiffany seemed unaware that Parker would have anything against her. "Okay, Tiffany. I need to talk to you about the stolen song."

Tiffany's face registered her confusion. "What?"

"The song you recorded. 'Altar Ego.'"

"What about it?" Her bewilderment seemed sincere.

"I wrote it. Your recording of it is copyright infringement. Serene Stevens recorded it first, for her new album. Then all of a sudden it's playing on K-Love, and you're singing it. I have proof that Brenna stole it off my computer."

"What?" Tiffany kept the sheet clutched to her chest as her feet slid off the table. "Are you accusing my dead daughter?"

Parker almost couldn't breathe, but she forced herself to go on. "All I know is that I wrote the song and now it's on the radio with your voice. I don't want to hire a lawyer and drag you through the mud, damaging your career and mine, and letting all the world think of us Christians as hypocrites."

"You're out of your mind!"

Parker struggled not to cry. "No, I'm not. If you didn't steal it, then how did you get it?"

"My husband bought the rights to it like he does all the others."

"But you're credited as the songwriter."

Tiffany looked confused. "I don't know. I don't handle those details."

"He didn't *buy* the rights to that song, Miss Teniere." She stopped for a second, tried to pull herself together. "I just came here to ask you if you would consent to Christian mediation so we can get this worked out. Your husband doesn't want to talk about this, but somebody's going to have to."

"My husband? You talked to him about this?"

"No, I didn't, but the people from the mediation firm did."

Tiffany gaped at her with her mouth open. "What did he say?"

"He denied stealing the song and said that I was crazy."

Tiffany stared at the wall, as if replaying scenes in her mind. Parker got the intense feeling that reality was dawning on her. "You said you had proof?"

"The police found my songs on Brenna's computer."

Tiffany's voice was a whisper now. "That doesn't mean she stole them."

"They were my demos. The only place she could have gotten them was from my computer." She hesitated as she saw tears filling Tiffany's eyes. "Maybe you didn't know where the song came from. Maybe it's not your fault. I'm not accusing you. But I might be sued, so we need to settle this. Serene's label wants the money they spent on recording the song — "

Serene's name seemed to summon Tiffany's anger again. "You're accusing my daughter. Brenna was not a thief. She was a victim."

The door came open, and the massage therapist stared at Parker.

Parker lifted her hand. "If you could just give us a minute."

"No," Tiffany said. "Get out."

Parker hesitated. "Please! I just want us to talk to mediators. I don't want to get lawyers involved."

Tiffany's teeth clamped together. "I want her out of here, now!"

The therapist leaned into the hall and yelled, "Security!"

Just what she needed. "No need, I'm finished," Parker said. She pushed past the masseuse, into the hall, and to the front door. Her face was hot, blood pounding into her head.

She slipped back inside her bug. Adjusting her mirror, she looked at her reflection. Her face was blotched with what looked like pink handprints. No, Tiffany hadn't slapped her, but she might as well have.

She started her car and backed out of her parking space. As she put it in Drive, she saw a man sitting in a white Corolla a little farther down, in the second row from the shops. She glanced in at him as she passed — it was the man she'd seen at McDonald's a few days ago. Same car, long brown hair, and a Volunteers baseball cap.

She looked away as she passed him, then glanced in her rearview mirror. He was pulling out behind her.

She told herself to calm down. Nashville wasn't a huge city. You tended to see the same people over and over again. Maybe he lived in this area, as she did. Maybe it was a coincidence.

She wasn't thinking clearly. She tried to compose herself, to focus. Her stomach felt sick. She needed a bathroom.

She pulled out into traffic, glancing in her mirror to see if he followed. A couple of cars were between them. She decided to turn right, onto an equally busy street. A block down the road, she saw in her mirror that he turned too.

That was it. She wasn't imagining it. Her mouth was dry, her heart pounded, and her hands shook as she reached into her purse, feeling for her cell phone. The car in front of her stopped, and she slammed on the brakes, knocking her purse off the seat. Her phone slid to the passenger door.

She forced herself to calm down and think. Somehow, she had

to get the guy's tag number. That was impossible as long as she was in front of him. But if she could get behind him …

She drove slower, and the cars between them passed her in the left lane. She saw him coming up behind her. With his cap and sunglasses, she couldn't see his face. He could be anybody.

She saw a small parking lot up ahead. Breathing hard, she swerved into it. He didn't have time to follow, so he passed. Quickly, she grabbed her phone off the floor and pulled back into traffic. A horn blasted behind her, but she ignored it and sped up, getting close enough behind the man to read his tag.

She pressed her speed dial for Gibson, waited as it rang.

"Hey," her brother said.

"Gibson, write this down! ULM 346."

"What?"

"ULM 346. Write it down! It's the tag number of the guy who's been following me."

"Somebody's following you?"

"No, I'm following *him*!" The man must have seen her — he turned off onto a less traveled road. She had no intention of following him there. "Did you get it?"

"Yes. Where are you?"

She stepped on her accelerator and raced away, in case he pulled a copycat and came after her again. "The better question is where is *he*? He just turned from Hillsboro Pike onto Woodmont. He's in a small white sedan. Send somebody, Gibson! Quick!"

"Is this the guy on the security tape? The one who may have called you?"

"Yes. He has the baseball cap, the long brown hair. I've seen him following me before."

"Are you safe now?"

"Yes, I lost him. Or … he lost me." She searched her mirror. "I don't see him anymore."

"Okay, give me a minute." He put his phone down, and she

prayed he was sending a squad car. He came back to the phone. "Very interesting."

"What?"

"You're not going to believe who this guy is."

She swallowed the invisible cotton in her mouth. "I'm dying to know."

"It's Mick Evans. Nathan Evans's son."

CHAPTER
THIRTY-TWO

Gibson sat in his Bonneville in the parking lot of Mick Evans's apartment, waiting for his sister's stalker to get home. Mick showed up not long after Gibson arrived and ambled up the steps to his apartment, hands in his pockets.

Gibson got out and yelled up to him. "Mick?"

Mick turned at the top of the stairs.

Gibson showed him his badge. "I'm Detective James with the Nashville Police Department. Can I have a word with you, please?"

Mick shrugged. "Yeah, sure." He came down the steps and shook Gibson's hand. "Want to come in?"

Gibson assessed him. Long hair, baseball cap. He looked a little like his father — and nothing like Brenna. "Yeah, if you don't mind. I just want to ask you a few questions."

"About my sister's death?" Mick asked.

"Yeah, mostly."

Mick shrugged. "Sure, come on up."

Gibson followed Mick up the stairs and waited as he unlocked it. As he turned the knob, the door flew open. Marta, Brenna's roommate, stood there.

"Hi!" She looked startled at the sight of Gibson. "What are you doing here?"

Mick looked just as surprised to see her in his apartment. "He wants to ask me some questions. What are *you* doing here?"

She looked a little troubled as she backed away from the door. Her eyes seemed to signal Gibson. Was she worried he'd tell Mick that she'd been the one to turn Chase in? She turned back to Mick and answered his question. "I wanted to talk to you, so I used my key."

Mick didn't seem happy. "You should have called."

Following Mick inside, Gibson felt tension rippling on the air.

"Do I need to go?" Marta's question seemed addressed to both of them.

Gibson thought about asking her to leave, but she'd been pretty forthcoming already. Maybe having her here would help them get to the bottom of things. "You can stay, as far as I'm concerned."

Mick ignored her question and went to the couch, gesturing for Gibson to have a seat.

There wasn't much furniture. Just a couch and a chair, a couple of beat-up end tables, bare white walls. A framed picture sat on one of the tables, the only picture in the room. It was a blown-up snapshot of a woman who looked like she didn't want to be photographed. Gibson nodded toward it as he sat down. "Pretty lady. Who is she?"

Mick didn't even look at it. "My mother."

"Tiffany?"

"Tiffany's not my mother."

Was that hostility in his tone? Gibson looked up at Marta. She wore a T-shirt with the neck cut out; it lay in a wide, frayed smile across her shoulders. Her hair was spiked, and the ring on her lip caught the light from the window. "His mother died."

Gibson looked at Mick. "When?"

"When I was twelve."

Gibson locked onto Mick's eyes — they were several shades of gray. "Did you live with her until then?"

"Yes."

Mick clearly wasn't a talker. He leaned forward, elbows on his knees. "So why don't we cut to the chase?" Mick asked. "We both know why you're here."

Did they? Were they talking about Brenna or Parker? "So why do you think I'm here?"

"My sister, of course."

Gibson decided to go with that. "Could you tell me what your relationship was like with your sister?"

"Half-sister," he corrected. "We didn't get along very well. I'm sure you already know that."

Actually, no one had mentioned it. "So how is it that you're friends with her roommate?"

Mick looked at the floor. "We met at a party at my dad's house."

Gibson didn't give keys to *his* friends. "So are you guys going out?"

They answered simultaneously.

"Yes."

"No."

Mick looked uneasy as he denied it. Marta's fragile smile faded.

"Mick, how did you hear about Brenna's murder?"

He looked at the floor and rubbed his mouth. "I was at work with my dad when Tiffany called and said the police were there, that they wanted to talk to him. He left and I stayed."

"Why didn't you go with him?"

"I didn't figure it was anything big. I thought Brenna might have gotten into trouble."

"Had that ever happened before?"

"No, but there's always a first time. She wasn't perfect, like some people thought."

Yes, definite hostility.

Mick went on. "She'd been involved in some things …"

"Like what?"

He shrugged. "Just … lies, now and then. I don't know."

Gibson wondered if he was referring to the song.

"Do you know why she was working at Colgate?"

Mick was quiet then. "I think you need to talk to my father about that."

"Did it have anything to do with the song 'Altar Ego'?"

Mick's chin set, his lips tight. "Like I said, you need to talk to my father."

Gibson pressed on. "That night, did you think the police were there to talk about the theft of the songs?"

"I sure didn't think it was about murder."

Marta, sitting on the arm of the couch, rubbed Mick's back.

"Were you in on that scheme? To have your sister infiltrate Colgate and steal Parker's songs?"

He looked up at Gibson at the mention of Parker's name. "I wouldn't take part in anything like that. We're in the Christian music industry. I believe we should act like it."

That sounded good, Gibson thought. But he wasn't buying it. "So you knew about the plot?"

Mick got up then. "That's not what I said. Do I need a lawyer?"

Gibson didn't want to shut him up. "I'm not accusing you of anything."

Now Mick didn't meet his eyes. He stared at the floor, his chin set again. His Adam's apple moved as he swallowed hard.

Marta met Gibson's eyes. "They didn't get along, but she *was* his sister. It's hard for him."

Gibson let the quiet settle between them.

Finally, Mick turned back. "I guess it was Chase, wasn't it? I wouldn't have thought so. He seemed like a good guy. But since he had the gun — "

Marta met Gibson's eyes again.

"Yeah, he had it all right." Gibson walked across the room, glanced through the opening into the kitchen. His kitchen was spotless, seemingly unused. "How long have you lived here?"

"I've had the apartment for a year. Sometimes I stay at my dad's, though."

That explained it. He didn't really *live* here. Gibson walked back to Mick. "Well, I guess I'll go now. Good to see you, Marta."

She nodded.

"Sorry I caught you just as you were coming in."

Mick shook his head. "No problem."

"Been at work?" Gibson asked, shaking his keys around, as if he couldn't remember which one started his car.

"No. I was just out running some errands."

"You didn't happen to be in the Green Hills Mall area, did you?"

Mick's eyes got dull. "Why?"

"My sister might have seen you over there." He looked down at his keys again. "You know, my sister and I ... we're pretty close. You might say I'm protective of her. And she has the idea that you keep turning up wherever she is."

Marta rose from the couch, her eyes narrowing. "What do you mean?"

Tension hung thick in the air. Mick slid his hands into his pockets. "I went to the Elite Salon to look for my stepmother. Her car wasn't there, so I was waiting for her. She was supposed to have an appointment." He took a step toward Gibson, got close to his face. "I know who your sister is. I saw her coming out of the salon. But I wasn't there for her."

Gibson stared at him for a moment. "So you haven't been following her? Calling her with cryptic messages?"

Mick wet his lips then, his eyes locked on Gibson's. "No, I haven't. But this is the end of this conversation. If you want to talk to me more, it'll be with my lawyer present."

Gibson hoped the warning was enough.

As he headed back out to his car, he heard Mick's door open and close again. "Detective James?"

He turned. Marta was hurrying down the stairs toward him. He waited until she reached him.

"I just wanted to ask ... what's the deal with him following Parker? I mean, I'm kind of in a relationship with him, and if there's something I should know ..."

Gibson glanced back at Mick's door. "If I were you, I'd steer clear of that whole family."

"But why? I mean, you seem to think he's been stalking her. But he wouldn't. He's not like that. What he told you is true. He doesn't lie."

"Marta, you seem like a nice girl. You've been a big help in this investigation. But you're a little vulnerable right now. Be careful who you get involved with."

He looked up. Mick was standing at the window, looking down at them. Tossing him a wave, Gibson backed toward his car, leaving the girl standing alone.

CHAPTER THIRTY-THREE

The studio needed new carpet. Parker had never noticed the dirt and stains until she'd sat on it for twenty minutes at two in the morning, waiting for the band Half Moon to vacate Studio H. Her whole family sat with her — her brothers on either side, her parents on either end.

Nothing was right. Her spirit had been unsettled ever since she'd spotted Mick following her a few days ago. She'd been completely distracted, which had thrown off her writing and preparing to record. Though she had quickly rewritten "Ambient" for Serene, her work on her own album wasn't coming as easily.

The fact that Gibson had warned Mick away didn't make Parker feel better. If Chase was innocent, as she believed he was, then the killer was still out there. Mick's behavior made him a suspect, at least in her mind. But Gibson had nothing on him. Even if he had been the one who called her, he hadn't threatened her in any way. In fact, he'd done just the opposite — he'd promised to protect her.

So was he the one who'd broken into her house to leave the song sheets? According to Gibson, he seemed to know about the theft. Would he have done something so stupid to tip her off?

She imagined herself sitting on the witness stand in court,

answering questions about his guilt. What would a jury think about his threatening calls to protect her? His breaking and entering to leave a message?

It was just too weird. The whole thing was driving her crazy.

Even Serene's phone call telling her that she was definitely still on the tour hadn't eased the burden. And now she sat here like some kind of idiot, her family lined up like ducks in a shooting booth, waiting for another band to keep their word and surrender the studio.

Pete had already gone back out to his car once, where he must have had alcohol waiting. He'd come back in, staggering slightly. "This is asinine," he said now. "*We* have the studio." He got off the floor, dusting his seat, and stepped closer to the studio door.

"What are you doing?" Parker asked.

"I'm gonna bang on the door."

"No, Dad. They're our clients. I can't run them out."

LesPaul sprang up, too. "That's ridiculous, Parker. Dad's right. We can let them know that they have to leave. That we have the studio now."

"But they're paying clients. *We're* not."

Her younger brother wasn't in the mood for logic — at least not her brand. "You work here for the sole purpose of getting studio time. So it costs you more than anybody else, when you get right down to it."

She looked at Gibson. His head was back against the wall. He was sound asleep. Her mother had her head on his shoulder.

Parker just wanted to go home and go to bed herself. How would they record in this condition?

LesPaul banged on the door, startling them awake. It opened, and Half Moon's producer leaned out.

"Your time's up, Griff," LesPaul said. "We have this studio now."

"We'll be out in a minute." Griff slammed the door.

LesPaul looked back at her. "Parker?"

"I can't do anything. He said a minute. We can wait a little longer."

Pete wouldn't listen. He banged on the door again. The door opened, and the producer looked angrily out. *What?*

Pete was a large, imposing figure — an asset in this situation. "Define *a minute*, pal."

"We just need a few, okay?"

"No. You have sixty seconds to get out, and then we'll come in and clear you out ourselves."

"Dad!" She scrambled to her feet. "I have to work with these people!"

She stepped forward and tried to diffuse the situation. "Griff, it's fine. We scheduled the studio at two because you said you'd be out by then. But if you need more time —"

"That's it," LesPaul said. "I'm going home. My time is valuable even if nobody else's is."

"No, wait. Les, please!" She turned back to Griff. "Here's the thing — I'm going on tour with Serene, and my album's not finished. The only time we can get in the studio is in the wee hours, since everybody's trying to make up for lost time …"

He just stared at her.

She winced. "But, like, if it's a problem …" Her voice faded, and she hated herself for being weak. "It's okay if you need more time."

Griff glanced back at the band members. "Oh, forget it. We'll get our stuff and go."

"Really? Thank you, Griff. I owe you one."

"No, you don't," LesPaul said. "You don't owe him anything. He's doing what he agreed to do. You book time, and you honor it. That's how it works."

The security guard came around the corner from the lobby. "Anything I can help with?"

"No, we're fine." She shot her brother a beseeching look. "Come on, Les, I have enough enemies."

Griff shot LesPaul a threatening look. "Don't worry about it. I said we're going."

Parker and her family waited as the band rounded up their gear and finally left the room. Groggy, Gibson and Lynn got up from the floor. "Mom, you really should go home and get some sleep," Parker said. "You have to work tomorrow."

"So do all of you. This is a family affair. It's not every day you get to see your daughter blossom into a star."

Parker knew that her mother worried about Parker's mental state, what with the murder, the break-in, and the stolen song. Lynn James had no musical ability, but she was great at encouragement. And tonight, they might need that even more than they needed caffeine.

Parker deliberately hadn't asked Daniel to play with them tonight. The early morning hour was too much to ask of a non-family member with a daytime job. Besides, she wasn't confident enough of the song they were recording to let him hear it just yet. And she was glad Daniel wasn't here to see their bad moods.

LesPaul's mood didn't get any better after they got into the studio. "Gibson, I suggest you throw down a Red Bull to wake you up. We have work to do."

"Les, you make things so fun."

Parker prayed that the irritable moods would be lifted from them before they started recording.

By six a.m., the recording of her new song was going as Parker could have hoped, but as she listened to playback, she felt that something was still missing.

"Parker, I think this number needs an orchestra behind it." LesPaul sat in the control booth, watching her through the glass.

"Forget it," she said into the microphone. "You know I can't afford that."

He folded his hands in front of his face and peered at her. Gibson was leaning back against the wall in the control booth, his feet propped up on another chair. She saw him mutter something to LesPaul, then LesPaul said into the mike, "We could ask the orchestra at church to do it."

She thought for a moment. That was one solution ... but could she expect them to come in the middle of the night? Not many people would do that for her.

"Whatever time we get in the studio, we need to spend it recording the rest of the songs. I think we'd better make do with what we've got."

"Yeah, I guess."

The fatigue was starting to work on her vertebrae, making her neck stiff and her back ache. Even her feet hurt. She felt old. She didn't know how many more sessions like this she could manage. But time was running out. She had to get the tracks down so she could get the records pressed. She had a million things to do. Once she got the recording done, she'd start worrying about money to finance it all.

When they finished recording her vocal tracks, it was almost morning. The sun had probably already come up. She hung her headset over the mike and went through the door into the control booth. Her family looked like the walking dead.

"I really appreciate you guys doing this. Nobody else in the world would do it for me."

"Yeah, well, when we get a shot at the big time, you'll do it for us," Gibson said.

She grinned. "You're kidding, right? I'm never sacrificing sleep for you people."

Gibson took off his cap and threw it at her. She ducked.

"Seriously, guys, thanks a lot."

"Well, don't thank us until you hear the finished mix," LesPaul said. "It may be the worst thing you've ever heard."

"I've got utmost faith in your abilities."

"At least your voice is strong enough to carry it. And the songs are killer."

She didn't often hear praise like that from her younger brother. Smiling, she crossed the control room, took LesPaul's face in her hands, and kissed his cheek. He badly needed a shave. "See, I knew you were a sweetheart under all that huffing and puffing."

He grinned and pulled away. "Somebody needs to huff for you, Parker, or you'll get blown away."

CHAPTER
THIRTY-FOUR

A week after LesPaul had finished mixing the album and they had tested the sound on speakers from Bose stereos to boom boxes and car systems, Parker took the chance of giving a copy to George Colgate. Her hope was that, even though he'd passed on signing her with one of his labels, her boss would still give her a pressing and distribution deal. That way, she wouldn't have to use her own funds to make and package the CDs. It was a couple of days before he listened to it, but her constant reminders forced him into it.

Finally, he called her into his office. "It's good," he told her. "Way more professional than I expected on a shoestring."

"Really?"

"Yes. You're a genius songwriter, Parker. And you chose the title song well."

Nothing about her vocals. Taking what she could get, she sat down across from his desk. "I'm really glad you liked it, George. It means so much coming from you. But I need a huge favor. I need a pressing and distribution deal."

He sighed. "Parker, we've been over all this."

"I know, but before, we were talking about a recording contract. I just need money to help me get it pressed. I only need a print run big enough to sell at the tour dates. And I need money for printing and packaging, and tour expenses. I have a great opportunity with Serene, and it would launch my career. It's almost a sure investment."

The pause that followed was awkward. "Parker, I do see potential here. You're a good singer. Your voice is ... kind of different."

Hope shattered at her feet. "Different ... in a good way ... or a bad way?"

He shifted and crossed his legs. "It depends on your perspective. I really like your sound, but it's a little risky."

"I'm not trying to be risky."

"No, it's not anything you're trying. It's just ... your sound."

Her *different* sound. Different from Serene and Tiffany Teniere. Different from all the pretty-voiced artists who pleased program managers in radio stations. "But why wouldn't you *want* someone different? Someone who stood out?"

She knew as she blurted the question that she shouldn't. It was asking for too much honesty. She felt it coming before the words hit her ...

"Parker, I think if I invested in you as a performer, I'd lose money."

"Wow." She felt like an idiot sitting here like this, forcing him to go on. But she couldn't seem to move. Somehow, she made herself swallow. Clearing her throat, she said, "Well ... thank you for your honesty."

"Parker, I'm sorry. I know this is a let-down."

Her cheeks were burning. She rubbed them, hoping to hide the pink. "No, no, not at all. I'm a professional. If I can't take criticism, how will I ever grow?" Her heart pumped blood into her face so fast it almost hurt.

"All I can say in the way of advice is ... well, don't invest more than you can afford to lose. You're a fabulous songwriter, Parker. That's where your future lies. In fact, I have artists right now who would love to record some of these songs. I know Serene gets first shot at them, but you could be making more money on them. You shouldn't have to work as a receptionist with such a marketable talent."

She tried to remind him that she worked here to get studio time, so she could record. But the words got caught in the knot of her throat. The words *different* and *risky* reeled through her mind in an endless loop. She managed to stand. "Okay, then. I'd better get back up front. Can't quit the day job, as they say."

The phone was ringing as she went back to her desk.

CHAPTER
THIRTY-FIVE

When five o'clock came, Parker gathered her things and hurried out to her car. Between eight and five, it seemed a thousand hours had passed. Holding her laptop and purse, she unlocked the car.

"Parker."

She swung around and saw Marta getting out of her car. "Marta, I didn't see you."

"I need to talk to you."

"Sure." Parker opened her car door and set her things on the seat as Marta came toward her. Her face was wet, her black mascara smeared. "Are you okay?" Parker asked.

Marta shook her head. "Why did you tell your brother that Mick was following you?"

Parker stiffened. "Because he was."

"No, he wasn't. He hardly even knows who you are." She wiped her tears on the sleeve of her black knit shirt. "Did he tell you we're going out?"

"Who?"

"Your brother, the cop. Did he tell you?"

"No. Gibson doesn't tell me everything."

"Well, we are." Her eyes rounded, and she stepped closer to

Parker. "He's not like that. He's been through a lot. The last thing he needs is to be accused of being a stalker."

Parker touched the girl's shoulder and made her meet her eyes. "I can see that you're upset, Marta. But with everything that's happened, you're extra vulnerable. Maybe you shouldn't be seeing him right now."

Marta shoved her hair back. "You've got this so wrong. He's not what you think. He's not at all like his family."

Parker wondered if Marta knew about the song. "Did he tell you about 'Double Minds'?"

Marta laughed bitterly. "This is so much more important than a stupid song."

So Marta did know. "What did he tell you?"

"What did he tell me? He told me that he found his mother dead when he was twelve. It was suicide."

Parker caught her breath. "Suicide?"

"So tell your brother the truth. Mick wasn't following you."

"Marta, I'm sorry about the suicide. That's horrible. But you shouldn't be with someone just because you have compassion for him. This case is still unsolved."

"No, it isn't. They have Chase."

"He hasn't been charged with murder, and frankly, I'm not so sure he did it."

Marta looked stunned. "But … the gun."

"Someone else could have put it in his apartment."

Marta's mouth came open. "Not Mick."

"We don't know who."

Marta hugged herself, her sleeves still clutched in her fists. "Maybe you deserved to have your stupid song ripped off."

She left Parker standing there and went back to her car. Parker didn't get into her own until the girl had driven away.

CHAPTER
THIRTY-SIX

Gibson stared at his computer screen and pressed Print. *The Tennessean* story of Katrina Evans's suicide ten years ago rolled out.

> Katrina Evans was found dead at her home at 3016 Meadow Drive in Brentwood on Thursday. Police have ruled it a suicide. Her twelve-year-old son discovered her body and notified police.
>
> "I didn't know her very well, but she seemed like a good person," Barbara Sulwer, her neighbor, said. "It's so sad to think that she was that disturbed and nobody knew it."
>
> Another neighbor, Linda Boykin, said she's in shock. "She and her son were so close. I can't imagine why she would leave him this way."

Gibson turned back to his computer and did a quick search on her cause of death. He pulled up all the public records he could find in her name.

Her Death Certificate reported it as Suicide. He studied the Autopsy Report. Toxicology indicated that she'd died of an overdose of sleeping pills.

He sat back, rubbing his eyes. Finding his mother dead at the age of twelve had to traumatize the kid. That was a decade ago, long enough for Mick to heal ... or harden.

He pulled up the public records associated with Nathan Evans. He'd divorced Katrina when their son was seven. Three months later, he married Tiffany, twenty-three at the time. Fourteen years younger than his first wife. Twenty years younger than Nathan, himself.

A Google search of Nathan Evans produced an article dated six months before Katrina's death. It was about a lawsuit filed by Katrina Evans against the record producer, demanding back child support.

> According to Katrina Evans, her ex-husband only saw his son twice a year, even though they lived in the same town. She stated that her son Mick had never even been invited into the mansion he shared with his current wife, Christian recording artist Tiffany Teniere, and their five-year-old daughter. Child support was not increased, but Evans was ordered to pay $50,000 in back payments.

Gibson looked around the office for his partner. He was standing at the coffee pot, his favorite hang-out, stirring sugar into a Styrofoam cup. "Rayzo, check this out."

His partner ambled over. "Whatcha got?"

He showed him what he'd found. Rayzo pulled up a chair and put on his reading glasses. When he'd seen it all, he leaned back and regarded Gibson. "It doesn't prove that Mick Evans did anything. Just that he had a crummy father and a lousy surprise when he was twelve."

Gibson thought about all those portraits and framed snapshots he'd seen of Brenna in her parents' home. Mick might have been bitter, especially if he felt replaced. But bitter enough to want his sister dead?

For once, he thought Rayzo might be wrong. "I don't know, Rayzo. Looks to me like a motive."

CHAPTER
THIRTY-SEVEN

The loan officer's smile didn't match his eyes, and a psychologist would have had a field day with his body language. To Parker, everything about him said no. "Well now, Miss James, what collateral do you have to offer?"

He said it like it was a trick question, as if she were a college student trying to buy a yacht. "I have some equity in my home," she said. "I've had it for three years. I didn't put much down, but it's probably appreciated in value."

He looked at her address on the application, and his smile turned into an apologetic wince. "Yeah, in that area, not so much. Of course, it depends on what you paid and the condition of the home."

She told him what the house had cost her. "It's in excellent condition. I've made a lot of improvements. The backyard is beautiful. I've done a lot of landscaping."

"Landscaping might help you sell faster, but it doesn't increase the value."

"Well, I've painted, put in new floors."

He made a notation in her file. "That could help. Do you have a current appraisal?"

"No — do I need one?"

"Before we could give you a home equity loan, we'd have to have that." He leaned forward in his chair. "I can give you the names of some appraisers, if you'd like."

An appraiser? That sounded expensive. "So, how much does that cost?"

"Could be two or three hundred dollars."

She swallowed. "I can't afford that unless I'm sure I'm getting the loan."

"Well, we can't assure you of the loan until we see the appraisal."

Checkmate. It looked like an appraisal was in her future. "Okay. How long does it take?"

He glanced over her shoulder, probably at a client who had a little more promise. "It'll take a couple of weeks to get someone to look at it, another week or so for them to write up the appraisal."

"I can't wait that long. I'm kind of in a hurry."

"Then I'm sorry. Your house is probably not the best collateral. Do you have anything else?"

"My car. I might have a few thousand dollars of equity in that." She told him the model and the amount she owed.

He turned to his computer and typed something in. "I'm sorry. With the Kelley Blue Book value, your equity in the car is very small. Really only a thousand dollars or so."

Her mouth fell open. "But I bought it new. It's nearly paid off."

"You lose thousands when you drive it off the lot."

Again, she felt he was lecturing her like some kid who needed her dad's signature. "What about a song? Could you use that as collateral?"

He frowned. "A song?"

"Yes. I wrote every song on Serene Steven's new album. There'll be money coming in. Just ... not for several months, till they pay royalties. I could give you my contracts, and you could use that ..."

He held up a hand to stop her. "I'm sorry, Miss James. While

I'm sure your songs will make you a nice profit, there's no way for us to measure that now. I'm afraid I wouldn't be able to get that approved."

It had to be the house, then. She got the number of a few different appraisers and called each one, begging them to come soon. The earliest she could get was the week after next. Apparently home appraisals were big business. Maybe she should go into that if her performing career didn't work out.

And at the rate she was going, it wouldn't. Until she could get the money for the pressing of her records, everything was at a standstill. The tour expenses wouldn't make sense if she didn't have CDs to sell. Short of a miracle, she wouldn't even be able to pay for her hotel rooms.

She might have to bow out of the tour, after all.

CHAPTER
THIRTY-EIGHT

Parker didn't have time to have lunch with her mother, and she dreaded the inevitable pep talk. It wasn't enthusiasm she needed — it was money. Still, Lynn had insisted on treating Parker for lunch at the Spaghetti Factory, and Parker never liked to disappoint her mother.

The smell of garlic bread wafted over the restaurant as Parker made her way between the tables. The place was decorated like a train depot, with a passenger car at the center of the room. Every entree was served with spaghetti, a basketful of garlic bread, and sorbet. The last thing Parker needed was more carbs. She'd already gained five pounds in the last couple of weeks. Stress hormones were fattening, and so was the food she choked down when she was too busy to think. She'd have to enlist Omar the tent-maker to costume her for the tour, if this kept up.

Her mother, on the other hand, looked lovely and sleek in a coral-colored blouse and a slim black skirt. She exuded confidence and peace ... so unlike the feelings coursing through Parker today.

They made small talk as they waited for their food. Parker tried to feign happiness, but her mother read her too well. Finally, she said, "Honey, you look miserable. Tell me about the money."

Parker rubbed her tense forehead. "Do I have to? I really don't want to talk about it."

"Yes, you have to. Come on, it's just me."

Parker sighed. "I'm waiting for the appraiser to come. He said he might come tomorrow or the next day. I'm kind of at his mercy. I've called about some of the other properties in the neighborhood, gotten their square footage and listing prices. Estimating from those, I'll only have half the equity I need to get the CDs pressed. And I still won't have money for the tour." She picked a cherry tomato out of her salad. "I've thought about asking Serene for a loan, but her father's always trying to squeeze money out of her."

"That horrible, cruel man has the gall to contact her?"

"Occasionally. Her gatekeepers help her avoid him most of the time. I don't want to take advantage of her like he does. Besides, she's already given me such an opportunity."

Her mother leaned on the table. "So what happens if you mortgage your house and go on tour, and you don't sell as many CDs as you hope?"

Parker put her hands over her face. "Mom, you're supposed to be the one who's positive and encouraging."

"I'm not being negative, honey. I think you're wonderful. You know that. I'm just worried about your future. I don't want you to lose your house."

Parker slid her hands down her face. "So you think I should cancel? Just give up?"

"No, of course not! How could you think I meant that?"

"Because I know my voice isn't like everybody else's. It's different. Maybe too different. I thought God was opening these doors, but maybe the door's not really open. Maybe it's just a tiny little window with the glass broken out."

"Stop it!" Her mom took Parker's hand and leaned toward her. "Parker, you've worked too hard on your album to give up. I have faith in your songs."

"Faith in the songs," she said. "That's just it. I have faith in the songs, too. But no one has much faith in my performance ability."

"You're letting George Colgate get to you," she said. "He just wants a sure thing. But Carole King wasn't a sure thing, and neither was Bob Dylan. The problem with these record labels is that they don't rush to embrace people who are different."

"You're right, Mom. That's my problem."

Lynn leaned in, fixing her gaze on her. "Honey, did God bring you this far, or didn't he?"

Parker rubbed her eyes. "I don't know, Mom. I honestly don't."

"Well." Her mother sat back. "I didn't expect to hear that from you."

"I know." Parker tried not to let her tears fall. "I want to believe he did bring me this far. The thing is, he's provided so much for me already. Maybe I shouldn't be asking for more."

Lynn smiled then, and crossed her hands under her chin. "Jesus said, 'You have not, because you ask not.' He gifted you. Why wouldn't he equip you to use your gifts?"

Parker stabbed at her pasta. "Maybe he has equipped me. Maybe the performing stuff is not my gift."

"I believe it is. And I can prove it." Her mother leaned over and got her purse, set it in her lap, and began to dig for something. "Parker, I don't want you to get that appraisal, because you're not going to need that loan. I want you to call the bank and tell them you've changed your mind."

Parker breathed a laugh and shoved a bite of spaghetti into her mouth. "Why would I do that?"

"Because I'm about to give you my face-lift fund."

Parker snapped her eyes up. "Your what?"

"My face-lift fund," she said in a loud whisper.

Parker almost spat out her food as laughter welled up. She grabbed her napkin and pressed it to her mouth.

Her mother looked from side to side. Keeping her voice low, she said, "Make fun all you want, but when a woman reaches her fifties, she looks in the mirror and doesn't like what she sees. I put a little money away so I could do something about my face."

Parker managed to gather herself. "Mom, I didn't know you were worried about the way you look."

She threw up her hands. "Of course not. Why would I broadcast it, so that everyone's thinking, 'Mom's a hag. Her face is drooping, her features are blurring, her eyelids are heavy, her jowls are like a hound dog's.'"

Now Parker let her giggles roll out. "Mom, that's ridiculous. You're beautiful."

Lynn waved the objections away. "That's beside the point. What I'm trying to tell you is that I have ten thousand dollars saved up for that and I'm giving it to you."

The laughter died, and Parker stared at her. "Ten thousand? Mom, I can't take that!"

"Oh, yes you can, and you will. Not only that, but I just sold some of Grandma's property, and I'm giving you the proceeds. I told God that if he let me sell it quickly, I'd give it to you. Sold right off the bat ... so it's yours." She slipped the check out of her pocket and slid it across the table.

Parker stared down at it. It was a few hundred more than she needed. "Mom, you're kidding me."

"I expect to get the money back when you finish the tour, at which time I can proceed with my face lift."

Parker gaped down at the check.

"This is my investment in your talent, Parker. I believe in you, and I know you're going to recoup the investment."

Suddenly Parker wondered if she was worthy of this kind of investment. "And if I don't?"

"And if you don't, well then, I guess that's God's way of telling me I don't need a face lift. I'll just find one of those expensive skin-tightening lotions." She set her chin on her palm. "They don't work, so I really hope you'll earn the money back. But I know you're going to sell every CD and come home with a list of backorders. The record labels are going to be competing to sign you. In fact, I bet Jeff Standard will be begging you to sign with him."

Parker's fatigue lifted, and she found herself invigorated with new energy. She smiled at her mother. "I won't let you down." Parker got up to come around the table to hug her.

That was when her phone rang. Wiping her eyes, she reached for it. Gibson's number came up. She slid her thumb across the screen to answer. "Gibson, you're never going to believe — "

Gibson stopped her. "Parker, I just got a call from the department. Tiffany Teniere was just found dead."

CHAPTER
THIRTY-NINE

Tiffany lay on her back in the center of her bed, a gun in her hand. Gibson stood over her, studying the position of the gun, the clutch of her fingers, the entrance wound. The first responders had been right to report it as a homicide instead of a suicide. The entry wound was right in the front of her forehead. It wasn't easy to pull the trigger from that angle, and her arm probably wouldn't have fallen in just that way.

Someone had posed her, put the gun in her hand, closed her eyes, and laid her flat. But there was blood higher on the wall, as though she'd been sitting up when she was shot.

"Who found her?" he asked one of the cops who'd called him in.

"Her husband."

"What was his demeanor when you got here?"

"He was hysterical, crying, shaken up. Looked authentic to me."

"Did you swab his hands for gunpowder?"

"Yes. They were clean."

"Are you sure?"

"Pretty sure, but we'll send it off to the lab."

Gibson stepped closer to the body. "Did he recognize the gun?"

"He said it was his own gun, that he kept it in his gun cabinet downstairs."

"Any signs of breaking and entering?"

"None that we could see."

Gibson pulled out his own camera and began taking pictures. Though the ones the crime-scene investigators were taking would be clearer and more detailed, it always helped for him to have his own shots, and the earlier, the better, before too many people had come into the room and moved things around.

"Did Nathan Evans think it was a suicide?"

"That's how he reported it. He said his wife had been really depressed since their daughter's death."

"I want to talk to him."

He found Nathan Evans downstairs on a couch, blowing his nose on a handkerchief as he talked to the cop. Gibson sat down on the coffee table facing him.

"I know you've answered a lot of questions," he said to the distraught man, "but I need you to start over from the beginning and tell me everything that's happened tonight."

The tears were real. Gibson had seen enough fake ones to know the difference. He may have been a detective for only a few months, but he'd been a cop for years.

"I was at work," he said. "Tiffany was supposed to come to the office for a meeting. She didn't show up and wasn't answering the phone, so I came home for lunch. I called out to her. She didn't answer, so I went upstairs. I found her ..." His hands were shaking as he wiped tears from under his eyes. There was dried blood on his hands. "Why would she do that? She could have gotten through this. They could have given her more medication. Why would she end it this way?"

"Mr. Evans, did you move her at all?"

He looked down at his blood-stained hands. "I shook her, trying to revive her. But the blood ... I knew ... so I called 911."

"When you shook her, did you pick her up?"

"No. I found her just like that. The gun in her hand."

Gibson studied the man, knowing he couldn't trust him. Evans was a liar and a thief. But was he a killer?

"What time exactly did you leave the office?"

Evans stared at the air. "I don't know. Noon, I think."

"Was there anyone there with you?"

"Yes, of course. I had people in my office with me." He gave them the names, and Gibson wrote them down. Tiffany's publicist, her manager, a secretary. Plenty of people to confirm his alibi. "I called her when I started home, and there was no answer."

"Was anyone else in the house with her today?"

Evans looked up at him. "No. The staff had the day off. She didn't mention anybody else coming." He looked at Gibson with questioning eyes. "Wait a minute. It was suicide. You don't think ..."

Gibson shook his head. "It's not a suicide."

Evans's brows came together. "Are you sure? I thought ..."

"Whoever killed her wanted it to *look* like a suicide."

"Whoever *killed* her?" Nathan stood up, his face blanched. "She was murdered?"

Gibson wasn't moved by his shock.

"My daughter murdered, and now my wife? Was Chase McElraney let out of jail?"

"No, he's still there."

"Then who did this?"

"That's what we're trying to find out. If you'll sit down, I have a few more questions."

Evans's face changed. "Do I need to get a lawyer?"

"You're not under arrest, sir."

"No, not yet. But I know what you guys do with grieving husbands." He stormed across the room, picked up the phone.

"Sir, I really wish you wouldn't disturb the evidence. You need to move around as little as possible. There could be prints, trace evidence, anywhere in the house."

Gibson watched him punch the number into the phone, heard him muttering something into it. He couldn't blame the man for calling his attorney. News networks went crazy with husbands of murdered wives. But Gibson doubted that Evans would be a prime suspect for killing both his daughter and her mother. Tiffany was his cash cow — his only hope for saving his company. And from the looks of the pictures all over the house, he loved Brenna.

But Mick's pictures were conspicuously absent.

When Evans got off the phone, Gibson said, "Mr. Evans, have you notified your son?"

Evans shook his head. "Not yet."

"Do you know where he is so we can contact him?"

"I haven't seen him today. I tried to call him, but he didn't answer."

"He works with you, doesn't he? Was he at work this morning?"

"He didn't come in."

"Why not?"

"I don't know. He doesn't always tell me his schedule. He has his own responsibilities with the company. He may have had a meeting."

"Has he been staying here with you and Tiffany?"

"He has his own apartment, but lately he's been staying here a lot ... until a couple of days ago."

"What happened then?"

Nathan's face shut down. "I'm not saying anything else until I get a lawyer. I'll notify my son myself."

CHAPTER FORTY

Tiffany's murder stabbed Parker with shards of guilt. How could this happen? As angry as she'd been at Nathan Evans, her compassion for him now came with surprising strength.

She called in sick for the afternoon, unable to tell George what had happened. Nausea rolled in her stomach. Soon Tiffany's death — the apparent suicide of a major Christian star — would dominate the news, local and national.

Had Mick Evans done this? Had his childhood been so traumatic that he'd resolved to get even with his stepmother and half-sister?

Parker's mother took her home from the Spaghetti Factory, held her as she cried, then prayed with her, reminding her how blessed she was to have the family she had.

To Parker's dismay, her father showed up. She didn't like appearing vulnerable with him, her nose clogged with grief and her eyes swollen. *She* was the caretaker, and in so many ways, he was the child.

He came back to the bedroom where she lay curled under a blanket, and sat next to her on the bed. "Hey, sweetheart."

She breathed in the scent of cigarette smoke tinged with

whiskey — her dad's unique smell. Somehow, it comforted her. "Hey, Dad. What are you doing here?"

"Your mother called. I came." He stroked her hair. "I don't claim to always know the right thing to do. Sure don't now."

His honesty warmed her. She sat up and hugged him. He clung longer than she would have. When he finally released her, he pulled six tissues out of the box next to the bed and handed her the wad.

She took one and blew her nose. "Strange things going on in that family," she said.

"Despite the song, those things have nothing to do with you."

"It just seems like I'm somewhere on the fringes of each one of these deaths. Like I'm connected in ways I don't understand. I saw her the other day — Tiffany, I mean. I harassed her about the song. Maybe I should have just let it go."

"She ain't dead because you tracked her down, Parks." He tried to change the subject. "Your mom tells me she gave you the money."

She nodded. "Yeah, that was amazing."

"I really want to do the tour with you. I missed a lot of milestones in your life. I want to be there for this one. I mean, *really* be there."

She didn't answer. What was there to say? She'd heard his apologies and remorse before. But his actions never matched.

"I'm checking myself into detox for a few days."

That was different. He'd never checked himself in before — not without a lot of coercion from the family or the courts. "That's good, Dad."

"I know the proof's in the pudding. What does that mean, anyway? What does pudding have to do with proof?"

"Probably some Betty Crocker phrase," she whispered.

"Anyway, I'm gonna try not to let you down this time. I'm gonna try not to let *myself* down."

Silently, Parker said her millionth prayer for God's deliverance for her father. One of these days, that prayer would be answered. Maybe it would be now.

When Parker finally relaxed into sleep, Pete covered her with the comforter. He found Lynn on the back porch, sitting on the swing.

He sat down next to her, the swing groaning under his weight.

"Is it true?" she asked. "About the detox, I mean?"

"You were listening." He smiled. "Yeah, it's true."

She patted his knee. "That's good, Pete."

"I want to be a better man for you, Lynn," he said quietly. "And for Parker. She's got a real shot at the big time, and I want to be there for her."

"You can be, Pete. All you have to do is make up your mind."

"I can't even protect her. I can't do anything for anybody I love."

"Yes, you can." She patted his leg. "You can, Pete. You can be everything you should have been."

He smiled. "Remember back before? When we were together without the alcohol? We would laugh at the silliest things. Dance when there wasn't even music."

"You'd sing to me."

He gazed at her. "You have *such* a smile. You're a lovely lady, Lynn James."

She needed that. "Well, that's nice to say to a lady who just gave up her face-lift fund."

His look told her he was sincere. "You don't need any help."

When he leaned over to kiss her, she stopped him, pressing her fingertips to his lips. "Six months sober," she whispered. "That's the way it has to be."

He pulled back, sorrow glistening in his eyes. That sorrow bled into her. She had never stopped loving him. But her hope that he would one day be sober had always broken her heart. She stroked his stubbled jaw. "Go home, sweet Pete. You're making me weak."

"Can't have you not sticking to your guns."

"Where would I be if I let you in and out of my life at the drop of a hat?"

His smile still worked its magic on her. "That's one of the loveliest things about you. That you do."

He had her figured out. "Not all the way. You're just so good at wedging your foot in the door." The swing creaked as she stood up, putting some distance between them. "You go now. I'll look after Parker."

He drew in a deep breath and stood. "I'm going to do this for you, Lynn. And for Gibson and LesPaul and Parker."

"You do it for *you*," Lynn said. "No one else has been able to rescue you. Look to God. He'll give you strength. You know, our church's recovery group meets on Friday nights."

"I may be out of detox by then. Maybe I can find a sponsor there."

"This time, find someone who doesn't want to party with you."

She wished she hadn't said it. He straightened and rubbed his jaw. She'd forgotten how tall he was when he wasn't in his drunken slump. "I'll try to do it right this time."

"I know you can."

"If I do, will you come on the tour? You'll be out of school by then."

Lynn tried not to let herself want. "I was planning to go anyway. It would be a pleasure to travel with you sober."

"Then count my six months as starting tonight."

CHAPTER
FORTY-ONE

The media frenzy around the Evans mansion was in full swing by the time Chief Sims showed up. Gibson stood inside at the window, taking inventory of the news vans surrounding the place — FOX, CNN, NBC, ABC, CBS, and dozens of others. That made it harder to investigate the murder. With so many reporters snooping for dirt, keeping evidence under wraps was almost impossible.

Chief Sims had a look around. Gibson went with him to see the condition and positioning of the body. Then they went into the room Mick Evans used when he was staying here. There were no clothes in the closet. The drawers were empty. Either he lived out of a suitcase when he was here, or he'd moved out entirely. Nathan Evans had indicated that, but his attorney had effectively shut him up.

When they came back downstairs, Sims peered out the window. "I'll have to make a statement," he said. "But we need to iron a few things out first."

Gibson nodded. "Iron what out, sir?"

"The fact that you're on this case. Until now, I let you stay on it because you were doing good work. But your family connection to all this could blow up in our faces. I'm taking you off the case."

Gibson's mouth fell open. "But Tiffany's murder *must* be connected to the Brenna Evans case. I've done so much work on that already."

"The press will say that Chase McElraney clearly wasn't involved in this one, because he's in jail. And they would be right. They'll be sniffing things out before we can think of them. They'll learn about the song theft and try to convict your sister of these murders."

"My sister? Parker couldn't have done it! She has a confirmed alibi for the first case, and today she's been either at work or at lunch with my mother. She hasn't had the opportunity."

"They'll say she had the motive."

Gibson lowered his voice. "Chief, Mick Evans had both opportunity *and* motive. And he'd been in Chase's apartment after Brenna died, so he could have left the gun there."

"I'll have Carter and Stone look into that. But do you see the position I'm in with you investigating the case? The press will cry foul."

Gibson didn't want to let go. "I didn't think you cared about the press."

"I don't, except when they're about to launch their own investigations. I shouldn't have let you have this case from the beginning. But now, you're off. I've already told Rayzo."

Gibson wasn't going to change the chief's mind, so he sat and read through his notes, making sure they were legible enough to hand over to his colleagues.

CHAPTER
FORTY-TWO

A couple of weeks later, Mick was still missing. Parker tried to put it all together in her mind — the murders of Mick's half-sister and stepmother, the break-in at her house to leave the song sheets, the phone call promising to protect her, the way he'd followed her. Dreading another appearance in her life, she forced herself to finish recording the rest of her songs. While LesPaul forfeited sleep to mix the songs in the edit suite, she finished designing her album cover, got it to the printer, and made arrangements to press the CDs as soon as her brother thought the album was ready.

She was almost ready to leave work one afternoon when a phone call came with a familiar voice.

"Parker, my love, it's grand to speak to you again."

Nigel Hughes. She had almost forgotten him. "Can I help you?"

"Yes, I think you can. I'd love to set up a meeting and interview you, if you have time. Starbucks after you leave Colgate today?"

"I'm busy," she said.

"That's a shame. You see, I'm investigating several stories at the moment. Nashville is a journalist's treasure trove. And it seems that three of these stories connect with you in ways that I find delightful."

Her stomach tightened. "I have nothing to talk to you about. If you look for dirt in anyone's life, you'll probably find some."

"Even the lives of Christians?"

"Of course. We're sinners saved by the grace of a loving God."

"I don't think I can agree with you on that, my love, because I haven't found any dirt on you."

"I'm not famous enough. And I don't have any lewd pictures or dark scandalous secrets that anybody would be interested in. I have to go now."

"Aren't you interested in hearing about the three stories that intersect with you?"

Maybe she'd better listen. "Go ahead."

"The first is regarding your friend Serene Stevens. The anorexia angle, of course."

Heat warmed Parker's cheeks. "You don't know anything about her."

"Actually, I do. As a matter of fact, pictures of her say it all. She stands in her concerts speaking of the, quote, transforming power of Christ. Yet she doesn't seem able to garner that for herself, does she?"

"Don't write about her," Parker said. "She deserves better than that."

"And the second story that intersects with you concerns this allegedly stolen song."

She caught her breath. "Who told you about that?"

"Never mind. I find it fascinating that the third story, the one of the song thieves being murdered ... well, you can see why I stay in Nashville. I'm considering relocating here."

Parker's heart sped into triple-time. Swallowing, she said, "I have nothing more to say to you." She hung up the phone and turned it off so he couldn't call back.

So he knew about the song, which she'd managed to keep quiet until now. But those who knew — cops and Serene's people — had probably shared the secret in confidence with people they trusted. Those people had shared with others, until it got into the hands of Nigel Hughes.

There was no such thing as confidentiality. Secrets couldn't be kept.

CHAPTER
FORTY-THREE

Parker was glad to get out of town when the first tour date finally arrived. The police still hadn't been able to locate Mick Evans. But since Gibson was no longer involved in an ongoing investigation, he was able to take a leave of absence for the tour.

They headed out in Parker's father's beat-up van, following Serene's tour bus. The CDs had been pressed, the liner notes printed, the jewel cases filled and shrink-wrapped. They carried the boxes of them in the back of the van, along with their instruments. Thankfully, they didn't have to bring their own sound equipment, since they'd be using Serene's, which would already be on stage when Parker came out.

Her dad had completed detox as promised, and her brothers had signed on as Serene's roadies to help pay their way. That meant they would have to work hard setting up and breaking down the set at each concert. There wouldn't be much time for rehearsal.

Parker's mother had opted out of teaching summer school and come along to work Parker's table at each venue, selling her CDs.

Though Serene had offered Parker the chance to ride in her elaborate tour bus, there wasn't room for her whole family. Even though she would have liked the chance to get to know Daniel better, she could hardly allow herself to be treated like a diva when her brothers and parents were rattling along behind them. So she chose to ride in the van.

The first stop was Atlanta, just a few hours south of Nashville. After they checked into their motel, Parker went with the guys to set up at Phillips Arena, one of Jeff Standard's additions to the tour. As they assembled Serene's elaborate stage set, Parker walked around the concourse. Tables were set up for sales of CDs, Serene T-shirts, and all sorts of paraphernalia related to her songs. Tomorrow the people who worked the tables would be swamped with business. She hoped her own table, stuck in an obscure place with no flow-through traffic, would garner even a fraction of Serene's business. The home of the Atlanta Hawks basketball team, the arena had recently hosted Bon Jovi.

Though Serene's concert wasn't sold out, twelve thousand tickets had already been sold, and more could be sold by tomorrow. Tomorrow when Parker sang, it would be to thousands of Serene's fans who'd never even heard of Parker.

The astonishing opportunity overwhelmed her. She dropped into a seat and tried to see where she'd be on the platform. The grand piano she'd play had not been placed on stage yet. The people working looked so small from this vantage point, but the Jumbo-Tron screens would magnify her face, her fingers on the keys ...

She should have had her nails done, as Serene always did. She should have had a facial and gotten hair extensions and hired a makeup artist. What was she thinking, to play in arenas like this without being ready? She must be crazy!

Then a thrill shivered from her neck down her backbone, reminding her that it wasn't about her. God had been preparing her for this all her life. She was ready.

Tears overtook her at the magnitude of it all. "Look how gracious you've been to me, Lord. Tomorrow my biggest dream's coming true."

She prayed for the men and women and teens who would fill

this place tomorrow night. There would surely be people in the audience who needed Christ. Would her songs — either the ones sung by Serene or the ones she performed herself — have any effect on their eternal lives?

"Lord, let me do that for you," she whispered. "Give me the talent and skill to reach those people for you. Please, Lord, that's all I ask."

Parker's emotions were raw, hovering wet in her eyes, as they left the coliseum when her brothers were finished. Cleansed from the tears and the prayers, she was just walking into her motel room when her phone rang. She saw that it was Butch.

She clicked on the phone. "Hey, Butch. What's up?"

She heard a siren in the background. "Parker, we've got a problem," Butch yelled into the phone. "Serene just collapsed. We've got an ambulance taking her to the hospital."

Parker sucked in a breath. "What do you mean, *collapsed*?"

"Passed out cold. The paramedics revived her, but I don't know what's wrong with her. She's asking for you. Can you come?"

Lynn came out of the bathroom with a mud mask on her face. "What's going on?" she asked.

Parker put her hand over the phone and quickly told her. "What hospital is she in?" Parker asked Butch.

"Emory."

"I'll be right there."

Parker got the van keys from her dad. She had no idea how to get to Emory University Hospital, but she used the GPS on her iPhone to get directions. She almost wrecked, trying to read the small screen while driving, but finally found the hospital and its emergency entrance, and pulled into a parking place reserved for doctors. She'd move the van later.

Her mind raced with possibilities. Serene could be dead. She could have had a heart attack, like those anorexics who starve their organs so badly that they just shut down. Had it finally come to that?

She fought tears as she made her way in. No one was at the desk, but a security guy sat in a booth near the door. "Can you help me?" Parker asked. "My friend was brought here in an ambulance. Can you tell me where she is?"

"What's the name?"

"Stevens," she said. "Serene Stevens."

The guard stood and yelled back to a nurse in another room, who poked her head out the door. "Take this lady to Serene Stevens," the guard said.

Parker wanted to ask him to hush. If this was about Serene's eating disorder, the quieter they kept it, the better.

"Sure, honey," the nurse said. "Are you family?"

"I'm about the closest she's got." Worried that they might not let her in, she added, "She had someone call me."

The nurse had a star-struck smile as she led Parker halfway down the hallway, then pointed to the room. "We're big fans of hers. We're all very excited that she's here."

"Then she's okay?"

"She'll be all right."

Serene was lying on a bed, dark shadows around her eyes, her face white as kindergarten paste. Technicians and nurses buzzed around her, setting up monitoring equipment.

"Serene!"

Serene saw her and started to sit up. "Oh, Parker. Thank goodness you're here." She reached for Parker's hand, then winced when her IV pulled.

"What did they say? What's wrong?"

Serene sank back. "I don't know. I just started feeling real sick and got chills. My chest was hurting. I thought I was having a heart attack, and then I just fainted." She burst into tears and pulled Parker into a hug.

"But it's not a heart attack," Serene went on. "It's just exhaustion, I guess."

That made Parker angry. "Serene, it's not exhaustion. It's malnutrition, and you know it."

Serene waved her off. "I'm not malnourished. Just a little dehydrated. Right, doctor?"

The doctor gave Parker a knowing look. "We're going to start putting some liquids into her system. Hopefully she'll feel better in a few hours." He touched Serene's arm, patted her. "Listen to your friend, dear. We're sending a meal in. I hope you'll eat it."

That was all the confirmation Parker needed.

When he and the nurses had left the room, Parker said, "Is there anything I can get you?"

"No. I don't want to eat before the concert."

"The concert's not until tomorrow night, Serene. You've got to eat."

"But I'll look fat. Once I finish the drip I'll be fine. I was just dehydrated because of all the stuff leading up to leaving on the tour. I haven't been drinking enough water."

Parker suspected that Serene had been throwing up so much that her electrolytes were down to nothing. "Serene, there isn't going to *be* a tour if you don't eat. Don't you understand? Your anorexia is going to kill you."

Serene looked like she could slap her. "I don't *have* anorexia."

"You go for days without eating and then you eat six peanuts or three bites of cantaloupe, and throw *that* up. Do you know what that does to your organs? Do you have any idea what it's doing to your teeth? You can't keep funneling stomach acid through your esophagus and think it's not going to affect your voice. You're a big star. You have everything going for you, but you're going to ruin it."

Serene looked so small lying on that bed. She covered her face and closed her eyes. "You don't understand, Parker."

"Understand what?"

"*None* of this would be happening if I were thirty pounds heavier! Fame has its price. You might as well get that through your head."

"Is it worth your death?"

"I'm not dying."

"You will if you keep this up. Haven't you ever heard of Karen Carpenter? She died of this very thing!" Parker didn't know how to get through to her. "So you're telling me that I won't make it unless I lose thirty pounds?"

Serene couldn't meet her eyes. "No, you look fine."

"No, I don't. You think I look fat."

"I never said that!"

"You say it every day by living your life as if breaking a hundred pounds is the end of the world."

"It's not, for you. It just is for me. Jeff Standard won't see me as a gold mine if I don't look thin and sexy."

"Then Jeff Standard has a problem."

"We all have problems, Parker. All but you."

Parker couldn't believe Serene would say that. Where had she been? "Okay, now you're starting to tick me off. I've had nothing *but* problems lately and you know it."

Serene's face twisted as tears worked at her eyes. Parker never could stand up to Serene's tears. This wasn't the time to yell at her. This was the time to be a friend. "I love you, Serene. I want you to be okay."

"I will be," she whispered. "Soon as I get some liquids in me."

"And food. You're going to eat, Serene, if I have to put it in your mouth and move your jaws myself."

Serene laughed and wiped her face. "Okay, maybe a few bites, if you'll get off my back."

Serene reached for another hug, and Parker sat down on the bed and clung to her. Serene wasn't the big, thriving star right now. She was the motherless child of a cruel father. A girl who couldn't control anything but her weight. Her God-gifted talent had been her vehicle out of her earthly hell.

"I'm glad you're here with me," Serene said. "Will you stay until they let me go?"

"Of course," Parker said. "I have to make sure you're all right, don't I? Somebody has to watch over you so you don't sabotage your own tour."

They brought Serene a ham sandwich. She ate the meat but refused to eat the bread. Thankfully, she didn't fight to go to the bathroom and throw it up.

Parker sat quietly beside her bed, praying silent prayers for healing for her friend as Serene drifted into sleep.

At one a.m., someone knocked on the door. "Come in," Parker called softly.

Nigel Hughes stopped in, camera in hand. "Parker, my love, I might have known you'd be here. So good to see you again. I'd love to get a picture of our friend here."

As Serene rose up, the camera flashed. "Who are you?"

"I told you to leave her alone!" Parker launched across the room and tried to get the camera, but he was taller than she and held it out of reach.

He looked at Serene. "I'd love a statement about your eating disorder, my dear lady. Have you been diagnosed?"

Serene crossed her hands over her gown. "I'm not making a statement. Get out of my room!"

"Just a few words, Miss Stevens, before my column is published."

A nurse pushed into the room. "What is it?"

"Please call security and get this man out of here," Parker cried. "And no more reporters!"

"Reporters? How did you get in here?"

Nigel smiled. "It's not exactly a secret when ambulances are involved, now is it? And I've made some rather good friends here tonight."

The nurse grabbed his sleeve and tried to muscle him out.

"Do you intend to go for treatment?"

"Exhaustion," Serene said. "I'm here for dehydration and exhaustion. That's all!"

Two security guards rushed in and dragged Nigel out.

"That's it." Serene got out of bed and reached for her clothes. "I'm leaving."

"No, you're not ready. Wait until the bag of fluids is empty."

Parker made her lie back down. Serene lay there, stiff, staring at the ceiling. "Who does he write for?"

"*New York Times.*"

She closed her eyes. "And he's writing about my weight?"

Parker didn't want to tell Serene, but she needed to know. "He's been snooping around asking about you. I think he's just feeling his way to see if there really is a story here. Your job is to prove there's not. All you have to do is start eating."

Tears came to Serene's eyes. "It's not that simple."

Now they were getting somewhere. "Then you admit you have a problem?"

Serene seemed to catch herself. "A problem with my weight."

Parker wanted to slap her. "Serene, you're skeletal. Don't you see it? Your ribs poke out. Your knees are getting bony. You're starting your tour tomorrow. Do you want that to be what people remember about you?"

"Stop it or I'm leaving, Parker!"

Parker didn't want Serene to leave before those life-sustaining fluids were in her, so she gave it up.

They didn't release Serene until three in the morning. Butch took her back to her hotel, rehydrated and looking healthier, but still weak. Parker feared that the chest pains Serene had been having didn't bode well for her heart. If she lost any more weight, her heart might give out. Parker told Butch to make sure she ate and not to let her purge, but she doubted he would heed her warning. Despite his complaints about her disorder, he liked the thin, lean Serene Stevens as much as Jeff Standard did.

Skin and bones was worth a lot more than a few pounds of flesh.

CHAPTER
FORTY-FOUR

Despite everything, Serene was brilliant onstage the next night. From backstage, Parker watched her friend perform. Serene had been as weak as a sick kitten just last night. Now she danced and shouted and had the energy of a star as she brought the house down.

Parker waited backstage, jittering like she had the DTs. After two more songs, Serene would do Parker's introduction, then change costumes while Parker performed her three songs. Her armpits were perspiring, but it didn't show through her outfit. She wiped the bubbles of sweat from her top lip with the back of her sleeve, then realized she'd wiped makeup onto her shirt. Panic spilled through her, and she turned around, searching for something, anything, to get it off. Maybe someone had one of those sticks that erased careless marks. Why had she done that? She needed to erase *herself*. She was so stupid.

She saw Serene's makeup lady standing in the hallway, waiting for Serene to come off. She almost tackled her. "I'm sorry to bother you, but do you have anything that'll get this off?"

The woman smiled. "Sure, hon. I have everything." She ran back up the hall, and Parker followed.

"Hurry, please. I'm about to go on. The camera's going to show my hands on the JumboTron as I play piano. My sleeve will show."

"Calm down, baby." The woman popped her gum as she got out one of those Tide sticks and began rubbing the tip on her sleeve. "It might look a little wet, but the spot'll be gone."

Relieved, she saw that the stick worked. Parker heard Serene transition to the next song — "Trying."

The woman whose name she didn't know grabbed her hands. "Honey, you're shaking and you're all out of breath. You've got to relax. You can't play piano like this."

How true. But Parker had no time to get a massage or do yoga.

Parker thanked her and headed back to the darkness of the backstage area. Her father and brothers were there now, decked out in jeans and shirts that looked unintentionally showy. She glanced at her father to see if he looked drunk. Her brothers had promised to keep him away from alcohol tonight.

He looked fine.

Thank you, Lord.

All three turned to her as she came back to the curtains. "Ready, Parker?" LesPaul asked.

Parker's lungs felt like a tightly shut cage. "No. I'm gonna faint."

Her father set down his guitar and came to her. Taking her hands, he said, "Look at me."

She did, nodding. The chorus of "Trying" rose and fell. The music faded, and she heard Serene's clear voice asking the audience to sing with her. She heard the sheer number of people who would see her perform tonight, their voices filling the place.

Thousands and thousands, more than she'd ever sung for at any other time in her life.

Pete bent down to her face. "Breathe, sweetheart," he whispered.

"I don't have time to breathe."

"In, long breath, hold it.... out, long breath ... Come on, do it with me."

It wasn't working. She grabbed her brothers' hands. "We have to pray. Hurry!" They formed a circle, eyes closed, as Serene resumed singing the chorus, and the band started back in.

"Father, help us. You've brought us this far. Calm me down, steady my hands. All I ask is that I do my best." She hadn't expected tears. Now what would she do? She opened her eyes, dabbing the corners, and tried to breathe again.

Gibson took over the prayer. "Lord, remind Parker that you gave her these songs. You're letting her deliver them. Fill her up. Calm her down."

They waited, listening, as Serene sang the fourth and most passionate verse of "Trying."

"Listen, baby," her dad whispered against her ear. "That's your song they're singing."

She felt the warmth of answered prayer wash over her, steadying her hands.

"You're ready for this," LesPaul said. "You've been preparing your whole life."

She banished the fear that they wouldn't like her sound. If she sang like Serene, she wouldn't have this chance. It was precisely *because* of her unique sound that Serene was bringing her along.

She stepped to the side curtain, looked in and saw her best friend, in all her skinny glory, lit up and moving across the stage, the long, filmy pieces of her top blowing like her hair in the air flooding the stage ...

Serene was born for the stage. Parker stood there for a moment, forgetting her own nerves and smiling at the mastery of her friend. That motherless little girl who had sat alone in the lunchroom had become a phenom.

Look what God can do.

The thought came like a whispered encouragement into her heart. He could do it with Parker, too. There was no limit to what he could do.

The song was winding to an end. "Let's go, guys," LesPaul said, and as the lights fell to darkness, illuminating only Serene, her father and brothers took the stage, transitioning with Serene's musicians. Parker waited to be introduced. She looked down at her hands. They were steady.

After a moment of all the musicians playing together — Serene's and Parker's — Serene's musicians moved off the stage. Not a note was missed. Daniel Walker came off, his guitar in his hand. He smiled as he spotted her standing there, and he leaned close. "Break a leg, Parker," he said. "We got them all warmed up for you."

She couldn't speak. He stood there with her, his hand on her back, waiting as Serene made the introduction that would bring Parker out.

"And now, I have a special surprise. I want you to meet my best friend, the girl who writes all my songs. The force behind 'Trying' and 'Ambient,' and all of the other songs I've recorded." The crowd burst into applause. "She's not only a fabulous songwriter, she's also a gifted performer. I think you're going to love her. Please welcome my friend ... Parker James."

Parker sipped in a breath as her brothers and father began to play "Inscribed." She walked out to the stage. As the crowd applauded expectantly, she took her place at the grand piano. A light came on directly over her, casting a glow on the keyboard ... and lighting her up like a star.

Serene disappeared off-stage into the darkness as Parker began to sing.

Three songs later, Parker played the last note, and sat silent for a second. Tears stained her face. She hadn't expected that, but as she'd sung, she'd felt the Holy Spirit taking over. Calm had enabled her to do her best.

For seconds after the note stopped resonating through the arena, she heard silence. Then, a smattering of applause that seemed to be contagious. It spread across the arena, growing slowly. Not wild applause, demanding an encore, but the kind of applause that happened after a passionate performance in church, when people were caught in prayer that they didn't want to end.

Serene's band members came back onstage, her keyboarder playing the transitioning chords. As Daniel walked past her, she saw tears on his face. He mouthed the word "Perfect."

And it had been — as perfect as she could do with what she'd been given. Floating on gratitude, she went off the stage as Serene came back out, dressed differently for her second set. Now the crowd went wild.

Pete lifted her up in his arms. "That was fabulous, baby!"

LesPaul and Gibson hugged her, too, and she could see the joy on their faces.

"That was *awesome*," Gibson shouted, punching the air.

"All the hard work," LesPaul said. "It paid off. Now go find your table and autograph your heart out."

CHAPTER
FORTY-FIVE

Parker's nerves took a rest the following day as they hit I-20 and made their way to Jackson, Mississippi. Her mother had sold three hundred CDs the night before, and Parker had autographed dozens. While she'd hoped to sell more, it had been a good start. Three hundred people had found her worthy of shelling out fifteen bucks for their musical pleasure.

The fact that Jeff Standard was coming to the Jackson Coliseum to watch the show made Parker nervous all over again. She told herself the tycoon wasn't here to see her, but Serene.

But that night, before she played, he stood backstage, watching without emotion as Serene blew out all the stops. Parker felt his censure as she sat down at her piano to do her part of the show.

But like the night before, she felt the Holy Spirit's presence as she performed her three songs. Again, there was a moment of silence after she played her last note, then a crescendo of applause.

When Serene took back the stage, Parker floated off. Jeff Standard stood in her way. She decided not to try to dodge him, and stuck out her hand. "Mr. Standard, I'm Parker James. Nice to meet you."

His smile was cool. "Good show," he said. "You have a real way about you."

She didn't know if that was a compliment. Somehow it had the ring of George's comment about her "different" sound. But she thanked him and pushed past to her father and brothers, who were celebrating again. Then she hurried toward her table to sign autographs. As she walked the perimeter of the coliseum, she basked in the sounds of her songs coming from Serene's gifted pipes. There weren't many people trolling around on the concourse. They were all in their seats, hanging on Serene's every note.

Parker glanced through the door and caught a glimpse of Serene at her best. She stepped inside and observed the audience from the last row, saw the joy on the faces of those whose rapt attention Serene held. Her gaze swept out over the backs of the heads in the crowd.

And then she saw him.

One man, looking back at her. He looked like Mick Evans.

She sucked in a breath and backed away from the door. Her heart slammed against her ribcage. Stepping outside into the concourse, she tried to catch her breath. Was that Mick? She had to know.

She stepped back in the doorway and looked in the section where she'd seen him. Her eyes scanned the backs of the heads. She couldn't find him. Maybe she was wrong. Maybe the pattern of lights and shadows had created an illusion.

She backed out again and ran back around the way she'd come, down the steps to the backstage area.

She'd forgotten her access badge, so the bouncer standing there wouldn't let her past.

"I'm sorry, you have to have a badge."

"I'm Parker James. I just performed. Didn't you see me?"

"Sorry, ma'am. No badge, no access."

She didn't have time to change his mind. "Could you please radio security in the backstage area and get someone to come and clear me? I have to get in touch with my brother. He's a cop."

She waited as the security guard made a call, then decided to let her through. She ran into the area behind the stage, searching for her brothers. She found Gibson back in their dressing room.

She bolted in and leaned back against the door. "Mick Evans might be here!"

Gibson sprang to his feet. "Where?"

"I thought I saw him in Section 14C. I'm not sure it was him, but is there some way you could find out?"

Gibson bolted out to talk to security. After a moment, someone who looked in charge appeared. She couldn't hear what Gibson was saying to him, but they motioned for Parker. "Come with us, Parker. Show us where you saw him."

She led them up the stairs to the concourse and out into the hall. She ran around the building, seeing Serene and the crowd every few yards as the hall opened into the auditorium. She took them to 14C, and pointed to where she'd seen him.

Gibson went in and walked, unnoticed, down the steps, pausing at the section Parker had pointed to.

The lights were down, and it was difficult to see. Parker began to despair. She must have been mistaken. Why would he be here, when the police in Nashville were searching for him? Why would he come out in public when his face had been flashed on the national news in connection with two murders?

Gibson came back shaking his head. "He may have seen you and left."

She felt like an idiot. "I'm probably wrong. The lights were low. It probably wasn't even him; just someone who looked like him." She sighed. "Should I go ahead to my table?"

Gibson looked unsure. "I'll come with you."

"Don't tell Mom. No need to get her all upset." She led him around the concourse, glancing inside to the people at every opening into the concert hall.

"I won't. But I'm going to go talk to security."

By the time they reached her table, Parker was certain she'd made a mistake. It would make no sense for Mick to come out in public when he was wanted for two murders. That would be ridiculous.

She stepped behind the table and plastered on her smile for the people waiting for her autograph. Her mother was jubilant and threw her arms around her. "Great show, honey. I've never been prouder!"

CHAPTER
FORTY-SIX

Gibson withdrew the weapon from his ankle holster. He'd thought of leaving it in his hotel room and leaving security to those who knew their way around the Jackson Coliseum. But he'd been right to bring it.

He hoped Parker had made a mistake, that the lights had distorted her vision, that she really hadn't seen the killer in the crowd. Still, he followed the security director back to his office, where screens lined the walls with camera shots of various angles of the building.

"Like finding a needle in a haystack," Roy, the director, said. "Short of locking the place down, I don't see how we'd ever find him if he was here."

"Can you just show me the exits?" Gibson asked. "And rewind it about ten minutes. Maybe he left after Parker spotted him."

Roy pointed out the screens with those shots, rewound, then sped through the footage. Only a handful of people were leaving. A woman with two children. Four kids who looked like they were middle-school aged, probably sneaking out for some mischief before their parents picked them up. Several scattered couples and small groups.

If Mick was among them, Gibson couldn't spot him. He stood there with Roy, watching the screens capturing activity in every part of the coliseum. Mick could have blended into the crowd, and they'd never see him. If he left when the crowd flowed out, it would be almost impossible to see him.

"Any way we can lock all but one exit so I can watch as people leave?"

Roy gave him a look like he was deluded. "No, man! I can't do that without orders from our police department. We got over ten thousand people in there who'll be trying to get out all at the same time. No way I'm blocking the exits."

Gibson knew he couldn't convince them to do that. Knowing it was a long shot, he left Security and went to the front exit himself, hoping that if Mick Evans were here, he'd come out this way.

CHAPTER
FORTY-SEVEN

When the concert ended and the crowd thinned out, and she'd sold all the CDs she was going to sell, Parker helped her mother pack up the boxes. When Gibson showed back up at the table and told her they hadn't been able to find Mick, she decided to venture back to her dressing room to get her things. Gibson went with her, eyes scanning the dark corners, his gun tucked into his jeans under his untucked shirt.

"I'm sure I made a mistake," she said. "He wouldn't come here. I'm just jumpy, that's all. I shouldn't have said anything."

"Yes, you should have. You did the right thing. If it had been him, we might have caught him. I'm still not convinced you didn't see him."

She went into her dressing room, gathered her things, and loaded them into a duffel bag. She slung the bag over her shoulder. "What about your guitars?"

Gibson shook his head. "We'll get them after we help break down the set. Just leave them here for now. Listen, I don't want you and Mom alone. Ride the shuttle bus back to the hotel." He opened the door and looked out into the hall. "Daniel."

Parker looked past him and saw Daniel Walker coming toward

them, guitar case in hand. "There you are," he said when he saw her. "My favorite part of the concert."

She managed a smile. "Your favorite part? Don't lie, Daniel."

"I'm not lying," he said with a laugh. "There's something about the way you perform. You can just feel the Holy Spirit all over the place. I hope you sold a ton of CDs."

Warmth flushed through her face. "I sold a few. I was a little distracted, though, because right after I performed I thought I saw Mick Evans in the crowd." She told him about her close encounter.

Daniel looked concerned. "Serene wanted me to ask you to come to her dressing room. But if you want to get out of here, I can tell her you had to leave. She was crying, though, so it must be kind of important."

"Crying? You don't know why?"

"No. She was talking to Butch and Jeff Standard, so I guess it could have been anything."

Parker glanced at Gibson. "Guess I'd better go see what it is."

"We'll walk with you," Gibson said.

Daniel walked beside them as they headed back to Serene's dressing room. When she reached it, she saw Jeff Standard and Butch standing outside it, talking to several other men she didn't know. None of them looked her way. She reached the door and gave her familiar knock, and heard Serene call, "Come in."

She opened the door and leaned in. "Hey, it's me. The show was fabulous.

"Parker, I have to talk to you." Daniel was right. Serene had tears on her face, mascara dripping like some teenaged Goth. "Come in and close the door."

Parker glanced back at Daniel and Gibson. Frowning, Gibson said, "I'll wait here for you."

"Me, too," Daniel said.

She stepped inside and closed the door. "What's wrong? Didn't Jeff like the concert?"

Serene ripped a tissue out of its box, dabbed at her eyes. "Yeah, he liked it. It's just ... he wants to make some changes."

Parker's throat tightened like a fist.

"Parker, this is hard."

She could already guess what the change would be. "Tell me."

"Oh, Parker, I'm so sorry. He wants you out of the show."

Was that her heart beating in her ears? Parker tried to breathe.

"He just thinks that your part brings the mood down. That it's too Christian — too serious. He doesn't get it. He says that your style and mine aren't compatible."

Parker finally found her voice. "Not compatible? I *wrote* your songs. That's not compatible?"

"I know. I told him that it was a worship thing, the mood that you bring, but he's not a Christian. That doesn't even make sense to him."

"But don't you get any say at all?"

"No, I don't." She sucked in a sob. "You don't argue with him. My contract gives him a lot of authority."

Bottle rockets seemed to flare in Parker's head. "So that's it? I'm out, just like that?"

"Please don't hate me."

She couldn't hear her heart anymore, and her lungs were shut tight. She'd spent her mother's money ... her grandmother's property had been sold. There was no way to recoup that investment if she didn't finish the tour and sell out of her CDs ...

Her dreams of a record deal spun to the earth. She could almost hear them splat. Parker felt the blood draining from her face, pooling down in her fingertips, her toes. "I don't care what your stupid contract says. You should have fought for me. He's not going to cancel the tour over it. He has too much invested."

"What do you expect me to do?" Serene grabbed another tissue. "Walk? Threaten him? My career's on the line. I have to do what he says." She pressed the tissues against her eyes. "I was so up after the concert. It was so great. I thought it had gone off perfectly. And then this."

Did Serene expect her to comfort her? Setting he jaw, she went to Serene's chair, leaned over it. "You can't do this to me. Do you know how much money I've invested? I pressed enough CDs for the whole tour. If I don't have the opportunity to sell them, I'm sunk. What about the contract you have with *me*?"

"There was an escape clause, Parker. It said that you were on the tour unless things didn't work out — "

"They *did* work out."

"Jeff doesn't think so."

Parker hated the tears rushing to her eyes. She pursed her lips, trying not to blubber like a child. How would she tell her family?

"I told him it would ruin our friendship. He didn't care."

"And you didn't care, either?"

Serene grabbed her hands. "It won't, will it, Parker? If I succeed, you will, too, as my songwriter."

Parker jerked away from her. "It wasn't about fame, Serene!" But even as she said it, she knew it wasn't true. It *was* all about fame. Parker wanted to follow Serene's rising star. She wanted to be one, too.

"If you need a loan to pay all this back, I'll help."

Now she offered. Where had she been before? If Serene had invested her own money in Parker's part of the tour, this wouldn't be happening. "I don't want your money!" she shouted. "I want you to honor your commitment. I signed a contract, trusting you. I rewrote the songs! My brothers took leaves from work. My mother gave me all her savings!"

A knock sounded on the door, and Parker wanted to scream that they were busy, to leave them alone. They had things to work out.

But she was kidding herself. Nothing was going to be worked out. Serene was cutting her loose. It was a done deal. They might as well end this conversation with an interruption, rather than an explosion.

She went to the door, flung it open.

Butch stood there with a copy of the *New York Times*, opened to Nigel Hughes's column. A picture of Serene in her hospital bed, with Parker beside her, filled the top half of the page. Butch's over-white teeth were set together. "Why wasn't I told about this?"

Parker had nothing to say to him. She bit her lip so hard she thought it might bleed.

"Oh, no." Serene took the newspaper and read the headline. "Anorexic Christian Star Serene Stevens Collapses."

Parker couldn't help the spontaneous indignation firing in her chest at Nigel's audacity. But then a small, distant voice whispered that Serene deserved it.

Anger propelled her out of the room.

Daniel was waiting, a look of concern on his face. Gibson was gone. "Everything okay?" Daniel asked.

She didn't want him to see her cry. "Did you know about this?"

"About the article? No, I just saw it when someone brought it to Jeff."

She stormed up the hall. "Not the article. The tour!"

He was right behind her. "What about it?"

He would know soon enough. The whole world would know. The humiliation would bleed far and wide. She swung around to face him. "I got cut from the tour."

His jaw dropped. "No way! Why?"

"I'm not good enough," she said through her tears. "I'm bringing the crowd down. Jeff Standard hates me." Her voice broke and she swallowed. "Where's Gibson?"

"Talking to the stage manager. He's decided not to help with the set tonight. He's afraid to leave you alone."

More breached contracts. She wanted to get out of here but didn't dare leave without Gibson's protection. "I have to finish help-ing my mom pack up the CDs." She sniffed. "Maybe we should just leave them. Maybe the janitorial staff will enjoy them." What would she ever do with that many CDs she couldn't sell? All the money spent . . .

Daniel touched her arm and stopped her. "Parker, what happened? What did she say?"

"I told you."

"That Jeff hates you? That's impossible. You were phenomenal. I wasn't just saying that."

"What Jeff thinks is all that matters. He's calling the shots now. Some guy who doesn't understand a thing about glorifying or praising God. How ironic that he'd sign a Christian star and then make judgments about the spiritual content of her show!"

She didn't want to be near him with tears staining her face. Her mascara was probably smeared like Serene's. That's what she got for wearing so much makeup, thinking she was somebody. Why had she ever wanted to put herself out there for everyone to judge?

"Where is Gibson?" she cried as she headed back for the stage area. "I just want to go back to the hotel and be alone."

Daniel grabbed her arm again. "Stop and sit down here with me, please. I just want to pray with you, all right?"

She paused and dug into her bag for something to wipe her face with. She found the T-shirt she'd worn over to the Coliseum today. She used it to wipe the black under her eyes, then her nose, then her cheeks . . .

"All right," she said. "Just . . . let me go into the bathroom for a minute."

He checked out the restroom before letting her go in, then he waited outside the door. She went in and stood in front of the mirror, looking at her reflection. She looked like a vampire. She hated the sight of the smeared mascara and thick matte makeup. She filled the sink with water and bent over it, allowing herself one last, good cry. Then trying to pull it back in, she washed her face.

Daniel was outside waiting for her, waiting to pray. Even now, he was probably praying. Why couldn't everyone on the tour be like him?

She washed off her tears and told herself to stop crying. She didn't want Daniel to remember her self-pity.

Daniel was still quietly waiting when she came back out. Gibson, who'd probably expected her to spend more time with Serene, wasn't back yet. Daniel pulled her into a corner in the backstage area, where two folding chairs sat catty-cornered. She sat down with him, arms folded on her knees. She couldn't meet his eyes. "I'm fine, Daniel. I know you're tired. I just needed a good cry, but I'm over it now. Time to move on."

"You have every right to cry." He took her hand, laced his fingers through hers, and began to pray without a prelude or a note of warning. As he talked to God about her situation, she found her sadness pinching her face again. She fought to hold back another meltdown.

He asked God to help her with her sorrow, to lift her spirits, to remind her that it wasn't over, that there was still a plan. He asked him to do his perfect will in her life. When he finally ended the prayer, she was a wreck.

He handed her a handkerchief. She looked down at it, hating to mess it up. "I didn't know guys still carried handkerchiefs."

"Helps onstage under those bulbs. Can't have sweat dripping into our eyes. That one's clean, though."

She smiled and looked down at it. "I wasn't worried that it was used." She blotted her eyes again, saw more black. How much of that stuff had she caked on tonight, anyway?

"Parker, this is wrong. They shouldn't have done that to you."

She shook her head and stared at the white cloth. "It's just business."

"Not good business."

She breathed a bitter laugh and sat back. "Oh, Daniel. That's nice of you to say, but I know what you think of my talent."

His eyes softened. "What do you mean?"

She swallowed the dryness in her throat. "That night I was performing for your group? The night Brenna died . . . I got the phone call from Gibson and I had to step out. Then I heard you tell the kids that I just slipped away so I wouldn't get the glory."

He looked embarrassed. "Oh," he said. "Yeah, I remember. I didn't know you were listening."

"But I'm not really that pious, and I'm not that selfless." She smiled and shook her head. "I really wanted the applause."

He stared at her for a moment, then laughed. "That's okay. We all want applause. That's why we perform."

"Yeah, but I let you go on thinking that was why I left."

His smile faded. "Well, after the news came out, I figured it out."

"But the point is that I didn't even want to set the record straight."

"You've been kind of busy." He took her hand, held it, looking down at it.

She knew she shouldn't go further, but she felt the need to unload all her baggage — to lay it down and walk away from it. "That night, I heard you telling them that I didn't have a voice that could draw crowds."

"Parker, did you hear the rest of what I said? That you can take your audience right to the throne of God? You did that tonight, too. Who says you don't have talent? Just because some record executive doesn't get it, doesn't mean you're not gifted."

She fingered the handkerchief. "I went with Serene to the hairdresser one day and watched how they pampered and fawned all over her. I thought, *Someday I'll have that, too*. How stupid."

"I don't believe that's what it was about for you," he said. "I've seen you worship with your songs. God smiles when you write, and when you sing."

She wanted to believe it, but right now her head swirled with humiliation and failure.

"Ready to go, Parker?"

She turned and saw Gibson. "Yeah, guess so." She'd have to tell him about the tour. Maybe she'd wait and tell him with her family.

She turned back to Daniel. "Thank you, Daniel. I appreciate your waiting with me."

He clung to her hand a moment longer. "I'll be praying," he whispered.

CHAPTER
FORTY-EIGHT

Gibson plugged one ear and tried to hear David Carter's voice on his cell phone. He was having problems hearing the detective who'd taken over the Evans/Teniere case because the conversation in the adjoining hotel room was getting heated. His family was incensed that Parker had been cut from the tour, but Gibson couldn't help thinking that it might be a blessing in disguise. With Mick Evans still at large, and Parker's possible sighting of him tonight, he was glad she wouldn't be sitting like a piano-playing bull's-eye at the center of the stage tomorrow.

"We've learned some interesting things about Mick Evans's background," Carter was saying.

Pete's voice was rising in the adjoining room. He wasn't taking Parker's news well. Gibson went to the door between the rooms and closed it. "I'm listening."

"We already knew his father left his mother for Tiffany when Mick was seven. Father basically ignored him as he was growing up. Mother struggled. She wasn't very well educated, married Nathan when she was seventeen and pregnant. She wound up working two jobs to support Mick."

"But she took Nathan back to court, right? Tried to get more money."

"And lost the suit. Nathan and the judge were golf buddies. So not too long after, the mother offs herself."

"Yeah, I know all that. Mick found her."

"This part you don't know. His dad's stuck with little Mick all of a sudden, so he moves him into the mansion, where he lives with Tiffany and the child they had together."

"Brenna."

"And apparently Tiffany doesn't like having him around. So a few weeks later, they pack him up and send him to a boarding school in Colorado."

Okay, so Mick was a traumatized kid. No excuse. Lots of kids had traumatic lives and didn't wind up murderers. "But he told me he's lived with them off and on lately. He works with his dad."

"Yeah, after he graduated from college with a 4.0, his dad let him come home. Put him to work in his record company. But we've interviewed his friends and coworkers, and they all say that it was no secret that Mick and Tiffany didn't get along. And he was hardly on speaking terms with his sister. He hated her, and the feeling was mutual."

Gibson ran all that through his mind. It was helpful. Maybe now that Tiffany and Brenna were dead, Mick had no further agenda involving Parker. For the thousandth time since Parker had alerted him, Gibson wondered whether he was making too much of this.

Gibson lowered his voice. "Can you think of *any* reason he'd be following this tour?"

"Not unless he has some kind of vendetta against your sister. We know her house was broken into, and that he was following her. And that he's probably the one who called her."

None of it made sense. The man who called Parker from the pay phone had promised to protect her. And the person who broke in hadn't stolen anything; instead, he'd left the song sheets. In hindsight, it was clear he'd been warning her about the stolen song, before anyone else even knew it had been taken.

"I'll keep you informed, but you do the same," he said. "No kidding. I need to know what I'm dealing with here."

"My guess is that he's still in Nashville somewhere, James. Don't sweat it. He wouldn't put himself out there like that."

Gibson hung up the phone and sat on the bed for a moment, staring into space. *God, please let that be true.*

He heard his dad's voice booming through the wall. He had to get back in there. He opened the adjoining door and leaned in. Parker was hunched on one of the beds, arms around her knees. Lynn sat on the edge of the other one. Pete and LesPaul were standing.

"What hotel is Jeff Standard staying in?" Pete bellowed.

"You can't go to his hotel!" Parker cried.

"Yes, I can, and I will!"

LesPaul looked ready to punch someone, himself. "Dad's right. At least maybe we could recoup the money invested in this tour. Or scare Standard into putting Parker back into the concerts."

Parker covered her face. "I don't want to force my way onto that stage. That's not how it was supposed to be!"

"You rewrote your songs because she promised you this spot," LesPaul said.

"Maybe that's where I went wrong. Maybe I just sold out."

Lynn got up and came to sit next to her. "Honey, you didn't sell out. You have a dream. You thought God was making it happen. We all did."

"We thought wrong."

"No, we didn't. You heard the people who bought your CDs for the last two nights. You drew them closer to God, they said. And if all the money we spent was to impact one person that way, then it was money well spent."

"What a crock." Pete set his hands on his hips. "Lynn, you're killing me."

"It's true, Pete. Music has power to impact people — I don't have to tell you that. To draw them closer to God. Don't tell me you didn't feel the Holy Spirit when you were playing with her onstage."

Pete looked at Parker, and his face changed. "No, I felt something. It was emotional, all right."

Quiet settled over the room as everyone absorbed Pete's admission. Gibson wondered if this disappointment would be enough to send his dad back to the bottle. He crossed the room and looked out the window. The parking lot wasn't well lit. Anybody could be out there.

"I'm so sorry, guys," Parker said. "You did so much to help me get ready. You put your own work, your whole lives, on hold. I wouldn't have asked any of it if I'd known it was going to turn out like this."

LesPaul's voice was softer as he answered. "How could you know? Come on, Parks. Nobody could have anticipated this."

"I should have," she said. "I know I'm not the best performer in the world. I'm no Serene. I thought maybe my voice was unique enough that I could pull it off."

"You did pull it off," LesPaul said.

"You sure as blazes did," their father echoed. He sat down beside her, touched her knee. "Here's what we're gonna do, sweetheart. I've given this a lot of thought. You've got to go country with some of these songs. Jesus gets good airplay on country stations. That'll get you into some venues that you haven't thought of."

Gibson's jaw dropped, and he looked at his sister. She unfolded from her knot, stretched her legs out in front of her. "Venues like honky tonks and mud races, with a few churches in between?"

"Parker, I'm not kidding."

Parker had the grace to smile. "Dad, I'm a Christian songwriter. I'm not changing." She sighed and grabbed the remote, turned on the television.

Mick Evans's face filled the screen.

The sight of him seemed to suck the air from the room, as Nancy Grace spoke of the search for the "person of interest" in Tiffany Teniere's murder.

"What did you find out, Gibson?" Pete asked.

He shrugged. "They don't have any reason to believe he's here in Jackson. Carter thinks he's probably still in Nashville, hiding somewhere."

"I sure hope so," Lynn said. "So what about tomorrow? We're going home, right?"

LesPaul shook his head. "Mom, I can't go home. I have a contract to help with the set."

"Surely you can't be expected to fulfill that when your sister was booted off the tour."

"I will be. They need both Gibson and me. I doubt seriously that Standard pulled the set designer in on the decision about Parker. He's counting on us. I don't want to be known as somebody who doesn't keep his word."

Gibson agreed. "We can tell him tomorrow that we need to quit, and we'll be close enough to Nashville for him to get replacements. But it would be bad business to leave him holding the bag."

"I don't want to pay for another night in a hotel," Parker said, "but I sure don't want to go to the coliseum and sit through the concert. It's humiliating."

"We'll put it on my credit card, sweetie," Lynn offered. "Your dad and I will stay behind with you, and we'll wait for Gibson and LesPaul. Then we'll all head back to Nashville after the concert."

CHAPTER FORTY-NINE

Parker lay in the dark in the room she shared with her mother, and stared at the ceiling. The events of the night should have left her sapped of energy, but her mind was wide awake, full of recriminations and fears.

Fear for her future loomed close to her fears of Mick Evans. How had her life come to this? Here she was without a job, in a hotel room she couldn't afford, after pouring her life into a set of songs that no one would ever hear.

And a killer might still be stalking her.

Her telephone blared out, its mad piano ringtone bringing her off the bed. Heart racing, she grabbed it and looked at the clock. It was two a.m.

Serene's face filled the screen.

"Who is it?" her mother asked from the other bed.

"Serene." She tossed the phone on the bed and lay back down. "I don't want to talk to her."

The piano played again and Lynn got up and reached for it. "Answer it. Maybe she changed her mind."

Knowing that wasn't it, Parker answered the phone. "Hello?"

"Parker, what room are you in?"

Parker rolled to her back and shoved her hair back from her face. "Why do you want to know?"

"Because I'm here in your hotel. I need to talk to you."

Parker sighed. "It's two o'clock, Serene. Everybody's asleep."

"It's important. Tell me what room."

How had Serene gotten here from her ritzy hotel a few miles away? Had she come in a cab? A limo? "Are you alone?"

"No, I brought Sam, my bodyguard."

Oh, yes. She'd forgotten about the bodyguard for the tour.

She heard Gibson in the adjoining doorway. "Parker, what is it?"

"Serene's downstairs. She wants to come up."

He groaned. "Let me get dressed, and I'll go down and make sure nobody's following her."

Parker told Serene to wait. She turned on the lamp as Gibson went down to get her. She looked back at her mother, who was blinking as her eyes adjusted to the light.

"She has a lot of nerve waking me up at two in the morning, after what she did," Parker said.

"You weren't even sleeping," Lynn pointed out.

"That's beside the point. I was up all night with her two nights ago, and what thanks do I get?"

"I'll bet she's had a heart-to-heart with Jeff Standard, and he's changed his mind. I'll bet you're back on the tour, and tomorrow everything will be back like it was."

If only that were the case. But Parker didn't dare hope.

After a few minutes, Gibson led Serene in. "It looks all clear," he said. "Call me if you need me. The bodyguard's in the hallway."

He went back to his room, leaving the adjoining door slightly ajar. She heard the mattress squeak as he lay back down. She could hear her father's snore softly ripping in the other room. None of the activity had awakened him or LesPaul.

Serene stood just inside the door and stared at Parker. The star looked like the girl she'd befriended at the lunch table so many years ago. Her face was clean of makeup, her eyes swollen.

She stood before Parker and her mother. "I know you both hate me."

Parker threw up her hands. "Hate you? Is that why you woke us up? Because you're worried what we think of you?"

"Yes, sort of."

The tiny bit of hope her mother had incited faded to nothing. "That figures."

Serene came farther into the room and sat on Parker's bed. "Tonight I went back to my hotel, and I've never been so lonely in my life. I'm sick over what happened with you, Parker. I wanted you with me on the tour. It's no fun to do this alone."

"You're not alone. You have a whole entourage. Managers and makeup artists and bodyguards and record executives."

"But I need a friend."

"So is that why you wanted me on the tour in the first place? So you'd have somebody to hang out with? Because that little luxury for you cost *me* a lot of money."

"Of course not. You know I wanted to showcase your talent. I thought you were doing great, and I know the crowd loved you."

Lynn sat on the side of her unmade bed, holding her robe closed. "Maybe you could talk to him again. Tell him how much time and money Parker has put into this."

"I did talk to him. He was so nice before, but now he's criticizing my hair and the band and the things I say on stage. Oh, and the article in the *New York Times*? Butch thinks Jeff was behind it."

Now she had Parker's attention. "What do you mean, *behind* it?"

"Butch found out that Jeff and Nigel are old college friends. He thinks this article was Jeff's way of breaking me away from the squeaky-clean Christian girl image as we got started on the tour. If he could have dug up some compromising pictures, he would have, but there weren't any."

"You really think Jeff would tell the press you have an eating disorder?"

"It's publicity, and in today's culture, it's not all that negative. Butch thinks Jeff's the one who called Nigel when I collapsed."

Parker couldn't believe what she was hearing. "Well, you can't let him get away with it. He can't treat people this way."

"Oh, yes, he can." Serene's face twisted as tears filled her eyes. "What am I supposed to do? Lose everything I've worked for? He owns me, lock, stock, and barrel."

"Oh, my word," Lynn muttered. She went into the bathroom and came back out with a box of tissue.

Serene blew her nose. "He came in after I saw the article, but Butch wouldn't let me say anything to him about giving Nigel the story. He didn't want me to make him mad, so I had to bite my tongue."

"Why? He's not going to drop you, Serene. He has way too much money invested in this tour."

Serene grabbed one of Parker's pillows and rammed her fist into it. "I'm a coward. I want to succeed so I can show my father and all those people who thought I'd never amount to anything ..."

That was the one thing she could have said to soften Parker's heart. Parker met Lynn's eyes. "You don't have to prove anything to them."

"You don't know what it's like," Serene cried. "You have this great mother, and a family that would drop everything to support you in your dream. I have nobody. Nothing but my talent. If my career is pulled out from under me, what will I do? Who will I be?"

Parker sat back down next to her. "You were successful without Jeff Standard."

"But now I'm legally bound. There's no turning back."

Lynn sat down on the other side of Serene. "Isn't there, sweetie?"

"No. I'm stuck. And I'm confused. I don't want out of my contract. Part of me likes where he's going to take me. I've never played to such huge crowds."

"He didn't get you those crowds, Serene. You got them because you have a hit song!"

"But he's taking me to the next level. Soon I'll have a bunch of hit songs, and not just on the Christian charts. Is it wrong to want that? I mean, I've been working at this my whole life."

Parker stared at her friend. She thought of finding the passage in the Bible about being unequally yoked, and pointing out that going to the "next level" for Jeff Standard might strip away who Serene was. But was it Parker's own bitterness leading her to those conclusions?

She lay back on the bed, wishing she could hold onto her bitterness a little longer. But her love for her friend had melted it away. "I don't think it's wrong to play music outside the Christian arena, Serene. Heaven knows, not everybody in the Christian music industry is authentic. There are people in it for money, and some are using it as a stepping stone. I've seen egos gone wild at Dove Award shows, and concerts where musicians stand up and trumpet the cause of Christ, then get drunk or high in their buses on the way to the next stop."

"That's the thing," Serene said, wiping her tears. "Singing to only Christian crowds doesn't mean I'm all that spiritual. But to sing onstage in arenas where not everyone is a Christian — isn't that a truer test of my faith?"

"Of course it is, sweetie," Lynn said. "You just have to make sure your faith is solid enough to deal with Jeff Standard and others like him. People will be watching you especially hard. They'll want to see you shaken from your faith."

"But there are people on your tour who can help," Parker said. "Like Daniel Walker. He can help you keep your focus."

A smile broke through Serene's tears. "Yeah, Daniel's great. Did you know that yesterday he went to a local homeless shelter and played a private concert?"

Parker smiled. "He did? He didn't say anything about it."

"He wouldn't. He's not doing it for anyone's approval but God's."

Parker was glad Daniel would be an influence for Serene. She just hoped Serene didn't fall in love with him.

"Serene, you get to decide how you conduct yourself. Jeff may make decisions about your career, but he's not in charge of your life … or your soul. You have to make sure that the choices you make are *God's* choices, not Jeff's."

Serene stretched out on the bed and balled up Parker's pillow. "Do you think I can have a secular career and live a Christian life?"

"Of course you can," Parker said. "Normal, nonmusical people do it all the time."

Tears again. "Remember the first song of yours I recorded? How fun it was the first time we heard it on the radio?"

Parker didn't want to remember. Her own eyes misted, and she looked at the ceiling. They had been a good team. She didn't want it to come to an end.

"Parker, I don't know if I can do any of this without you there."

"I'm not your keeper, Serene. Like you've said, you can glorify him from the stage in front of fifteen thousand fans, whether Jeff likes it or not. If you make him enough money, he'll have to accept it."

"And if I don't?"

"Then he'll cut you loose. It's a tough business."

"Maybe I don't belong here. Maybe I'm in over my head."

Parker sighed and lay down next to her. "No, Serene. I want you to have your dream. You've worked hard for it, sacrificed a lot."

"But not my best friend. I don't want to sacrifice you."

Parker wiped a tear gathering in her eye. "All right, Serene. I'll talk to you on the phone every day, on one condition."

"What?"

"That you get even with Jeff Standard by proving the anorexia story wrong. You eat, and gain some weight, and that story will dissolve. And Nigel Hughes will look like an idiot."

"That's a great idea," Lynn said. "And honey, if you can't bring yourself to do that, then you need to take some time off the tour and get help."

Serene sat up. "Okay, let's start right now. I'm starving. Let's order room service."

"Room service?" Parker gave her a smirk. "You're thinking of *your* hotel. Ours has a vending machine down by the stairs."

Serene went to the door, leaned out, and asked the bodyguard to get her some things from the vending machine. He came back with an armload of potato chips and Cheetos, peanuts and pretzels, and several cans of soda. Serene brought them all to the center of the bed and began reading the labels.

"No calorie checks," Parker said. "I mean it!"

"Okay." Serene took a bag of pretzels and tore the bag open.

"And you can eat on my bed, on one condition."

"What?"

"You will not throw up in my bathroom. Do you understand that? Whatever you eat, you're going to keep down."

Serene nodded. "If I don't, you have my permission to call that Nigel guy."

As Serene ate and drank, Parker could see that she was beginning to feel better. They turned on the television and leaned back against the headboard. Lynn channel-surfed until they found a black-and-white Cary Grant movie. They lay on the bed like girls at a sleepover, watching until the very last lines. Finally, Serene fell asleep next to Parker.

Lynn smiled and covered her up. "Well, we might as well get some sleep," she whispered.

Parker met her mother's eyes. "She has no intentions of getting help for her anorexia, does she?"

Her mother's smile faded, and she shook her head. "I doubt it. Not yet."

Parker turned on her side and looked at Serene, out like a child. Her hand lay open under her chin, and Parker could see the burn scars on her palms from her father's grill. Serene had other scars, too. Some external, others not so visible.

Parker turned off the lamp. "Good night, Mom."

"Night, honey. You did good, sweetheart. I'm so proud of you."

Parker knew she wasn't talking about her performance on the stage, but her performance just now. She lay in the dark next to Serene, listening to the gentle sound of her friend's breathing.

She'd always had trouble holding a grudge against Serene. If she'd had the same father, the same horrors in her childhood, she might be as clueless as Serene was.

Before she fell asleep, she prayed that the residual traces of her own resentment would go away. Silently, she interceded for her friend, asking that the scars of Serene's youth would be completely erased and that everything good God had planned for her would be fulfilled. Even if it meant leaving Parker behind.

The prayer gave her more forgiveness for the wounded star beside her, and finally, she fell into a restful sleep.

CHAPTER FIFTY

The Memphis concert was sold out the next night. Parker stood backstage as Serene sang in front of the crowd that wouldn't hear Parker's name or buy her CDs. Serene wasn't quite as "on" tonight as she'd been at the past two venues, but her fans didn't seem to know it.

Daniel seemed at his best, however. He got better with every show. She watched him for a few minutes, saw how adept he was at moving from one song to the next, allowing Serene the time she needed to speak to the crowd. Though the pianist seemed to lead the band, Daniel worked in perfect harmony with the others.

And he didn't look too shabby. Playing at homeless shelters had a way of making a man even more attractive, Parker thought. The memory of his comforting words last night helped soothe the pain of being cut from the tour. He didn't see her as a loser. Daniel had different benchmarks for success than Jeff Standard did.

Too bad she wouldn't be able to get to know him better on the tour. But he did live in Nashville.

Watching the concert was torture, so she ambled through the backstage area. It was filled with people helping in various capacities — stage hands, sound engineers, the makeup lady, a hair stylist, spouses or significant others of band members, local radio people, a caterer, and a number of VIPs who'd been given backstage access. She went back to the dressing room with the star on it and slipped inside.

Serene's casual clothes were wadded and hanging over a chair. Parker lifted her jeans, smoothed out the wrinkles, and folded them neatly. She got her blouse and hung it up.

What was she doing? She was supposed to be one of the performers tonight, yet here she was cleaning up after her friend. She sat down on the couch, looking up at the ceiling and wishing she wasn't here.

God, where will I go from here? I thought I knew your plan, but now I'm so confused.

She should never have thought she could be more than a receptionist. Who was she to think she could pull off a major concert tour?

A force as strong as gravity dragged her mind down a destructive path. She had to fight it. Maybe she'd just go sit with her parents in the audience and watch the concert.

She stepped outside the dressing room and was enveloped by the booming chords on stage. The dressing room wasn't far from the backstage area, but the corridor, which had been lit up moments earlier, was dark. Some building maintenance guy had probably turned the light off to save on electricity. But Serene would soon be coming off the stage for her costume change. She would need light.

Parker felt her way down the hallway toward the backstage area, looking for a light switch.

Then someone touched her shoulder. She jumped, pivoted ...

... and came face to face with Mick Evans.

CHAPTER FIFTY-ONE

Parker screamed, but Mick threw his hand over her mouth, muffling her. He spun her around, pulling her back against him. "I'm not gonna hurt you!"

She fought him, trying to break free, but he was bigger and stronger. Her muffled screams blended with the music blaring from the stage.

"Please, calm down," he said into her ear. "I just want to talk to you."

She knew if he got her into one of the dark, vacant rooms, he would kill her. He would end her life without thinking twice and leave her bleeding on the floor. She thought of those pictures of Brenna in her own blood, imagined Tiffany dead on her own bed.

There would be crime-scene photographs of her own body, from every possible angle.

She couldn't let that happen. She threw her head back, butting his chin, then elbowed him in the stomach and lifted her feet so she would fall out of his grip.

He lost his hold, and she screeched out her terror as she stumbled away.

"I don't want to hurt you!" he said. "Parker, just listen!"

If she could just get upstairs into the light of the concourse, she could get help. Someone … anyone … would hear her screams.

She stumbled and righted herself, reached the stairs. He was right behind her. "Parker, I'm trying to save your life. Stop fighting and listen! I know what you think of me, but you're wrong."

She rammed herself into the door, but it wouldn't open. He grabbed her as she pulled it. She slipped free again and got it open, slid out into the lighted hallway.

"Help me! Somebody help me!" she screamed.

"You'll get us both killed!" he shouted.

She turned and headed toward the merchant tables, searching, hoping, praying for someone to come into sight.

A gun fired. The bullet whizzed past her and she dropped, throwing her hands over her head. He had a gun! Frantic prayers rolled through her mind. *God, help me. I don't want to die!*

Then Mick was on her again. "Don't shoot!" he yelled.

Confusion sliced through her terror.

"You'll kill me, too," he said. "Drop the gun!"

His words didn't compute in her mind. The music coming from the auditorium now only crescendoed, masking the sound.

"Get her up!" Another voice …

Mick whispered into her ear, "Do as I say, and nobody has to die."

Trembling, Parker got to her knees and let him pull her to her feet. As she did, she saw someone up ahead, standing in the shadows of another dark hallway.

In a blurry rush of understanding, Parker realized that Mick wasn't the one with the gun. He was shielding her.

"Be still and quiet." His whisper was damp against her hair. "We're safe if I'm between you."

The shooter stepped into the light …

Parker gasped. It was Marta.

CHAPTER FIFTY-TWO

The security room at the Memphis Coliseum held a bank of screens on one wall that flashed video of key areas inside the building. Gibson and LesPaul sat scanning the screens, watching for any sign that Mick Evans had shown up again.

Gibson had had a talk with Vince, the security director, when they'd arrived to set up for the concert that morning. After checking with Nashville PD, Vince had agreed to allow Gibson and LesPaul to provide more eyes on the monitors as they sat the concert out with him.

So far, they hadn't seen Mick. They'd given pictures of him to all the security personnel in the building, and no one else had seen him. But Gibson knew it would be difficult to spot him in such a large crowd, even under the best of circumstances. If he'd cut his hair or changed his look in any way, he would be able to slip right past them.

Mostly, the cameras taped the comings and goings at entrances or exits within the building. There was some coverage around the concourse and some of the corridors. But the cameras weren't sufficiently spaced to show everything that went on in the building.

The phone rang, and Vince picked it up, mumbled something into it, then said, "Where?"

He gestured to Gibson and pointed to the screen illuminating the west side of the building, concourse level. "Probably something in the air conditioning system, but we'll check on it."

Gibson watched that area, trying to orient himself. As Vince hung up, he asked, "What is it?"

"Janitor says he heard something that sounded like a gunshot in that area."

Gibson came out of his seat. He looked at that screen and those around it with more focus. "Can you move those cameras?"

Vince flicked a few things on his control board, and the pictures slid a little farther along the concourse. They showed nothing. He bent down and got the gun out of his ankle holster.

LesPaul was on his feet now, watching the screens that showed the backstage area. "Where's Parker?"

"Probably in Serene's dressing room."

There were no cameras in there. Gibson's pulse pounded in his head. "I'm going to find my sister while you check out that sound. You have an extra radio?"

Vince grabbed one, checked that it was working, and tossed it to him. Then he radioed for the security detail on that side of the building to check out the area from which the sound had come.

LesPaul followed Gibson around the building and down one of the staircases that led into the backstage area, on the ground floor. He went down the hall toward Serene's dressing room. Why had the lights gone out in that area? He radioed Vince and asked him where the light controls were. Vince told him, and Gibson turned them back on. No one lurked in the hallway.

He reached the star's dressing room and opened the door. "Parker?"

No answer. He went in, checked the bathroom. No one was here.

LesPaul stood in the doorway. "These stairs over here lead up to the area where the janitor heard the sound."

It could be nothing, Gibson told himself. But where was his sister?

He pushed past LesPaul and went up the stairs. He pulled open the door at the top and looked both ways, then slipped into the brighter corridor. He turned to his right, toward the stage.

A security guard was stooping with his radio at his ear. A spent cartridge lay at his feet. Gibson's face went white. "The janitor heard right."

The security guard pointed up to the wall. "There's your bullet."

Gibson wiped sweat from his forehead. Thankfully, there was no blood. He spoke into the radio. "There's an armed gunman somewhere in this building. We have to find him. And I don't know where my sister is. Rewind some of the tape and see if you can locate her."

He turned and looked in both directions, then ran toward the merchant tables. No, this was wrong. No one holding a hostage would have come this way. He turned back, ran to the quieter end of the hall. Nothing.

"Call Mom and Dad. See if Parker's with them."

Their parents were sitting in the audience, watching the show. LesPaul pulled his phone out and pressed his mother's number on speed dial. "Mom, is Parker with you?" He put his hand over the phone and said, "She's not."

"Where are they?"

"In the C section, back row."

"Tell them to get out of the building. Tell them to wait in the van."

CHAPTER
FIFTY-THREE

Parker's breath came in gasps. Mick kept his arm clamped around her stomach, as if he were the hostage-taker. At gunpoint, Marta had moved them into a dimly lit equipment room.

The machinery in the room, probably meant to cool the coliseum, roared with the potential to mask voices and gunfire. Blue-painted pipes snaked around the room with words like *Chilled Water Return* and *Condenser* written on the sides. Parker scanned the room for a way out — or a weapon.

A spiral staircase went down a flight. She didn't know where it led, but if she could get to it, maybe she could escape.

"I don't want you to kill anyone else, Marta." Mick's arm was sweating through Parker's shirt. "Enough people have died. If you shoot her, you'll shoot me."

"Then move away from her."

"Why do you want to kill me?" Parker managed to ask. "What did I do to you?"

Marta's teeth ground together. "He has a strange attachment to you, and I don't like it."

Parker heard his unsteady breath. "That's not true," he said. "She has nothing to do with you or me." He spoke as if trying to calm a wild animal.

"Yes, she does," Marta said. "I had to kill Brenna because of her."

Parker sucked in a hard breath.

"Nobody had to kill Brenna," Mick said. "I had it under control. I could have talked them out of using the songs. I told you about it in confidence. I didn't mean for you to *kill* anybody."

"Spoiled little brat had it coming. Treating you like you were nobody. Treated me like that, too." She lowered the gun, and her face twisted. "I'm the only one who's ever stood up for you, Mick."

"I know you are. I ... appreciate that." Fear rippled in his voice. "Put the gun down and let Parker go, and we'll run away together. Isn't that what you want?"

Marta clenched her teeth and fixed her aim. She wasn't buying it. She glanced at the door of a room nearby. "In that room. Move, now."

Mick and Parker hesitated.

"Now, I said!"

Parker moved with Mick to the door. He turned the knob and they pushed inside. It was lit up and smelled of popcorn. A stainless-steel box filled most of the room, with an industrial-sized popcorn maker over it. It held crumbs and kernels, but no popcorn. Flattened popcorn boxes were stacked floor to ceiling against the walls.

Parker saw another closed door across the room. It probably opened into the hallway. Mick stayed close to Parker as Marta came in and bolted the door. Under the light, Parker saw the wildness in her eyes.

"This room won't do," Marta said. "They'll hear us. Let's go back."

Confusion. That was good, Parker thought. They could use that. On the other hand, confusion could cause Marta to act without thinking.

Mick didn't budge. "Marta, you're making this so much worse for yourself. Every killing is tangling this tighter. I know you think you're doing the right thing — the noble thing. Even when you killed Tiffany …"

Parker squeezed her eyes shut. So Marta had killed both of them. Marta's confidential meeting with Parker and Gibson was just part of the cover-up. She must have hidden the gun in Chase's apartment herself.

"Tiffany. Threw. You. Out." Marta bit off each word. "You should have killed her yourself. Who did she think she was? She was going to pin the stolen song on you and let you take the fall. She was going to tell them you killed Brenna. You would have gone to prison."

"I'm wanted for murder now," Mick said. "How much worse could it have been?"

Parker glanced around the room, looking for something — anything — they could use as a weapon. There were metal scoops in the popcorn box, but she wasn't close enough to them. On the floor was a fire extinguisher. She could use it if she could inch toward it.

Marta pouted like a scorned child. "I bring good things into your life, Mick. Not bad things, like you say."

"I know you do," he said, his voice wobbling. "I want to let Parker go and hold you. But I can't let you kill her. Come on, we'll open the door and let her go. Then you and I will leave through the chiller room. Before she gets help, we'll be long gone."

Parker held her breath. *Please, God.* Marta seemed to be considering it, but then her gaze grew feral again.

"No. You have this stupid infatuation with her. You were following her like you had some crush. He fought his father for you," Marta told Parker.

"Not because I had a crush on her," Mick countered. "I didn't even know her. I fought my father because he was going to send Brenna to steal. It was wrong."

The gun was aimed at Parker's face, dead center. Death would come the moment it went off. No chance of survival.

"He followed you, Parker," Marta spat out. "He obsessed over you. I can't let that go on."

Parker wanted to speak, but she knew the slightest thing could set Marta off. The slightest word from the person Marta loathed.

Mick spoke instead. "I followed her because I was afraid of what you were going to do next, Marta. You were stalking her, watching her every move. You broke into her house and left those song sheets. That wasn't rational. One minute you think you're helping her, the next you're trying to kill her."

"And that's the reason I have to kill her. Because of your protection of her. You've never protected me that way."

"I'm trying to protect you now."

Her laugh had a razor edge. "We can stay here all night like this, Mick. I'll stand here with this gun until you move out of the way. Or maybe I'll just kill you both. I could walk out of here. Nobody's even looking for me."

Sweat dripped into Parker's eyes. "Marta . . . ," she said in a shaky voice, "my brother, the cop, is in the building. He'll realize I'm not around. He'll come looking for me. There might have been witnesses, people who heard me scream. Someone may have heard the gunshot. They'll call the police." She stopped, tried to swallow the knot in her throat. "If you go now, while no one is here, they'll never find you." Her mind searched for things she'd read about hostage situations. *Talk to your captors. Help them to see you as a person. Draw sympathy.* "Marta, I liked you when I met you. We hit it off, didn't we?"

Marta didn't answer. "I was acting. I'm good at it."

"You are," Mick said. "You . . . we . . . should go to Hollywood. You could get auditions. Be in a movie."

"After I kill her."

Parker tried again. "My mom is out there, in the audience. Don't make her find me here. Please. My little brother, too. He's backstage. I don't want him traumatized."

"Your little brother is twenty-four. I know all about your family, so don't try to make me feel sorry for some kid who doesn't even exist."

"If you know about my family, then you know how close we are. If I die, it will affect so many people who don't deserve it. And I haven't done anything except listen to you and care about you."

Her pleading wasn't working. Marta wanted blood. Her eyes had a vicious glint. "Mick told me your songs spoke to him. *I* tried to write songs that spoke to him, but they stank."

Parker searched her memory for what she knew about Marta. She'd been in her room, seen her things. The picture of Mick ... it must have been hers instead of Brenna's. "But you sing, right? You're a vocal performance major. You must be good, or you wouldn't have gotten into Belmont."

"I am good," she said. "I could be doing what Serene Stevens is doing, only better."

That gave Parker hope. "If you let me go, I'll write some songs for you to record."

Marta's eyes were dull, uninspired.

"Choosing the right songs is half the battle. If you have good songs and a good voice, you could go far."

Marta's grip on that gun was steady. "I can go far without you."

Parker tried again. Every word bought a little more time. "The Bible says, 'I have a plan for you ... plans to prosper you and not to harm you, plans to give you hope and a future.'"

"Jeremiah 29:11," Marta said through compressed lips. "Don't quote the Bible to me."

"You don't think God has a plan for your life?"

"If he planned the family I came from, then I'll choose my own way."

So that was it. A damaged past. If Parker could get down to that, probe the inner workings of Marta's pain, maybe she could make her see that another murder wouldn't fill the void. Parker wiped her damp hair back from her forehead. Mick still stood behind her, holding her. "What kind of family did you come from?"

Marta's lips curled again. "The same kind he came from. Divorces and suicides and abandonment and steps and halves ..."

"It must have been hard."

"Yeah, you wouldn't know, would you? You have that close family, everyone intact."

"My parents are divorced." It was the first time she'd ever seen it as a positive. "My father's an alcoholic."

Marta gave a mirthless laugh. "Poor Parker." Her mocking tone turned to hatred, and her lips sneered. "Did you ever get molested by your mother's boyfriend? Did you ever get consigned to the basement because you're from a 'previous marriage,' and the real family had the run of the house?"

"No, I never had that happen."

Marta came closer with that gun, only a few feet away from her, just out of reach. Parker pulled her head back, as if putting more distance between her and the barrel would save her life.

Tears ran down Marta's face, her black eyeliner dripping like mud. "That's why I loved you, Mick. We were the same. I knew how you felt. I even knew why her songs spoke to you, because they spoke to me, too."

Parker thought through all of her lyrics, wondering which ones appealed to her. Maybe in some of the verses she'd written, Marta had found her story. Songs were sometimes like mirrors, speaking life or death into wounded minds.

"They spoke to you because God was using them," Parker whispered. "That's proof that he's been watching over you. Trying to comfort you."

"Where was he when they stuck me in a mental hospital?"

So there it was. She was mentally ill. It didn't matter which came first, the treatment or the disease. She wasn't rational today.

"What did they treat you for?" Parker asked.

"Depression, psychosis ... drugged me up, calmed me down, tucked me out of the way for six months or so ..."

Six months. Her family had her in a mental ward for six months?

"Just like Mick, only *he* got sent to boarding school. Shipped away where he wouldn't be a problem. Can't have anybody reminding the new spouse that there was a life before, can we? Even putting in all that church time — going three times a week, choir practice, teaching Sunday School, my mother couldn't bring herself to be a decent mother to her firstborn."

Parker's cell phone began to ring in its irritating riff, startling her. She went for it, but Marta cocked the gun. "Don't touch it."

Parker froze and felt Mick pulling her tighter against him, keeping Marta from shooting. As much as Marta wanted to kill Parker, she didn't want Mick to die.

"It's my family looking for me," Parker said carefully. "I told you. You won't get away with this if they find me dead."

"Give me the phone."

It was clipped to her belt. Parker pulled it off and glanced down. Gibson's picture smiled back at her.

"Give it to me!"

If she could drop it, Marta would have to stoop to get it, giving Parker the chance to kick the gun out of her hand. She tossed, and it hit the ground and skidded some distance away.

"Nice try." Marta's aim didn't waver. She backed over to the iPhone, then stomped on it, the heel of her shoe cracking the screen.

CHAPTER
FIFTY-FOUR

Back in the security room, Gibson stood with LesPaul and Vince Summers, the security director. "I rewound the tape, and here it is. Something right here."

Gibson saw someone pass across that screen. Parker, with a man holding her ...

His stomach flipped as they moved by again. He couldn't see where they'd gone. "They're out of the frame. Is there another camera that picked them up?"

"There's a short blind spot there." Vince pointed to another screen, backed the video up on that one. Nothing. "They must have gone into one of the rooms near there. There's no video of them leaving the building. They vanished right there in that area."

"What are the rooms?"

"There's a chiller room, a boiler room, a janitor's closet, a concession storage room, the popcorn room, a prop and stage set room —"

"Are there cameras in any of them?"

"No, no cameras."

Gibson addressed the cops who'd answered the call. "He's got my sister. He's killed two people, and he's probably armed and dangerous. We have to figure out where he's holding her." He turned back to the security director. "Lock the exits. Don't let anybody out. LesPaul, go get word to Serene to stretch out the concert to keep everybody here."

The cops were rallying, unsnapping their weapons, fanning out around the building. They'd been trained for terrorist activity, and this qualified. His heart pounded as he ran behind some of them toward the area where Mick and Parker had disappeared.

CHAPTER
FIFTY-FIVE

Lynn and Pete had no intentions of going to the van. The question LesPaul had asked on the phone was sure evidence that something had happened. If Mick Evans had come back, then Parker was in danger. Lynn got her All Access pass out of her purse and ran around the concourse, down to the backstage area. Pete was on her heels.

It was time for Serene's costume change — the part of the show when Parker would have done her three songs. Now they seemed to stretch out the time with the band playing a long instrumental, while Serene ran to change her clothes.

Lynn saw LesPaul, waiting beside the stage as Serene shot off. "Serene," he said, blocking her. "You have to extend the concert. Parker's in trouble. They're locking down the exits to keep anyone from leaving."

Serene's makeup artist stood waiting. "Come on, honey. There's not much time."

Serene didn't budge. "What do you mean, Parker's in trouble?"

Lynn pushed through the people beginning to gather around the star. "LesPaul, where is she?"

He gave her and Pete an irritated look. "Mom, we told you —"

Pete stepped between them. "We don't care what you told us. Where's Parker?"

He swallowed. "We can't find her. We think Mick Evans may be here."

Lynn's heart slammed to the pit of her stomach. "Does he … does he have her?"

He avoided the question and pointed in the direction where they'd found the shell. "Someone heard a gunshot in that part of the building on the main floor. Don't panic, Mom."

But panic spread like fuel-fed flames through Lynn's body. She turned and ran toward the dark hallway.

"Mom, don't! Dad, stop her."

Pete overtook her and passed her as they got to the stairs. "Let me go first."

LesPaul ran after them. "Mom, Dad, we found a shell at the top of those stairs. He's armed and dangerous."

"I don't care what he is!" she said. "My daughter may be with him!"

She got to the top of the stairs and opened the door, looking up and down the corridor. Police were already there, going from door to door, checking each room.

A cop stopped her. "Ma'am, we need you to go back downstairs!"

"I'm not going anywhere until I find my daughter!"

One of the cops looked around her. "Miss Stevens, we'd really appreciate it if you would get back on stage and keep the concert going. If people start to leave …"

Lynn turned and saw Serene standing behind her, tears on her face.

"The band will keep playing until I get back," she said. "Please … you have to find her."

CHAPTER
FIFTY-SIX

Sweat trickled through Parker's hair, down her temples. Mick was sweating, too. His shirt was wet against her back.

"Marta, I know your life has been hard," Parker said. "People let you down. They betrayed you. But *I* didn't do it. If you love Mick, don't leave another body for police to find. They'll think he did it. They'll come after *him*."

That seemed to give Marta pause. "I never meant for them to blame him. They never would have if it hadn't been for him following you. They would have assumed it was Chase. I made sure of that."

Mick's voice was louder now. "Marta, they knew it wasn't Chase when you killed Tiffany. And you'd made threats against Parker. I followed her to protect her from you."

It was all becoming clear. Mick had been the one to call Parker that night, to tell her that it was about her, but that he would protect her. Somehow, the stolen songs had prompted a fight in that family. Marta had taken their treatment of Mick a little too personally.

Marta moved to the side, as if trying to get an angle where Mick wouldn't be hit. Mick stayed glued to Parker. "You're not that good a shot, Marta. You shoot her, you kill me."

"Then let her go!"

"No. Just give me the gun. Come on, Marta. We have no future if you don't."

"I don't have a future anyway!" The noise from the nearby chiller room muffled her cry. "You don't love me. I had to hold you hostage to keep you with me. You tried to leave me, too! You said I was crazy!" Marta was crumbling. Her eyes shifted wildly back and forth across the room, as if puzzling whether it was worth it to kill them both.

Suddenly, someone jiggled the doorknob. Marta spun, and the gun went off.

Parker screamed and dropped to the floor, praying no one on the other side of that door had been shot.

CHAPTER
FIFTY-SEVEN

Lynn lifted her face from the floor where she'd dropped when the gun fired. *God, she's in there! Help her!*

Police backed away from the room, all of their weapons poised. Gibson was among them, right in the line of fire. She found LesPaul on the floor, getting to his knees. Pete was up and pulling her back to the staircase.

And then she saw Serene ... lying back against the wall in a growing pool of blood. "She's hit! Serene's hit!"

Chaos ensued around them as two cops fell to Serene's side. Others gathered around Lynn, Pete, and LesPaul, pushing them into the staircase, forcing them toward safety.

She heard one of the police officers radioing for paramedics. Someone radioed back that they were already in the building and on their way.

Lynn rushed to the bottom of the stairs and fell into Pete's arms. "Oh, Pete, we have to pray," she cried.

CHAPTER FIFTY-EIGHT

Marta swung back around, revolver clamped in her hands. "Now look what you've done!"

Mick shoved Parker against the wall and dove for Marta, tackling her. She kicked and thrashed, and Parker saw Mick grab Marta's wrist. The girl's finger was on the trigger, ready to pull. Mick gritted his teeth as his full weight pinned Marta down. He slid his hand up beyond her wrist to her hand, to the gun — and with a quick movement, he twisted the gun from her grasp and scrambled to his feet. "Against the wall, Marta!" he yelled. "Now!"

She lay crumpled on the floor in fetal position, hands over her head. Parker managed to get up and stumbled to the door. She opened it, and saw the guns aimed at her. Throwing her hands up, she screamed, "Don't shoot!"

She backed out of the way as the cops pushed in. Gibson crouched behind his own weapon. "Drop the gun, Evans!"

Parker screamed. "No, it's not him! Don't shoot! It's her!"

Mick tossed the gun toward Gibson so Marta couldn't get it again and weakly lifted his hands. Marta lay in fetal position, sobbing against the floor.

"Sis, you all right?" Gibson asked without taking his eyes from Mick.

She tried to catch her breath. "Yes. *She's* the killer. The one who shot Brenna and Tiffany and hid the gun in Chase's apartment. She did it all. Not Mick."

The local cops took over, and Gibson took Parker out of the room. The music was still playing onstage, an instrumental Parker didn't recognize. Serene wasn't singing. Then Parker saw that blood smeared the floor ...

As they pulled the gurney out of the staircase, she saw her friend. "Serene!"

"She was shot," Gibson said, holding her back. "Let them work."

Dizziness closed in. "Is she ... alive?"

"I don't know."

The music still played, the musicians oblivious to what was going on. The audience was beginning to shout and stomp, calling for Serene to come back out, bored with the instrumental. Some began to spill out of the auditorium and saw Serene's bleeding body being rolled out on the gurney.

Parker followed it to the ambulance and climbed inside with her. Serene was unconscious, and the medics were hooking up IVs and oxygen, and radioing stats in to the hospital.

"Are you okay, ma'am?" one of the medics asked Parker.

She didn't realize he was speaking to her.

"Ma'am?"

Startled, she looked up from Serene's face. "Yes ... I'm fine."

"You can ride with her, but is there anything we can do for you?"

She swallowed and forced her mind to focus. "Save my friend," she said.

CHAPTER FIFTY-NINE

The bullet that hit Serene had ricocheted off the concrete wall and torn through her lung. After hours in surgery, she spent two weeks in ICU on a ventilator. When they finally put her in a private room, Parker insisted on staying with her.

Parker sat on the edge of her bed, trying to make her friend smile by reading her fan email. There were thousands of them, all offering prayers and hopes for her recovery. She stopped reading when Serene's eyes began to glaze over.

"Tour's a wash," she whispered. "They're postponing all my dates."

"Doesn't matter," Parker said. "The publicity will sell more CDs than the tour would have. You're world famous now. The star who took a bullet for her friend."

"It wasn't like that," Serene whispered.

Parker stretched out on the bed beside her. "It sort of was. You didn't have to be there."

"Neither did your mom or dad, or Gibson or LesPaul."

"That's right," Parker said. "I have to say, Gibson really came through. I didn't have enough faith in him. But it's pretty clear that the rest of the family's insane. Including you."

Serene smiled at the implication that she was family. "This has taught me a lot, though."

"Oh, yeah? What?"

Serene paused, her face strained by emotion. Her lips pressed together, and tears rimmed her eyes. "It's taught me that I don't want to die. Not from a bullet, and not from anorexia."

Parker raised up on her elbow. "Yeah?"

"As soon as I get out of here, I'm going to that treatment center for eating disorders you told me about."

Parker caught her breath. "You are? Really?"

"Yes, really. I'm sick — sick enough I could have died from it. The bullet almost got me there first, but starvation would have, eventually. When I'm well, I'll talk about it onstage. Maybe it'll keep others from going down the same path."

Parker took her friend's hand and smiled. Could it be that God's hand had been on this whole crazy story from the beginning?

She thought of Mick Evans. She hadn't seen him since the shooting, but she'd given a statement to the police that she hoped would help him. Marta had been arrested for two counts of murder, two counts of attempted murder, and kidnapping, since she'd held Mick against his will in the basement of a mountain cabin for weeks. He'd managed to get away from her when she got him to the Memphis Coliseum. If he hadn't captured Parker and made himself her human shield, Marta would have murdered her for sure.

Mick was still being charged as an accessory, since he hadn't gone to the police as soon as he suspected Marta.

Parker had seen news reports of Nathan Evans bonding Mick out of jail. The two had a lot of fallout to sort through. She hoped they'd find a way to be there for each other as they navigated their way through their grief and trauma, and the legal minefield awaiting both of them.

Marta's attorney was making noises about an insanity plea. Parker prayed for the girl each day — that somehow, she would reach out to God and find the peace so desperately lacking in her life.

As Parker lay on the bed bantering with her friend, she said a silent thanks to God for seeing them through. Maybe it was time for a new beginning for all of them.

CHAPTER SIXTY

The audience smiled up at Parker with rapt attention, captivated by the words and melodies she crooned. Being held hostage had raised her celebrity a notch. Her case had made national news for several days. It wasn't how she'd expected her fame to hit.

But no one in this audience knew who she was.

She glanced at Daniel as she sang and played her guitar. The light spilling off the stage caught the pleasure in his eyes.

There were probably fifty people here, all homeless or desperately poor, who came to the Nashville soup kitchen for their one hot meal of the day. They hadn't expected a concert today.

They swayed to her music with tears in their eyes, wiping their wizened faces with stained fingers. Some of them closed their eyes and raised their leathered hands to heaven.

She'd never felt a greater thrill, not even in a coliseum with twelve thousand people. How could she have wanted more than this? The things she had once sought had a bitter taste now. They tasted like lost money, hurt pride, stress, and disappointment. She'd had enough of it.

Her mission as a writer was to lead people to Christ, to help them praise him and worship him and remember his glory, to help them understand their blessings and show them where to turn when things went bad … and when things went well. There would be no more watered-down songs with her name on them. She would only write those that had eternal value.

And her mission as a performer was to sing for those who couldn't give anything back.

As the chorus reached its crescendo and the raspy voices began to sing, she stopped playing and listened to the lovely sound of their voices singing without her. Closing their eyes in prayer, they sang off-key, some of them tone-deaf, but the sound had never been more beautiful.

Teary-eyed, she slipped off her stool and winked at Daniel.

The men and women continued to sing as she began to make her exit, but he reached out and grabbed her arm, pulled her back, and pressed a kiss on her cheek. Heat flushed to her face as it always did when he kissed her. He let her go, and she slipped out of the room. Her guitar case was in the hall where she'd left it. She packed it up.

The poor and needy were singing louder, their voices carrying down the long church hallway. She lifted her case and walked out to her car, comfortable in the knowledge that she'd performed her best for her audience of one.

She didn't need or want the applause this time. All she needed was the warm sun of God's good pleasure.

AFTERWORD

Parker James is one of my favorite characters, because her life is so similar to mine. Creatively, we're almost twins, telling stories in hopes of impacting lives. I think one of the things unique to the writer's life is that we do seem to be on a roller coaster. I finish a book! Hoorah! Everything's wonderful. Then I send it off and wait. Time passes. My spirits plunge. It's the worst thing I've ever written. Why, oh why did I send it when I did? I start scouring the newspaper for real jobs. Then I get the call. They love it and are really going to publish it. Yes! Life is grand! Woo-hoo!

Then I get the revision letter. It's horrible. They want me to rewrite the whole book, change the title, and think about a pseudonym. They hate the plot and think the wrong characters died. Oh, and they want me to add a dog and a baby. I plunge again as I try to pick up the pieces that are salvageable. But then it occurs to me how it can be done, and hey, that dog really does add to the suspense, and the baby will be worth a few boxes of tissue, so yahoo, I'm up again as I send it off. It's the best thing I've ever done, a guaranteed blockbuster.

But then I can't pay my light bill, and the checks are starting to bounce, and that check from the publisher never comes. So I plunge again. Finally, I get paid, and dance around singing, "I'm in the money!" Then I write a check to Uncle Sam, pay that late light bill, my late insurance premium, and wonder how I'm going to make it on what's left over until the next check. Spirits take another dive.

Book comes out, good review, I dance again and sing for joy and write all my friends and get copies for my mother. Then I go on Amazon and read one lousy review from some hostile reader, and I notice that I'm ranked 6,000,342,786, and I go around the house looking for my gun. But before I pull the trigger, I start thinking, "What if some guy had a gun, and before he offs himself a shot rings out and he hits the floor and suddenly wants to live, only others want him dead," and woo-hoo, my spirits soar and my eyes glaze over, and like a homing robot, I stumble back to that keyboard and start banging.

And it all starts over again.

That's the writing life.

But I love that roller coaster. It's the ride God gave me, and doing it for the Kingdom of God is a privilege. There's a ride for you, as well, one that He chose for you before the foundation of the world. I hope you're on it.

John 15:8: "My Father is glorified by this, that you bear much fruit, and so prove to be My disciples."

Find your gift and use it. Then enjoy the ride!

Blessings,
Terri Blackstock

DOUBLE MINDS STUDY QUESTIONS

1. Parker feels uncomfortable when Serene asks her to rewrite her songs to tone down the Christianity, but Serene argues that she can reach more people with the gospel if her music reaches a larger audience. Can you think of any Christian artists who have gone mainstream with their music? What did it do to their careers? How did their secular songs compare with their Christian ones?

2. Have you had times in your life when you've made compromises in the interest of success? Does success look the same to God as it does to the world? Discuss the difference.

3. What significance does the song title "Double Minds" have in the story? Which characters have a "double mind" that they must confront? Do all Christians struggle with this to some degree?

4. Discuss the friendship between Parker and Serene. In what circumstances did their friendship begin? How does each view and treat the other? What misconceptions does each woman have

about herself that work their way into the friendship? Are these eventually resolved?

5. Many of the characters in the story are deeply affected by their relationships with their families. How does Parker's family differ from the others portrayed in the novel? How are the characters shaped by their families growing up? Are there any characters who are able to rise above the negative influence of their families?

6. What causes Pete to finally decide to get help for his alcoholism? How does his family react? What does this say about the nature of trust? Forgiveness?

7. Throughout the novel, Parker fights to keep Serene's anorexia out of the public eye and urges Serene to acknowledge that she has a problem. Do you think Parker should have handled Serene's eating disorder differently? What would you have done in her situation? How do you think prominent Christian figures should deal with their personal struggles?

8. Parker criticizes the hypocrisy often found in the Christian music industry. What examples of this come up in the story? Is this a problem in high-profile Christian occupations? What standards should we expect of our "leaders?" What should be our response when they fail?

9. How do Parker's ambitions change throughout the story? Are you satisfied with her choices at the end? Can you see Parker's journey resulting in a more fulfilled life?

A Sample Chapter
from Terri Blackstock's Forthcoming Novel,
Intervention
Releases November 2009

Barbara Covington's rescuer stood on the sidewalk at baggage claim, smoking a cigarette and chugging a Red Bull. Barbara swallowed back the irony that the interventionist, as she was called, had promised to help rid her daughter of her addictions. Clearly, she had a few of her own.

Maybe she should drive past her, forcing her to get back on that plane and return to the drug rehab she ran. She could work this out herself. Lock her daughter in her room and take away her car keys and force her to stay sober. But hadn't she already tried that? Despite her best efforts to turn their home into a lockdown, Emily still managed to sneak out and get high.

How had this happened?

That familiar knot burned in her stomach as she pulled to the curb and waved at the woman. It had to be her. She was wearing the long red skirt she told her she'd have on, and a white peasant blouse that made her look more like a college student than someone who could escort an active addict across the country. What if Emily put up a fight? How would this petite thing handle her?

Barbara swallowed back her fears and pulled the lever under the dashboard, popping her trunk. Forcing a welcoming smile, she got out of the car. "Hi, are you Trish?"

"Sure am." The woman dropped her cigarette on the concrete and stomped it out with a sandaled foot, then thrust a hand out to Barbara.

Barbara hoped her hand felt warmer than it was. "I'm Barbara Covington."

"Trish Massey."

Barbara glanced at the small bag at the woman's feet. "Is this all you have?"

"Yeah, I won't be here long."

Barbara picked up her bag and set it in the trunk as Trish got into the car. She slipped back into the driver's seat. The car that she'd freshened with Febreze suddenly smelled of smoke.

Trish was all smiles. "So where did you tell Emily you were going?"

"To an Al-anon meeting."

"And that's okay with her?"

Barbara breathed a laugh. "Oh, yeah. She likes it when I'm working on her problem. She would love it if everybody she knew were going to meetings and wringing their hands. She loves to keep us playing the What-to-Do-about-Emily game."

There she went again, letting her bitterness spill out to a perfect stranger.

"Meetings are good," Trish said. "Have you been to any?"

Barbara pulled away from baggage claim and headed to the loop that would take them out of the airport. "I've been to plenty. I've done the workbooks and gone through the twelve steps, as if I'm the one with the problem. I've done everything they've told me to do. But she's still using."

"Al-anon meetings are to help the family members' sanity, not to give you some secret code to sober up your loved one."

Barbara knew that had been her mistake. She'd gone hoping to learn what would work. When she didn't get those answers, she'd lost interest. Her sanity would return when her daughter was sane.

Strange that a woman who couldn't be more than thirty would be counseling her now. And who was Trish to counsel an eighteen-year-old? Emily would take one look at her and declare her dominance.

What was she doing? Maybe this was all wrong.

"You're doing the right thing," Trish said, as though she'd read her mind.

Barbara didn't want to cry in front of the woman. "When Emily was going into preschool, I personally visited fourteen schools. I interviewed teachers. I even spent a day with her at the few I liked, to see how she fit in."

"I don't blame you. I'd probably do the same if I had children."

"It's no easy thing, sending her to a place like this, halfway across the country. I talked to at least two dozen places before I decided on Road Back. I chose very carefully."

"You won't be disappointed."

She was counting on it. She glanced at Trish. "She'll be locked in, right? Because if she isn't, she'll leave. I've tried treatment two other times — one time, she ran away. The second time, she smuggled drugs in and got kicked out."

"She'll be monitored at all times. Don't worry, we do this all the time. She'll be very comfortable."

Comfort wasn't her main concern, though she didn't want Emily to be miserable. Barbara bit the inside of her cheek as she pulled onto the interstate, headed for the hotel she'd reserved for Trish. She was sinking thirty thousand dollars into this rehab, money that had come from a second mortgage on her house. But being expensive didn't guarantee that it was good. Even the best rehabs had underwhelming success rates.

She wished the young woman inspired more confidence. "You seem very young. How did you come to own Road Back?"

Trish flicked her hair behind her ear. "I'm a recovering addict myself. I got clean at Road Back, and when I graduated, I stayed and worked there. I've been doing interventions for them for five years. A couple of years ago, the directors wanted to retire, so I decided to buy it. I couldn't stand the thought of it not being there anymore. That's how much I believe in the program."

That made her feel somewhat better. She wished she could go there herself to make sure it was safe. But once she'd made up her mind to do the intervention, there hadn't been time to take a trip to check it out in person. Waiting could result in Emily's arrest ... or worse. They had to act now.

And escorting Emily herself would never work. No, she'd made the decision that it would take a professional to convince Emily to go, and Trish had to be the one to escort her.

She had to stop thinking of Emily as that same little girl she'd raised. She had changed, and Barbara didn't like the person who'd replaced her. If only this rehab could exorcise the addiction within her and return Emily home in her former condition ...

It would be a miraculous answer to prayer.

But what if this failed too, and she never saw that little girl again?

Blinking back tears, she took the exit that was near her home. The hotel sign loomed up ahead. "I hope the room is okay. I went ahead and checked you in." She handed her the key card.

"It'll be fine. You should see some of the places I've had to stay." As Barbara pulled into the parking lot, Trish shifted in her seat to look at her. "So, did you write the letters?"

Barbara nodded. "Yes, I have them with me." She dug into her purse. "Here they are."

Trish took them and turned on the overhead light. "And who is Lance?"

"My son. He's fourteen."

"What about her father?"

"He died four years ago. When Emily was twelve."

"Oh." The word almost thudded between them. "Is that when Emily's problems started?"

"Not right away. But over the next year she got in with the wrong crowd. Bunch of thugs and criminals." She paused, letting Trish read. Those dreaded tears rimmed her eyes, spilled over.

"We're not like this. There was never even alcohol in our home. I've taken her to church every Sunday of her life . . ." Her voice faded out. Trish probably heard this same song and dance from every parent she dealt with.

"It's not your fault."

Then whose fault was it? Pursing her lips, she let Trish finish reading.

Finally, Trish looked up. "Is there anyone else who'll be there? Grandparents?"

"They're too far away, and they're not in good health. I've kept them in the dark about all this."

"Friends? A boss?"

"Her friends are like her. They don't want her sober. And she lost her job three weeks ago. Hasn't been sober enough to get another one, so there's not a boss who can get through to her." Barbara glanced at her in the shadows of the car. "Is it a problem that it's only my son and me?"

"No, we can work with that." She handed the letters back. "You both did a good job with the letters. The main thing is that you stick to your guns about what will happen if she refuses to go. You have to be willing to throw her out with no resources, to precipitate change in her."

Barbara said nothing. She had grappled with that issue for months now, and lain awake for the past three nights, begging God to give her a way out. Why couldn't he sweep down and deliver Emily, before Barbara had to send her away for help or throw her out on the street?

"Are you ready for that? Putting her out if she refuses to go?"

Barbara swallowed. "I don't know."

"Well, do you think she'll agree to go to treatment?"

Barbara's spine stiffened. "I thought you were here to convince her."

"I can only do so much."

So what had this extra thirty-five hundred dollar fee paid for? A free vacation for this woman? "She has to go with you. If she doesn't, she'll wind up in jail."

"Or dead."

Dead. No, she couldn't survive burying anyone else. "I can't let that happen. This has to work."

"Do you think she's sick of her disease yet?"

Barbara fought the urge to argue semantics. She hated the AA words like *disease* and *relapse*, like it was some kind of virus she had caught somewhere.

"I don't think she's at the end of her rope yet, like I am."

"Well, maybe she won't have to be at the end to want help." Trish opened her car door. "What time will you pick me up?"

Barbara tried to think. The flight was at three, and this whole thing could take hours. They had to start early. "Eight a.m. I'll get her up while you're there."

"Tonight, you need to take her car to a friend's house. Park it there and hide the keys. If it's not in the driveway, she can't talk you into giving her the keys. If she leaves, it'll have to be without the car."

That shouldn't be too hard. She could have one of her drug buddies there in minutes.

"Hopefully her connection with you and her brother will be enough to make her go. And I'll do my part to make her see the possibilities." She got out her cigarettes, pulled one out. "It'll be okay. Most of the interventions I do are successful."

"But there's no guarantee."

"I'm afraid not."

She'd have to pay her whether Emily went with her or not. Success was the only option.

Double Minds

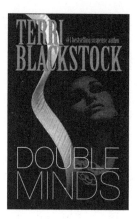

Terri Blackstock,
#1 Bestselling Suspense Author

As talented singer/songwriter Parker James struggles to make her mark on the Nashville music scene, she finds the competition can be fierce — even deadly.

When a young woman is murdered at the recording studio where Parker works, Parker is drawn into a mystery where nothing is as it seems. Unraveling the truth puts her own life at risk when she uncovers high-level industry corruption and is terrorized by a menacing stalker. As the danger escalates, Parker begins to question her dreams, her future, and even her faith. Does stardom even matter anymore?

Double Minds is a compelling suspense novel that unfolds in the middle of the Christian music industry in Nashville. Terri Blackstock, known for her Up All Night Fiction, grabs readers at page one and keeps them riveted until the final plot twist is untangled. This well-turned mystery is Blackstock's first stand-alone title in several years, and it was worth waiting for.

Hardcover: 978-0-310-31842-2
Softcover: 978-0-310-25063-0
Unabridged Audio CD: 978-0-310-28812-1
Audio Download, Unabridged: 978-0-310-28813-8

Pick up a copy today at your favorite bookstore!

A Restoration Novel

Last Light

Terri Blackstock,
#1 Bestselling Suspense Author

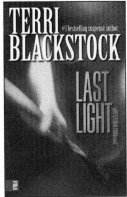

Today, the world as you know it will end. No need to turn off the lights.

Your car suddenly stalls and won't restart. You can't call for help because your cell phone is dead.

Everyone around you is having the same problem ... and it's just the tip of the iceberg.

Your city is in a blackout. Communication is cut off. Hospital equipment won't operate. And airplanes are falling from the sky.

Is it a terrorist attack ... or something far worse?

In the face of a crisis that sweeps an entire high-tech planet back to the age before electricity, your family faces a choice. Will you hoard your possessions to survive — or trust God to provide as you offer your resources and your hearts to others?

Yesterday's world is gone. Now all you've got is your family and community. You stand or fall together. Like never before, you must rely on each other.

But one of you is a killer.

Number one bestselling suspense author Terri Blackstock weaves a masterful what-if novel in which global catastrophe reveals the darkness in human hearts — and lights the way to restoration for a self-centered world. *Last Light* is the first book in an exciting new series.

Softcover: 978-0-310-25767-7
Unabridged Audio CD: 978-0-310-26880-2

Pick up a copy today at your favorite bookstore!

A Restoration Novel

Night Light

Terri Blackstock,
#1 Bestselling Suspense Author

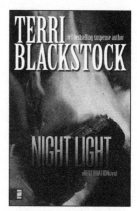

In the face of a crisis that sweeps an entire high-tech planet back to the age before electricity, the Brannings face a choice. Will they hoard their possessions to survive—or trust God to provide as they offer their resources to others?

Number one bestselling suspense author Terri Blackstock weaves a masterful what-if series in which global catastrophe reveals the darkness in human hearts—and lights the way to restoration for a self-centered world.

An era unlike any in modern civilization is descending—one without lights, electronics, running water, or automobiles. As a global blackout lengthens into months, the neighbors of Oak Hollow grapple with a chilling realization: the power may never return.

Survival has become a lifestyle. When two young thieves break into the Brannings' home and clean out the food in their pantry, Jeff Branning tracks them to a filthy apartment and discovers a family of children living alone, stealing to stay alive. Where is their mother? The search for answers uncovers a trail of desperation and murder ... and for the Brannings, a powerful new purpose that can transform their entire community—and above all, themselves.

Softcover: 978-0-310-25768-4
Unabridged Audio CD: 978-0-310-26921-2

Pick up a copy today at your favorite bookstore!

True Light

Terri Blackstock,
#1 Bestselling Suspense Author

The darkness deepens in a world without power.

But, daring to defend a young outcast, one family strikes a light.

In the face of a crisis that sweeps an entire high-tech planet back to the age before electricity, the Brannings face a choice. Will they hoard their possessions to survive — or trust God to provide as they offer their resources to others?

Number one bestselling suspense author Terri Blackstock weaves a masterful what-if series in which global catastrophe reveals the darkness in human hearts — and lights the way to restoration for a self-centered world.

Now eight months into a global blackout, the residents of Oak Hollow are coping with the deep winter nights. But the struggle to survive can bring out the worst in a person — or a community.

A teenager has been shot and the suspect sits in jail. As the son of a convicted murderer, Mark Green already has one strike against him. Now he faces the wrath of all Oak Hollow — except for one person. Deni Branning has known Mark since high school and is convinced he is no killer.

When Mark finds himself at large with a host of other prisoners released upon the unsuspecting community, Deni and her family attempt to help him find the person who really pulled the trigger. But clearing Mark's reputation is only part of his battle. Protecting the neighbors who ostracized him is just as difficult.

And forgiving them may be the hardest part of all.

Softcover: 978-0-310-25769-1
Unabridged Audio CD: 978-0-310-26922-9

Dawn's Light

Terri Blackstock,
#1 Bestselling Suspense Author

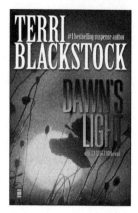

In the face of a crisis that sweeps an entire high-tech planet back to the age before electricity, the Brannings face a choice. Will they hoard their possessions to survive — or trust God to provide as they offer their resources to others?

Number one bestselling suspense author Terri Blackstock weaves a masterful what-if series in which global catastrophe reveals the darkness in human hearts — and lights the way to restoration for a self-centered world.

As the Pulses that caused the outage are finally coming to an end, thirteen-year-old Beth Branning witnesses a murder. Threatened by the killer, she keeps the matter to herself. But her silence could cost her life.

Meanwhile, as Deni's ex-fiancé returns to Crockett with a newfound faith and the influence to get things done, Deni is torn between the man who can fulfill all her dreams and Mark Green, the man who inhabits them.

As the world slowly emerges from the crisis, the Brannings face their toughest crisis yet. Will God require more of them than they've already given? How will they keep their faith if he doesn't answer their prayers?

Softcover: 978-0-310-25770-7
Unabridged Audio CD: 978-0-310-26923-6

Pick up a copy today at your favorite bookstore!

ZONDERVAN®
.com

Cape Refuge

Terri Blackstock,
#1 Bestselling Suspense Author

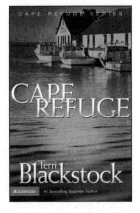

Mystery and suspense combine in this first book in this exciting four-book series by bestselling author Terri Blackstock. Thelma and Wayne Owens run a bed and breakfast in Cape Refuge, Georgia. They minister to the seamen on the nearby docks and prisoners just out of nearby jails, holding services in an old warehouse and taking many of the "down-and-outers" into their home. They have two daughters: the dutiful Morgan who is married to Jonathan, a fisherman, and helps them out at the B & B, and Blair, the still-single town librarian, who would be beautiful if it weren't for the serious scar on the side of her face.

After a heated, public argument with his in-laws, Jonathan discovers Thelma and Wayne murdered in the warehouse where they held their church services. Considered the prime suspect, Jonathan is arrested. Grief-stricken, Morgan and Blair launch their own investigation to help Matthew Cade, the town's young police chief, find the real killer. Shady characters and a raft of suspects keep the plot twisting and the suspense building as we learn not only who murdered Thelma and Wayne, but also the secrets about their family's past and the true reason for Blair's disfigurement.

Softcover: 978-0-310-23592-7
Audio Download, Unabridged: 978-0-310-30429-6

Pick up a copy today at your favorite bookstore!

ABOUT THE AUTHOR

Terri Blackstock is an award-winning novelist who has written for several major publishers including HarperCollins, Dell, Harlequin, and Silhouette. Her books have sold over 6 million copies worldwide.

With her success in secular publishing at its peak, Blackstock had what she calls "a spiritual awakening." A Christian since the age of fourteen, she realized she had not been using her gift as God intended. It was at that point that she recommitted her life to Christ, gave up her secular career, and made the decision to write only books that would point her readers to him.

"I wanted to be able to tell the truth in my stories," she said, "and not just be politically correct. It doesn't matter how many readers I have if I can't tell them what I know about the roots of their problems and the solutions that have literally saved my own life."

Her books are about flawed Christians in crisis and God's provisions for their mistakes and wrong choices. She claims to be extremely qualified to write such books, since she's had years of personal experience.

A native of nowhere, since she was raised in the Air Force, Blackstock makes Mississippi her home. She and her husband are the parents of three adult children—a blended family which she considers one more of God's provisions.

Terri Blackstock (www.terriblackstock.com) is the #1 bestselling author of the Cape Refuge, Sun Coast Chronicles, Second Chances, and Newpointe 911 suspense series, and other books.
With Beverly LaHaye, she wrote *Seasons Under Heaven*, *Times and Seasons*, *Showers in Season*, and *Season of Blessing*.

Share Your Thoughts

With the Author: Your comments will be forwarded to the author when you send them to *zauthor@zondervan.com*.

With Zondervan: Submit your review of this book by writing to *zreview@zondervan.com*.

Free Online Resources at

www.zondervan.com/hello

 Zondervan AuthorTracker: Be notified whenever your favorite authors publish new books, go on tour, or post an update about what's happening in their lives.

 Daily Bible Verses and Devotions: Enrich your life with daily Bible verses or devotions that help you start every morning focused on God.

 Free Email Publications: Sign up for newsletters on fiction, Christian living, church ministry, parenting, and more.

 Zondervan Bible Search: Find and compare Bible passages in a variety of translations at www.zondervanbiblesearch.com.

 Other Benefits: Register yourself to receive online benefits like coupons and special offers, or to participate in research.